WITHDRAWN

Life in The Family

NEW RELIGIOUS
MOVEMENTS

Gordon Melton, *Series Editor*

Life in
The Family
An Oral History of the Children of God

James D. Chancellor

With a Foreword by William Sims Bainbridge

 Syracuse University Press

Copyright © 2000 by Syracuse University Press

Syracuse, New York 13244-5160

All Rights Reserved

First Edition 2000

00 01 02 03 04 05 6 5 4 3 2 1

Frontispiece: "The Prophet." Poster. Courtesy of The Family.

Library of Congress Cataloging-in-Publication Data

Chancellor, James D.

   Life in the family : an oral history of the Children of God / James D. Chancellor.—1st ed.

     p. cm.

   Includes bibliographical references (p.) and index.

   ISBN 0–8156–0645–1 (cloth : alk. paper)

    1. Children of God (Movement) I. Title.

BP605.C38 C48 2000

289.9—dc21   00–022544

Manufactured in the United States of America

To Donna

James D. Chancellor is W. O. Carver Professor of World Religions and Christian Missions at the Southern Baptist Theological Seminary, Louisville, Kentucky. He is the author of articles on new religious movements and has contributed numerous entries to *The Evangelical Dictionary of World Missions.*

Contents

Foreword

William Sims Bainbridge

James Chancellor has written a rigorously researched but intimate view into one of the most remarkable religious movements of our era, The Family, or as journalists have often called it, The Children of God. This millenarian, communal, missionary movement emerged in the late 1960s as an amalgam of the youth counterculture and the Protestant Holiness movement, amid other novel Jesus People groups. Under the leadership of David Brandt Berg (earlier known as Moses David, later on as Father David, and revered within the group as "Dad"), The Family developed beliefs and practices that differed greatly from those of the standard churches. This book seeks to understand this unusual spiritual and human adventure by exploring the members' private experiences.

From its very first days, The Family existed in high tension with the surrounding sociocultural environment. It accused the churches of hypocrisy and worldliness, decrying their spiritless "Churchianity," and it expressed hostility toward the secular world of commercialism and bureaucracy. Members were the first victims kidnapped by deprogrammers and subjected to brainwashing attempts to destroy their faith and commitment to the group. The currently widespread anticult movement first came into existence to combat The Family, and ever since those stormy days in California it has remained the implacable enemy of The Family, attacking the group by all means, fair or foul, in many nations. What is it like to live outside the conventional system and suffer its constant disapproval?

Believing that America and the churches were both hideously corrupt, The Family has, from the very beginning, felt that the world was entering the Endtime. Unlike some other millenarian Christians, they believe that the followers of Jesus will not be raptured away early in the cosmic struggle but will experience the full horror of the Antichrist. The mark of the beast is a computer chip, implanted in the palm or forehead, identifying the followers of the Antichrist and allowing them to buy and sell. During this reign of terror, The Family will guide other true Christians to remain faithful and reject the mark until Jesus saves them. Having no roots in the Adventist tradition, The Family does not try to calculate the date of the Endtime but watches the signs of the times in the news and their own lives. How does it feel to expect the end of the world at any moment?

From the youth counterculture of the 1960s, the Children of God derived the value of liberation from society's unwholesome sexual inhibitions. For a decade beginning in the late 1970s, The Family included a sexual ministry among the ways that it communicated with love-starved potential converts, and today it continues to endorse erotic sharing among adult members, so long as no one is harmed. A central doctrine, the Law of Love, views sex as a beautiful gift from God that can be used sacrificially to express His love to others. More generally, the doctrine holds that acts performed in God's genuine love are good. What is the quality of family life, when love is not limited to marriage?

From the Holiness tradition, they derived the belief that a faithful Christian could have direct communication with the deity. From the death of his radio evangelist mother in 1968 until his own death in 1994, David Berg was the authoritative channel of God's words for the group. Subsequently, most members learned to receive messages from the spirit world, and they seek divine guidance whenever they face a difficult decision. How does a believer integrate constant prophecy into abiding faith?

Throughout its history, The Family has been the target of vicious attacks, chiefly from journalists and officials but often instigated by the local branch of the anticult movement. In 1978, for example, early hostile publicity about the group's sexual ministry triggered the brief arrest of several members in Mexico. From 1989 through 1993, a series of raids in Argentina, Australia, France, Spain, and other countries seized 600 of the group's children, often separating them from their parents for many weeks with the threat that they would be given up for adoption. But in each case, the authorities eventually dismissed charges of child abuse and returned the traumatized children. What is it like to be persecuted?

After an early period of celibacy when The Family was originally being formed, its acceptance of sexuality and its rejection of artificial birth control led to the birth of many children. Living entirely within the movement, largely being schooled at home, the second generation grew to adulthood with the difficult personal decision of remaining in the Army of God or defecting to conventional society. Whatever they may lack in book learning, those born and raised in The Family generally possess great skill in dealing with the immense practical challenges of a wandering missionary life, and most are quite capable of undertaking their own voyages of spiritual discovery. Can a radical religious group survive the death of its founder and the coming of a second generation?

For James Chancellor, the central question is, "Who are these people?" To answer this riddle, he invested much time, care, and energy developing familiarity with the group's culture and building trust with its members. His sensitivity was rewarded by many interviews in which members poured out their hearts and share often painful memories of their tumultuous histories. In the pages of this eloquent book, the Children of God reveal themselves to be profoundly religious people who have gone to the ends of the earth and the limits of human experience, as they believe, in the service of Jesus.

As a sociologist, I naturally wonder what the inherently fascinating story of The Family tells us about society and religion in general. It would be wrong to dismiss the group as merely one of the inconsequential residues of the radicalism of the 1960s. That colorful decade highlighted long-term trends, rather than being a fundamentally aberrant period. In every industrialized nation, a bundle of developments we call secularization—including science, cosmopolitanism, and bureaucracy—are eroding traditional religion. Two factors have minimized this trend in the United States. First, longstanding American religious freedom has encouraged the emergence of a vast array of competitive denominations, meeting the psychological needs of many social strata, and has helped religious traditions adapt to changing conditions. Second, successful superpowers develop implicit ideologies that strengthen them in their struggles against other powers, and by becoming the sole hyperpower on Earth, America has proven not only that it is a large and wealthy nation, but also that it has a greater cultural capacity to sustain belief than is possessed by the other major nations. However, America is not immune from secularism, and the dramatic collapse of faith in Europe is only more rapid and dramatic than the parallel erosion of faith in the United States.

Secularism does not herald the death of religion but its transformation. Weakness in the conventional, mainstream denominations encourages the emergence of sectarian religious movements that revive faith and renew commitment. In time, the most successful sects moderate into denominations, reduce their tension with the surrounding secular society, and unintentionally create the opportunity for new sects to arise. Thus over the centuries, the American religious economy has seen a circulation of movements, a balancing process of secularization and revival that leaves Christianity basically unchallenged as the primary supernatural tradition. It is possible to see The Family as one of the revival movements stimulated by secularization, returning to the early communal phase of the original Christian movement, and thereby contributing to the survival of faith.

However, extreme secularization unleashes religious creativity and the emergence of new religious traditions sometimes called cults. A cult is a small culture, noticeably different from the standard religious traditions of the society in which it arises. In social scientific terminology, a "cult" is by no means a harmful group but a culturally creative one. Because journalists and the anticult movement attach very negative connotations to the term "cult," many scholars prefer the neutral phrase "new religious movement," or "NRM." Whatever words we use, it is possible to see The Family as one of the more adventuresome of the culturally creative religious groups of the late twentieth century. Seen in this way, the group is a potentially healthy religious reaction to an advanced state of secularization.

But seen on its own terms, The Family is neither a sect nor a cult. Rather, it is a movement composed of living, feeling human beings who are willing to take great personal risks to fulfill the same values held by many more timid people in modern society. With conventional Christians, and especially conservative or Holiness Protestants, they share faith in the reality of God and they experience a direct personal relationship with Jesus Christ. Jesus does not tell them to work for a conventional bureaucracy all week and worship only for an hour each Sunday but to dedicate their entire lives to his service. With many humanists and cultural liberals, they share a general conviction that love between human beings is good and that sexuality can be a beautiful, pure channel for love. Missionaries that they are, they institutionalized nuclear family.

Taking some of the core values of Western civilization to their logical conclusions, members of The Family share sexual love within their movement, sometimes beyond its boundaries as part of their ministry, and they experience direct contact with the spirit world. Many readers may be understandably reluctant to agree that these features of Family culture have their roots in the larger culture of the Western world. But at the very least, all of us should be challenged to ponder whether we, ourselves, have given love sufficiently and are as open as we can be to experiences of the spirit.

This analysis is sociological, and I am not suggesting that James Chancellor endorses it. His aim is to document the history of the Children of God through their own experiences of life within The Family. Whatever intellectual context we readers may prefer to place around this fine book, we can gain immeasurably from reading it.

Acknowledgments

I owe a great debt of gratitude to Bruce Lawrence for his friendship, guidance, inspiration, and careful reading of my work. David Bromely and John Dever also gave thoughtful consideration, encouragement, and very helpful observations. Marsha Omanson corrected my grammar and pushed me to write as clearly as I can. I must thank the administration of Southern Seminary for their support during my research.

My family has been supportive and generous during the past five years. My wife, Donna, kept the home fires during my many months of field research. She consistently encouraged me to keep the manuscript accessible to "regular folks." This book is dedicated to her.

Most of all, I thank The Family. Noah and Claire have given a great deal of time and energy to this project. Maria and Peter Amsterdam trusted me with their Children. And I can never repay the debt I owe to the hundreds of disciples who poured out their hearts and lives to this stranger. They make up the portrait. If the image is out of focus or distorted, I can only apologize and say I did my best.

Introduction

The Children of God, now known as The Family, emerged in the late 1960s as the most controversial group to flow out of the Jesus People Movement. The call on young people to "forsake all" for the cause of Jesus by dropping out of conventional society elicited considerable response from concerned parents and the religious establishment. Their bitter denunciation of American cultural, economic, political, and religious values, and the confrontational style of the movement soon brought down the wrath of the secular and religious press. In 1971 a number of concerned parents banded together to form The Parent's Committee to Free Our Sons and Daughters from the Children of God, FREECOG. FREECOG was the first anticult organization in America. It began a legal and public relations campaign against the Children of God. David Brandt Berg,[1] founder of The Family, left the United States, and encouraged his followers to flee to more hospitable lands in Europe, Asia, and Latin America. Within three years, a substantial percentage of Father David's young disciples responded to this call. Those who remained went underground. The Children of God virtually disappeared from the American landscape.

In the late 1980s, the Children started to come home. The Family had gone through radical theological, organizational, and lifestyle changes. This small, North American countercultural movement had grown into a worldwide religious subculture of over ten thousand people. In the spring of 1993, I received an informational letter from The Family directed to academics interested in New Religious Movements. I made contact and was invited to visit a Family home in Washington, D.C., in the fall of 1993. On this first visit I met Noah,[2] who would

1. David Berg is known by several names within The Family: "Moses David" and "Father David" are the most common when speaking with outsiders. However, the internal term of reference by first-generation members is almost always "Dad," and "Grandpa" among the second generation. I will use "Father David."

2. Converts take "Bible names" and are generally known within The Family only by those names. Legal names are employed only for official use such as passports or drivers licenses. Members are free to change their Bible names, and many do.

prove to be a most valuable informant. Noah is one of several persons who assist in the interface between The Family and government agencies, the media, and the academic community. It was the beginning of a very productive relationship.

The next evening, Noah arranged a meeting with Peter Amsterdam and several other members of Father David's household.[3] We discussed a wide range of topics, but Peter was particularly interested in the possibilities for acceptance of The Family in the wider world of traditional Christianity. I offered little hope, but suggested a course of openness about the past and changes for the future. From my first encounter with the Children I departed intrigued and gifted with thousands of pages of Family literature, several audio- and videotapes, and a deep desire to know more.

Throughout 1994 I continued to visit Family communities, had a group of Family young people stay in my home, and began to talk with members about their life experiences. I also immersed myself in the scholarly literature on The Family, literature from the secular anticult and religious countercult movements, books and stories by hostile former members, and what seemed an endless stream of Family literature.[4] I began to see a gap. I envisioned an oral history of the movement from the perspective of persons who have chosen to remain loyal and committed disciples of Father David. I proposed the concept to Peter Amsterdam in early 1995. He offered his enthusiastic support and the promise of full cooperation from the highest level of Family leadership.

I devoted the major part of a sabbatical leave to The Family. I have visited over thirty homes in North America, Europe, and Asia, often staying for a week or more. I also had the opportunity to interview a significant number of Latin American disciples and several North Americans who spent their entire Family life in South America. I participated at virtually all levels of life in The Family including fund rais-

3. Peter Amsterdam was at that time second in command under Father David and Maria. Shortly after the death of Father David in October of 1994, Peter married Maria and now shares leadership with her.

4. For the perspective of generally hostile former members see Davis 1984; McMannus and Cooper 1980; and Williams 1998. For the anticult or countercult perspective see Enroth 1977; Hopkins 1977; Lynch 1990; and Patrick 1976. For academic study of The Family see Bozman 1998; Bromley and Newton 1994; Davis and Richardson 1976; Melton 1994; Millikan 1994; Palmer 1994), Richardson and Davis 1983; Shepherd and Lilliston 1994; Van Zandt 1991; Wallis 1976; Wallis 1981;Wallis 1987; Wangerin 1982; and Wright 1994.

ing, provisioning of food, social ministries, street witnessing, cafe singing, prayer meetings, Word studies, parties, fellowships, recreational activities, devotional meetings, and communion services. When possible, I did my share of cleaning, washing dishes, and other mundane duties necessary to keep the home running. I interacted with over one thousand disciples, formally interviewing at length over two hundred. I collected over 450 hours of audiotaped interviews and hundreds of pages of notes. With the exception of extensive interviews with Peter Amsterdam, this study avoids top-level leadership and concentrates on disciples at work in the field. The quest from the beginning was for "lived religion" in The Family—the everyday thinking and doing, the hopes and fears and dreams of the ordinary Child of God. I made every effort to gain as broad a perspective as possible, choosing informants from twenty-one nationalities who have served as Family missionaries in over eighty countries around the world.[5]

This work is an attempt to weave together the lives of a diverse group of people into a whole fabric. It is a cloth of many hues and colors. There are dark threads of suffering and pain and abuse, blended with the bright colors of joy and hope and the love of life. Since it is their journey, as much as possible, it is conveyed in their own words.[6] Chapter 1 provides a brief historical overview. This timeline will be

5. The relationship between academics and the adherents of New Religions has emerged as a contentious issue, particularly the acceptance by investigators of financial support or gifts. See Miller 1998, 8–15. Cognizant of this problem, I have maintained a very strict code of conduct with The Family. The Family has provided no financial support for this research, none. I have funded all of my travel and research expenses from sources outside The Family. Of course, I have stayed for months as a guest in Family homes around the world. In each visit, I left a "small donation" to cover the cost of my food and incidental expenses.

I have allowed Family representatives to read portions of the manuscript and have accepted their assistance in striving for historical accuracy. However, The Family has no financial investment in, and no editorial control over this work.

6. The Family has developed its own jargon. Distinctive terms will be explained when they first appear and are referenced in the glossary. I have edited the testimony of informants for redundancy, grammar, and syntax but have retained the language and tone as much as possible. On a few occasions I have merged the testimonies of closely related disciples when they offered complementary accounts of similar events.

The MO Letters are the primary authority of the movement. "MO" is short for Moses David, one of the various titles claimed by Father David. These letters were written by Father David and later by his consort and heir to the throne, Maria. They are viewed as divinely inspired and have authority equal to the Bible. The MO Letters are intended only for active disciples, but a few of them have been mass produced for use as evangelistic tools. The Letters are sent out on an individual basis to Family homes, then later gathered together and published in several volumes. These volumes are not generally available to anyone outside the movement.

useful as the story unfolds thematically rather than chronologically. Chapter 2 is the book of origins, exploring who these people were before joining and what motivated them to turn their backs on life as they knew it, "forsaking all" for the cause of Jesus and Father David. Chapter 3 focuses on the belief system that shapes and sustains life in The Family. There is no effort at theological evaluation of Family literature or the official Statement of Faith.[7] Rather, I have attempted to locate and explicate the essential theological and ideological commitments that bring focus and direction to the lives of the disciples. Chapter 4 explores the most distinctive and controversial dimension of the movement, "The Law of Love." Here I examine the shifting and evolving sexual ethos, the emergence of sexual allure as a means of proselytizing and financial support, and the most sensitive aspect of life in The Family, sexuality and children. Although I treat this topic at length in this chapter and reference it fully in other places, the intent is not to make this issue the central focus. Whereas sexuality is fundamental to Family identity, it is but one dimension of a complex corporate character. Chapter 5 focuses on the central aspects of life in The Family: religious experience, the missionary enterprise, and the life of faith. Chapter 6 deals with the cost of discipleship. Here we explore the emotional distress, physical hardship, and outright persecution that has often been a corollary of disciple life. Chapter 7 relates the life experience of Father David's grandchildren, the second generation who were born and raised as Children of God and have chosen to remain. The book closes with some brief reflections on the future of The Family.

Studying The Family

Religion is primarily discovered in the lives of religious people. The amassing, classification, and systematic analysis of religious data play a vital role in our effort to understand religious movements. But that mosaic must always include some consideration of how the data relate to the persons, what the institutions, symbols, doctrines, and rituals mean to those who are involved in the practice of religion. If under-

7. See Appendix A.

standing the personal quality of religious experience is the goal, we must somehow include adherents not only as informants, but also as interpreters. As Wilfred C. Smith has so clearly put it: "of the various ways of finding out what something means to a person, one is to ask him (1959, 40)." If we are to find the soul of faith, to discover the power of religious ideas, the depth and intensity of religious moods and motivations, and the complexities of the religiously centered life, then we must abandon an intellectual imperialism that denies faith adherents the right to interpret their own experiences.

This is no simple task. How does one immerse oneself in a religious community, seeing the world through the eyes of informants, while maintaining an "objective" view of things? How does one apprehend human religious experiences of an intensely personal nature and then translate those experiences into concepts that are accessible to those outside the community of faith? Psychoanalyst Heinz Kohut frames this issue in terms of "experience near" and "experience distant" concepts (Geertz 1983, 56–57). Experience near concepts are those that a religious informant naturally and effortlessly employs to define and communicate what she knows, sees, feels, and imagines. Experience distant concepts are those employed by an observer to enhance the understanding and apprehension of the world of the religious insider to a wider audience. "An openness to God's voice" is an experience near concept, whereas "religious system" is experience distant. Family disciples, though at times remarkably self-aware and self-critical, speak almost exclusively in experience near language.

My role is to play across the gap, to frame their religious discourse into a structure that is both coherent and meaningful to an outside world. Religious informants do not simply speak for themselves. I have attempted to be critically self-conscious of the manner in which my very presence and my framing of the issues might shape the responses of the disciples. Aware that the nature of questions posed can determine the results of any inquiry, I have approached the task with openness, patience, and genuine human sympathy. I have worked hard to help Family members find their own voices, then to blend those voices into a chorus that not only sings their song, but does so in a way that the wider audience can hear and understand.

The perception, selection, interpretation, and integration of those voices are conditioned by my values and my assumptions of the nature of knowledge and human experience. These assumptions and values are closely linked to my own identity. I am a seminary professor. More significant for this study, as a young man in the 1960s, I had a life-transforming encounter with Jesus of Nazareth. Though I spend considerable time peering through the "dark glass," this encounter remains at the heart of my own self-understanding. The trajectory of my life has been markedly different from the road Father David and his disciples have traveled. Yet, like the disciples, I speak the language of faith as an original tongue. This linguistic facility has enhanced my ability both to understand the disciples and to draw out the fuller story of their lives. Though shaped by my own values and my orientation as a historian of religion, I remain confident that what follows is a clear self-portrait of an intriguing and unique community.

Of course, two issues must be faced directly. First, is this the whole story? No, it is not. The complete "story" of The Family requires broader assessment and analysis of a wide range of other data by social scientists, as well as insight from the testimony not only of loyal members, but also of former members—both the relatively few hostile "career apostates" and the thousands of former Children of God who have little or no stake in the outcome.

The second is a much more difficult question. Is it true? In one sense, what follows is an attempt to construct a corporate autobiography. And perhaps George Bernard Shaw was right when he mused that all autobiographies are lies: not just omissions or exaggerations, but bold-faced and deliberate lies. It may be that everyone's personal history undergoes constant reconstruction. Also, from the earliest days in California, The Family has been a very closed and secretive community, holding most of their more extraordinary cards close to the vest. In the past few years, the organization has cautiously opened itself to academic inquiry. But tension between the Children and the outside world remains quite high. And given the pain and suffering from recent attacks, The Family leadership understandably would use every opportunity to paint as positive a picture as possible, and to minimize their vulnerability. Indeed, the first year of inquiry produced little beyond the public relations–oriented stories that are now available on the World Wide Web. After the top level of leadership authorized the study, however, the nature and quality of access shifted. And as I began to spend considerable periods of time living with the disciples, closets slowly began to open. Adults and young people alike found themselves with an opportunity to vent issues and episodes that had been consciously or subconsciously suppressed for years. Often, both the joy and the pain of old memories were thick in the air. The emotional intensity of many interviews is impossible to convey. One simply had to be there.

It may well be there are yet secrets of Family life hidden from this study. But, as I recently remarked to Peter Amsterdam, "What could they possibly be?" This work may not be the Whole Truth. Perhaps the Whole Truth of any religious community is simply unattainable. But what follows is an authentic story. It is their story.

Life in The Family

1. A History of The Family

The Family

The Children of God: 1968–1977

The life in The Family begins with David Brandt Berg. Born February 18, 1919, to itinerant evangelist Virginia Brandt Berg, by 1944 Berg had committed his life to full-time Christian ministry and had married Jane Miller. By 1951 he had four children. He was ordained to the ministry in the Christian and Missionary Alliance and spent twenty years in and out of various ministry positions, working a number of years for Rev. Fred Jordan with his *Church in the Home* radio and television program and Jordan's Soul Clinic training institutes.

Berg had several religious experiences that he interpreted as God's placing a special call on his life. He was to serve as a missionary to a lost and confused America, but not in the company or the pattern of the established churches. In 1966 he and his family left Jordan's Soul Clinic ranch and took to the road as an itinerant singing and evangelistic ministry. Along the way they added Arnold and Arthur Dietrich. By this time Father David had already begun to recede into the background as teacher and mentor, with the majority of public ministry and evangelistic witnessing falling to his children and new followers, now known as Teens for Christ. In early 1968 Father David and his extended "family" settled into Huntington Beach, California.

It was here that Berg grasped not only the vision for a new ministry, but also the initial insight for his grand role in God's Kingdom.

One dark night, as I walked the streets with those poor drugged and despairing hippies, God suddenly spoke to my heart and said, "Art thou willing to go to these lost sheep to become a king of these poor little beggars? They need a voice to speak for them, they need a shepherd to lead them, and they need the rod of My Word to guide them to the Light!" And that night I promised God that I would try to lead them and do everything I could to save them and win them to

1

*the Lord and lead them into His service. . . . They'd been churched to
death and preached to death and hounded to death by the System
and it hadn't done any good, so we just had to get out there and
somehow love'm back to life. ("I Will Set Up One Shepherd!" MO
Letter (hereafter ML) #1962, Jan. 1984)*

The Teens for Christ had been singing one night a week in the Light
Club, a Christian coffeehouse operated by Teen Challenge. They had
little success until, at the insistence of Father David, they discarded
their white shirts, ties, and three-piece matching outfits and began
dressing, talking, singing, and acting like the rebellious youth they
were attempting to reach. The first shot in the Jesus Revolution had
been fired. In no time the Light Club was full every night, and a good
number of young people were responding to the simple gospel message
of committing their lives to Jesus Christ as personal Savior. But Father
David's revolution was not only for Jesus. It was also against the
"System," the corrupt educational, political, economic, and religious
structures of contemporary American society that were soon to be con-
sumed by the full wrath of God. Those youth who received Jesus were
further challenged to "forsake all" by rejecting every tie to the evil
System, commit full-time as a disciple of Jesus on the model of the early church, and move in with Father David and his growing family.

By the spring of 1969 "Uncle Dave's Teens for Christ" now numbered almost fifty.[1] The growing antisystem rhetoric, aggressive evangelism on school campuses, and disruptive "church visitations" led to
considerable opposition and negative publicity. In April, acting on
prophecies that California faced imminent destruction, Father David
took his band of disciples on the road again. A young Pentecostal
church worker named Karen Zerby (Maria) joined up. She went to work
as Father David's secretary, and soon they began a sexual relationship.
In August of 1969 the majority of the group had settled temporarily at
a campground in the Laurentian Mountains in Canada. Here Father
David announced the foundation prophecy for the Children of God: "A

1. Statistical information comes from "The Family Key Statistics: 1968–1994,"
printed in an unpublished draft of "The Family History." This chapter is informed by
this unpublished document and extensive interviews with Peter Amsterdam and Noah.

Prophecy of God on the Old Church and the New Church" (ML #ħ, Aug. 1969). The old System Church had now been rejected by God in favor of His New Church, the Children of God. In conjunction with establishing this New Church, Father David also announced to his inner circle that he was ending his relationship with his Old Wife and taking Maria as his New Wife. Though Maria was to be far from Father David's only sexual partner, she remained unfalteringly loyal as wife and scribe. She gradually rose in stature within the movement, and eventually inherited the mantle of leadership upon Father David's death.

For the remainder of 1969 the Children traveled the eastern United States conducting sackcloth-and-ashes vigils, warning a corrupt and decadent America against impending doom. Father David organized the community into twelve tribes and established a hierarchy of leadership centered in his extended family. The disciples lived off the land, surviving on gifts from supportive family members, funds brought into the community when new disciples joined, and "provisioning" most food and necessities by direct appeal to the general public. By the time the COG (Children of God) settled on to Fred Jordan's Soul Clinic ranch in West Texas in February of 1970, they numbered nearly two hundred. In March of 1970 a second colony was established at Jordan's mission house in Los Angeles.

During this phase the basic patterns for COG life were established. Father David began to withdraw from direct contact with the disciples, guiding the community through his established leadership structure. The disciples settled into a routine of Bible memorization, Bible studies developed by Father David, provisioning, routine jobs to maintain community life, devotional and fellowship meetings, training in witnessing strategies, and witnessing ventures. After losing a power struggle with Father David, Fred Jordan evicted the COG from both his properties. This event facilitated the spread of the movement. By the end of 1971 some sixty-nine colonies had been established in the United States and Canada with almost fifteen hundred disciples.

The summer of 1971 also marked the beginning of FREECOG, the original anticult organization. The COG's strong antiestablishment rhetoric and demand that new disciples forsake all worldly possessions and ties to the system brought "blistering attacks from the religious press." FREECOG, started by concerned parents, began a propaganda campaign accusing the COG of criminal behavior such as kidnapping and drug use. Additionally, the COG was accused of psychological terror in the form of hypnotizing and "brainwashing" innocent young people. A number of parents attempted to kidnap their children and forcibly "deprogram" them. These attacks were met with a two-pronged response. On the one hand, Father David insisted that under-age youth must have legal authorization from parents or guardians before joining the community. In addition, some public relations efforts were made in an attempt to establish a more positive public persona. On the other hand, the Children became much more security conscious. Guards were established to protect the colonies from un-friendly visitors. Some colonies were designated "Selah" (secret). The attacks on the COG only exacerbated a fortress mentality that already laid heavy emphasis on the otherness of the outside world (Van Zandt 1991, 37–38).

In this formative period, Father David received two revelations that would dramatically shape the future of The Family. In December of 1970, while on a scouting mission for new colony sites in Europe and Israel, he recounts the following dream:

> I was praying about you and your needs there—your need of my help, supervision, and instruction, counsel, and leadership, and I became so burdened about your desires for me to return. . . . Suddenly I saw myself in a vision seated at a table with a pen in hand. . . . from my pen there shined rays of light in several directions. . . . And I'll never forget the peaceful, contented, happy, pleased look I had on my face. . . . While I was with you I could only be in one place at a time. . . . Now I'm equidistant from all of you and closer to all of you in spirit than ever before, with more pure light flowing from my pen by His Spirit, more light to lead and guide you than I have ever given you before. ("I Gotta Split!" ML #28, Dec. 1970)

From this point on, he withdrew from direct contact with most members, relying on written correspondence to the leadership to retain control and direction of the movement. Outside of the top level of leadership and his personal household, few of the some fifty thousand persons who passed through The Family ever had a personal encounter with Father David. He self-consciously channeled his charisma and authority through his correspondence, known as MO Letters. In "I Gotta Split!" Father David, for the first time, drew a direct parallel between his life and that of Jesus. In a very short time, the disciples begin to view the MO Letters as Scripture.

In the spring of 1972, Father David had a dream of mass destruction in the United States. In response, he urged his followers to flee America as soon as possible and to begin in earnest the missionary task of reaching the world for Jesus.

> The storm of God's judgments upon the ease and luxury of these nations, particularly America, is fast approaching. . . . God has warned us time and again . . . that His judgments were going to be soon poured out upon America, and we (the COG) should flee. . . . Those whose loyalty, love, faith, diligence and faithfulness has already been tried and proven and ready for new fields of battle, not those who just want to go along for the ride! ("The Great Escape!" ML #160, Apr. 1972)

By the end of 1972, missionary colonies had been established in much of Western Europe and Latin America, Australia, New Zealand, Japan, and India. The speed and level of response by the North American disciples demonstrate their strong level of loyalty and commitment to the COG, the degree to which Father David had established his charismatic authority through the Letters, and the effectiveness of the leadership structure.

With the migration out of North America, the overtly confrontational, antiestablishment component of the COG message dissipated. In part, this change was due to the new target populations of Europe and Latin America, where denunciation of American society as corrupt was hardly revolutionary. The change in posture also reflects the enlarged vision for a worldwide missionary enterprise. The shift is captured in an encounter with the World Council of Churches. It was the summer of 1972, and John was leader of the COG colony in Utrecht:

Sometime in the summer of 1972 I became aware of some kind of big meeting of the World Council of Churches there in Utrecht. We had a couple of disciples who had been with The Family back in the States. Someone came up with the idea of doing a sackcloth-and-ashes vigil against the WCC. I mean, who was more obviously the System Church? We all thought this was a great idea. We brought in the colony in Amsterdam. We really got into it. The girls got busy sewing our sackcloth robes and making warning scrolls, while the guys began to search the woods for staves. Word spread, and soon everybody wanted in on this thing. People from everywhere began showing up. A lot of top leadership came. It was really turning into a major production.

Somehow, Father David got wind of it. He sent us a letter. I can paraphrase: "Are you guys crazy? That meeting is filled with influential and powerful Christians from all over the world. We have a task to carry the message of Jesus to the whole world and there are lots of people at this meeting who could really help us do that. So don't make enemies out of these people, make friends."

Sort of took the wind out of our sails. But hey, we did what Dad said. We tossed away the sackcloth and staves, put on our best attitudes, and started going down to the meetings to help in any way we could. As usual, Dad was right. We made lots of important friends there, people who later helped us all over the world. And I don't remember hearing about any more vigils.

In 1973 Father David addressed two pressing problems within the COG. First, the explosive growth, rapid distribution, and overwhelming youth and inexperience of most disciples left the organization with serious leadership problems. He sought to slow the growth of the movement until adequate leaders could be developed. Second, though the evangelistic success of the COG was remarkable by any standard,[2] Father David saw that the effort would fall far short of reaching the entire world before The End. In June of 1973 he issued "Shiners?—or Shamers!" (ML #241).[3] Earlier he had urged disciples to move away

2. "The Family Key Statistics" reports that in 1972 the two thousand disciples personally led 142,503 people to receive Jesus as their Savior.

3. ML is the common abbreviation for MO Letter. Each is numbered for easy reference.

from direct personal witnessing toward distribution of COG literature, but many disciples did not respond well to this change. Peter Amsterdam recalled his experience: "It was really weird for me. For the first year and a half I was in The Family, we'd always said that we didn't work for money. We just trusted the Lord for income and witnessed."

"Shiners?—Or Shamers!" ordered the transition, establishing strict record keeping, quotas, and penalties for non-productive members. New disciples slowed to a trickle. By the end of 1973 more than 19 million pieces of literature had been distributed, mostly MO Letters carrying an End Time warning and a simple gospel message. The distribution of COG literature was termed "litnessing," and it quickly became the primary method of evangelism. Though disciples continued to witness personally where possible, "litnessing" became the primary task. Since the literature was exchanged for "a small donation," finances improved dramatically.

From the earliest days of "Teens for Christ," music had been a central aspect of Family life and witness. Almost every colony had disciples who played guitar and sang on the street as part of the witnessing strategy. Disciples have written hundreds of songs of protest, praise, and proclamation.[4] By 1974 several COG bands had achieved wide public acceptance. "Les Enfants de Dieu [the Chidren of God]," the French performance group, recorded a top-selling song in 1974. For several months, they appeared regularly on national television. Other groups in Latin America achieved a similar level of success. "Les Enfants de Dieu" and other COG singing troupes were common sights at pop and rock festivals across Western Europe. In addition, numerous discos, known as Poor Boy Clubs, were opened around the world. These clubs featured dancing, recorded and live music, and dramatic skits. They were an important means of witnessing and winning new disciples. Poor Boy Clubs foreshadowed the gradual shift in target away from the dropouts and toward the "up and outs" of society.

In 1975 Father David's dissatisfaction with the leadership structure reached a crisis point. The top level of leadership generally consisted of his extended family and a few long-term members. By this time, Father

---

4. A selection of Family songs is included in Appendix B.

David had developed an expanded sense of self. He was not only God's unique End Time Prophet, but King of God's New Nation. It appears that some top-level leadership began to chafe at this elevated status. In some cases they were not responding to his guidance and direction, or passing that direction down to the field colonies. By contrast, Father David was deeply concerned about the overly authoritarian approach of most leaders, and their general lack of concern for the welfare of the ordinary disciples. In the "New Revolution" of early 1975, Father David established a new "Chain of Cooperation." This new organizational format consisted of various levels of elected leadership, reaching all the way to the King. Some members of the Royal Family were given charge of special aspects of COG activity, providing them with substantial status and resources, but excluding them from direct control of the organization. However, the old guard retained primary authority over the movement. Most of the leadership under the Chain of Cooperation was appointed from the top rather than elected from the bottom. The Chain also functioned to further distance Father David from the vast majority of disciples. The Chain remained in place until 1978, and life for most of the ordinary disciples grew more difficult.

In the early 1970s Father David initiated the most significant and controversial dimension of his "Revolution for Jesus," a complete transformation of sexual ethos. Shortly after taking Maria as a second wife, Father David began having sexual encounters with other female disciples in his inner circle. By the early 1970s, the top level of leadership were following his example and experimenting with multiple partners. These activities were unknown to the vast majority of disciples, whose sexual mores continued to reflect the conservative Christian roots of the movement. But dramatic change was soon to come.

In late 1973 Father David and Maria began to frequent ballroom dance clubs for exercise and entertainment. Father David gave attention to the lonely persons they met and encouraged Maria to employ her feminine charms as a tool to "communicate the love of Jesus." She made friends with a young businessman named Arthur. Father David encouraged her to begin a sexual relationship with Arthur, making sure he understood fully that: "I'm loving you because God loves you! God wants me to show you how much He loves you and how much He cares for your needs" ("God's Only Law Is Love!" ML #537, Dec. 1973). Arthur was converted, joined, and remains a loyal disciple.

In March of 1974 Father David and Maria moved to the resort of Tenerife in the Canary Islands. He gathered a small group of trusted and attractive female disciples to begin a broader experiment in this new witnessing strategy, which he termed "Flirty Fishing," later shortened to "FFing." A series of MO Letters beginning with "The Flirty Little Fish" (ML #293, Jan. 1974) laid out the theoretical basis of this new direction. However, the Tenerife colony was "selah" (secret), and few field disciples were aware of the extent to which Father David was pushing the Flirty Fishing principles. In 1976 the "King Arthur's Nights" series came out. These Letters described the FFing of Maria and others in graphic detail, set the model for the larger community, and encouraged the disciples to begin this new "ministry." Slowly, a number of colonies throughout the world began to implement the new approach. But acceptance was by no means universal. Many disciples had strong reservations, and a significant but difficult to determine number left the movement.[5] A few of the leaders rejected Flirty Fishing and would not allow it under their jurisdiction. Other leaders viewed it as too dangerous or uncontrollable. They authorized the practice only for themselves or a few trusted followers.

Flirty Fishing marked some significant shifts. The hostile, confrontational approach was now gone forever, replaced by a strong emphasis on the love and compassion of Jesus. Additionally, the target audience had shifted almost completely away from the "hippies and dropouts" who were at the center of Father David's original vision. By 1978 a number of disciples had small children, and they began to employ those children in their witnessing endeavors. Almost all the children began singing and witnessing at a very early age, a practice that continues to the present. This strategy naturally led toward target au-

5. Significant numbers of children were being born into the COG at this time; the number of children increased from approximately 90 in 1971 to 1450 in 1977. Even though children counted as full-time members, the total number of disciples increased less than 300 in 1977, even as the number of persons led to receive Jesus as Savior skyrocketed to 1,259,927. It appears that at least in the early years, Flirty Fishing cost the COG far more disciples than it gained.

diences that appreciated and enjoyed children. The Children of God were coming of age. But the COG was also coming apart.

The Family of Love: 1978–1981

By the end of 1977, very serious problems were coming to the attention of Father David. A number of leaders in the Chain of Cooperation, including some members of Father David's immediate family, began to question his divine appointment as God's End Time Prophet. They also raised doubts regarding some of his teachings, particularly the radical shift in sexual mores. In addition, Father David became more aware of the extent to which many leaders were abusively authoritarian and were living in luxury by means of exorbitant taxes on field colonies. In January of 1978, Father David issued "Re-organization Nationalization Revolution" (ML #650, Jan. 1978). Known as the RNR, it is the most significant event in the history of The Family. The COG, as an organizational entity, was abolished. The Chain of Cooperation was totally dismantled, and some three hundred leaders were fired and ordered into the streets as ordinary disciples. Colonies, now termed homes, were to elect leaders who would be directly responsible to King David, who would establish a "very benign, liberal and loving dictatorship in which we are going to insist that the Colonies govern themselves!" The movement was renamed "The Family of Love." All those loyal to the King were welcome to remain.

Several key figures departed, including Deborah (Father David's oldest daughter). Timothy Concerned, his most trusted assistant, and Rachel, his most cherished disciple and consort, also left. Father David was deeply troubled by these losses. He became discouraged and depressed, and his discouragement led to alcoholism and serious health problems. He openly admitted his difficulties to his disciples. He would later reflect back on this time with sadness:

That was quite a blow when Rachel and Emanuele departed. Deb and Jeth had already departed, and a whole bunch of top leaders departed at the time of the RNR. I guess I got mad at the Lord and I said, "Well, Lord, if everybody else is going to quit, I might as well give up and quit too!"—and I drank too much. Lord forgive me, I was trying to drink myself to death. ("My Confession—I Was an Alcoholic!" ML #1406, summer 1982)

Membership fell in 1978, even with the birth of some six hundred children. After the Jonestown tragedy, King David anticipated a wave of "anticult hysteria" and issued the "Nationalize Reorganize Security-wise Revolution," the "NRS." Members were urged to go underground. A number of disciples returned to their homelands and blended back into the System. Many others "went mobile," traveling about in campers or caravans as itinerant missionaries. Most ceased to identify themselves publicly as Children of God. Their only direct connection to the movement was the MO Letters. Many disciples "infiltrated" the established churches, seeking opportunities to spread the message and to obtain financial support. By the end of 1979, the number of "souls won" plummeted by 80 percent from the high in 1977. Though the disciples continued to litness and witness, Flirty Fishing increased dramatically after the RNR. In some areas of Asia and Latin America, FFing became the primary means of witness and financial support.

In the years prior to the RNR, the sexual ethics of the COG grew increasingly liberal. The practice of multiple sexual partners (sharing) had filtered down from leadership to the colonies. In the RNR, Father David freed the disciples from any leadership constraints, and the "love bomb" exploded with full force. Sexual liaisons between members of each home and at interhome fellowships became common practice. As one disciple recalls: "I know of places where relationships started up within an hour of receiving the Letters."

In early 1979 The Family took a significant leap along this path. Father David had long held that sex was a beautiful, natural creation of God. In exploring how this principle might relate to children, he sent out Letters detailing his early childhood sexual experiences, the sexual curiosity and sexual education of Maria's three-year-old son Davidito, and directives for adults to allow children full freedom to express their natural sexual inclinations. Father David did not issue any clear instructions that mandated sexual contact between adults and children. However, from 1978 to 1983, he and the entire Family were exploring the outer limits of sexual freedom. Most disciples were aware that sexual contact between adults and children was occurring in the King's household. Some disciples interpreted certain MO Letters as encouraging sexual contact between children and allowing for sexual interplay of adults with minors. It is not possible to determine the extent or degree of this activity, but it was not merely a localized phenomenon.

Between 1978 and 1980, The Family was widely dispersed, with most disciples living in nuclear families. Many remained loyal, continuing to tithe and maintain contact through the Letters. Others slowly drifted away. The year 1980 saw the full-scale development of the *Music with Meaning* (MWM) radio shows. Father David commissioned his daughter Faith to spearhead a worldwide effort to develop quality radio programs that would reach millions of persons with the Family message. Production units were assembled in Greece, France, Thailand, and Puerto Rico. By 1983, Family radio shows were being broadcast on over thirteen hundred stations and *Music with Meaning* was receiving four thousand letters per week from responsive listeners.

By the end of 1980, The Family of Love had grown to almost eight thousand members. Dispersed throughout the world in small homes, most disciples were isolated from the larger community. In many areas of the world, disciples were out of touch with the sense of unity, sacrificial cooperation, and missionary zeal characteristic of the early years. In April of 1981, Father David initiated the "Fellowship Revolution" (ML #1001). Homes were ordered to begin weekly fellowship meetings with others in their area. A new hierarchical structure was established, consisting of local, district, area, national, and continental "Shepherds." These persons were elected. However, many individuals who held leadership positions in the old "Chain of Command" and had remained loyal after the purge of the RNR surfaced again as leaders in the new structure. The Fellowship Revolution also established "Combos" in each country, large homes that functioned as national headquarters. The Fellowship Revolution was accompanied by a renewed insistence that as many disciples as possible leave North America and Europe and move to the south and the east. The move was necessary to avoid a coming nuclear disaster and to bring the proclamation of salvation through Jesus to as many people as possible before The End.

The introduction of video equipment was another significant aspect of the Fellowship Revolution. In 1980, the *Music with Meaning* community in Greece recorded various aspects of their life and ministry and sent these videos to World Services. Father David, who had lived in seclusion for over ten years, was delighted to have this access to his "kids." He encouraged all the Homes to obtain video equipment and begin sharing a video record of their lives with him and other homes. Videos functioned to break down the isolation and played a significant role in pulling The Family back together.

In keeping with his desire to explore fully the limits of sexual freedom, Father David requested that MWM and other homes make "Love Videos," which would involve musical background and: "Our beautiful women could dance in a very artistic and soft and loving way. . . . I don't mean a lot of porn . . . any kind of porn, but just plain beautiful beauty and artistry just the way God made you in your natural beauty" ("Nudes Can Be Beautiful!" ML #1006, Mar. 1981). Numerous Love Videos were produced. They mostly consisted of women dancing topless or fully nude, often covered by a sheer veil. On rare occasions, younger girls would join in the dancing, usually topless and attempting to mimic the movements of their mothers.

Father David also offered a suggestion that some homes might film some romantic or erotic scenes between couples. MWM in Greece and a few other homes responded by producing videos that depicted sex acts between couples, usually men with women, but a few women with women. These more explicit videos were sent to Father David and circulated among some leadership homes. Most disciples were not involved. Some of these videos went beyond even Father David's spirit of sexual exploration. After seeing one of them, he wrote:

Sex can be ugly if you don't approach it from the right angle and in the right way, in the right spirit, and with the right know-how. Some places it's against the law to even have such materials in your possession, so it could endanger your family, and we don't want to hurt the Lord's work or you. So let's cancel those outright love-making sexual-act videos and let's put more emphasis on displaying the beauty and music and attire of our lovely women's dance videos, shall we.

("Glorify God in the Dance!—Caution & Importance for Your Erotic Videos!" ML #1026, July 1981)

By the mid 1980s, the novelty had worn off, and Maria was becoming more sensitive to the possible negative effects of these videos. In April of 1984 World Services put a number of restrictions on the dance videos. Within a few years the disciples were instructed to stop altogether and erase any of these recordings in their possession.

By the end of 1981, The Family of Love had begun to pull back together into a cohesive movement. A new leadership structure was in place, and large numbers of disciples were moving from marginal levels of involvement in North America and Europe toward greater unity and commitment on far-flung fields in Latin America, Africa, and Asia. Another significant transition overtook The Family. In 1971 there were 15 adults for every child. In 1981 there were 719 births, and the ratio had fallen to 1.3 adults per child. From this point on, children constituted the majority of members. The care, discipline, and education of children would soon require an increasingly significant portion of energy, time, and resources.

The Family: 1982–Present

From 1982 to 1984, The Family reordered itself back into a tightly knit organization. The disciples also began to renew the original vision of communal living. The average home size increased from four to ten. Disciples responded in significant numbers to Father David's warning of imminent nuclear disaster in the North and his call to carry the message of Jesus to the "Third World." By the end of 1982, 34 percent of the disciples were in Latin America and almost 40 percent in Asia.

In 1982 children became the majority of full-time members. The emphasis on sexual freedom combined with a strict policy against any form of birth control produced an annual birth rate of 75 per 1000 adults. The trend was obvious. The Family responded in several ways. Children began to play an even greater role in outreach ministries. An ever increasing amount of attention was given to child rearing and a substantial portion of the literature turned toward issues of family life and the care and education of the children. Most significantly, The Family began to see the youth as the hope of the future, the disciples who would carry the message to The End. There was no direct or conscious effort to de-emphasize the recruitment of new disciples from the outside, but this was the trend. New disciples did join, particularly in Asia. However, the total number of full-time members reached ten thousand in 1983 and hovered around that mark for the next ten years, despite averaging over 700 births per year. Many of the new disciples proved to be short term, and The Family began to lose more people than were joining through evangelism and recruitment.

In 1982 the children began to turn into teenagers. At that time, age twelve was considered entry into adulthood. Most parents had no experience with adolescents, had a good number of younger children to care for, and were busy in their work. Several "school homes" were established to care for the education and discipleship of the growing number of teens. These specialized homes established a trend that continued until the mid-1990s. The majority of young people spend most of their teen years apart from one or both of their parents.

In 1983, Father David received disturbing reports of misconduct at one of the teen homes. Word came of fights, vandalism, lying, and disrespect for adults. His response was quick and decisive.

> Belonging to this Family is a privilege and a blessing and an honor!—And anybody that dishonors this Family like that doesn't deserve to be a member. . . . Their parents ought to be ashamed.
>
> We are not going to have any kids or parents of that kind of kids who are going to reflect on the message we preach, the Jesus we are supposed to manifest. . . . Any more reports of such behavior, and that family is out—Excommunicated. Incorrigibles will be expelled from The Family. ("Teen Terrors!" ML #1512, May 1983)

This letter set the tone for the next decade. Teenagers were to be strictly guided, with high expectations for their personal conduct.

Though the disciples became more absorbed in child rearing and family responsibilities, evangelism was still the central focus. The primary outreach strategies remained personal witnessing, literature distribution, musical groups, and Flirty Fishing. In Asia and Latin America, a few homes experimented with large public evangelistic meetings. This method was successful, but Father David was not comfortable with mass evangelism. With the April 1983 Letter "Mass Evangelism," he moved the disciples back to the direct, personal approach.

Do we want to blow the whole thing by going so public that we offend the System and the scribes and the Pharisees and the Chief Priests and they go to the System and insist that they get rid of us! As far as I am concerned, the only safe, sound, permanent, effective, efficient and fruitful evangelism, is personal evangelism! ("Mass Evangelism!" ML #1510, Apr. 1983)

Flirty Fishing had been opened to all members and was strongly encouraged. By the early 1980s Flirty Fishing was widespread and becoming increasingly central to the life of many communities. "FFing" was originally envisioned and theologically justified as a witnessing strategy, a method of reaching persons who were not open to the message under any other circumstance. Family records indicate that from 1978 to 1983 an average of nine thousand persons a year were led to Jesus through FFing. Yet according to these same records, this number is only slightly more than 1 percent of the total conversions through Family witness. Flirty Fishing was not a useful tool to recruit new disciples. Very few male disciples were "FFed" into the movement. Though men were not as effective in FFing, they did participate and occasionally were able to bring in new female disciples. I have encountered only one man who was FFed into The Family.[6] Far more disciples were lost to the System as a result of Flirty Fishing than were ever gained.

Witnessing and disciple winning were by no means the only focus of Flirty Fishing. Even before 1978, FFing had become a primary source of financial support and political protection. Many female disciples established long-term relationships with wealthy or influential men. These men often provided money, food, clothing, housing, and other needs, including legal advice, help in immigration, and protection against social and political repression. It was not uncommon for some women to spend considerable amounts of time with their "fish," sometimes leav-

6. However, this disciple was quite a "catch." He was a director of an international manufacturing concern. He forsook all, and brought roughly $400,000 into The Family. This was the money that established the tape ministry in Latin America and the Video Ministry in Japan.

ing their husbands and children for weeks or months at a time. In some areas of Asia, Europe, and Latin America, female disciples went to work for escort services, providing sex for a fixed fee. Though conceding that escort service work (ESing) perhaps crossed the line, Family leadership insists that Flirty Fishing was not prostitution because the ultimate goal was always to bear witness or support the witness for Jesus.

Flirty Fishing was characteristic of growing sexual liberality and the increasing role that sexual activity was playing in Family life. After the RNR in 1978, FFing and sexual "sharing" were opened to all disciples. In the spring of 1980, Father David sent out "The Devil Hates Sex!— But God Loves It!" In his own iconoclastic and "revolutionary" style, Father David made very clear his view that the disciples served a "sexy God" and that God loved sex and wanted his Children to enjoy it fully "God made them male and female, not the Devil! God blessed them and said "Be fruitful and multiply!"—in other words, "Go to it, start fucking!—Right out here in the open, in public, in the Garden, on the grass" ("The Devil Hates Sex!—But God Loves It!" ML #999, May 1980).[7] Nudity and open sexuality became common features of life. Father David had spelled out the full implications of the "Law of Love"; anything done in love was above the law. Sexual sharing grew to the point where some Shepherds made out and posted "sharing schedules" on a weekly basis. But by 1983, problems were surfacing.

During the early 1980s, sexually transmitted diseases (STDs) began spreading through The Family. Flirty Fishing introduced STDs, and open sexuality resulted in widespread contamination. It was also common practice to have a considerable amount of sexual sharing at area fellowships, facilitating the spread of STDs from home to home. In March of 1983 Father David issued ML an MO letter, "Ban the Bomb!" (#1434). He halted sexual activities at area fellowships, restricted visiting leadership from sexual contact in the homes, and limited all sexual relationships to persons residing within the same home.[8] The signifi-

7. Father David's use of "earthy" language is a manifestation of his full rejection of System values and what he perceived as the hypocritical and evil approach of the conventional church to the issue of human sexuality.

8. Father David exempted himself from this rule, and top-level leadership also was exempt, using condoms to prevent the spread of disease.

cance of "Ban the Bomb!" goes beyond the control of STDs. It is the first point at which Family leaders began to face the negative spiritual consequences of unrestricted sexual freedom.

So, let's do a little sex-fasting at area fellowships! It's not going to hurt you, it'll keep your minds more on the Lord & off of the carnal & the flesh & more on the spiritual, which I think is far more important! . . . You'd get through the meeting in better shape & not so tired & not having to stay up so late every night! You'd get more rest & wouldn't become so totally exhausted & hardly able to even stay awake in the sessions! (Maria: That's true!) Let's keep our minds more on our main business of figuring how to evangelize the world . . . & not how to infect the world. ("Ban the Bomb!" ML #1434, Mar. 1983)

In December of 1984 Maria wrote "Sex for Babes?" (ML #1909). This Letter prohibited new members from any sexual encounters during their first six months. The pendulum of sexual freedom had reached its apex, and began the slow swing back toward a somewhat more conventional sexual ethos.

In 1984 two lasting changes in outreach strategy also occurred. In 1983 Father David had a vivid, futuristic dream of Heaven and the New Jerusalem, which he termed "Space City." Family artists produced a colorful poster of that vision with a message on the coming kingdom printed on the back. In 1984 a whole series of posters were produced for use as evangelistic tools. The posters have messages on the End Time, heaven, love, and peace written on the back. The message always closes with an appeal to the reader to pray and receive Jesus as Savior. Posters soon became a primary outreach tool, and as of 1996 more than 100 million had been distributed in over forty languages

Also in 1984, Maria commissioned the *Music with Meaning* home to produce a series of audiocassettes for the general public. The songs were appealing to a general audience, bearing themes of love and peace and hope and forgiveness. However, each tape closed with a direct appeal to receive Jesus. The tapes were an immense success and soon became a central focus of outreach. They were also an additional basis of financial support, distributed for "a small donation." The Family has produced scores of cassettes and CDs. Over 8 million copies have been distributed worldwide.

As The Family reconfigured toward a more tightly structured organization of large communal homes, problems developed. A number of disciples had lived independently for years, and in some places the level of conduct, spiritual life, and missionary commitment had fallen off considerably. Additionally, local and mid-level leadership began to take on more and more responsibility and authority. Many disciples still carried scars from the early years, and they were reluctant to be drawn back into a similar authoritarian environment. These were not idle fears. In 1985, World Services received reports of harsh and oppressive leadership practices in Japan and other areas. They responded with a flood of literature urging local and area leaders to carry out their duties as servants, dealing with disciples under their care with love and understanding. World Services, under the direction of Peter and Maria, conducted leadership conferences to establish a more caring and uniform leadership structure. In time, these conferences evolved into permanent training centers for leaders, teens, and adult disciples who needed help in regaining or maintaining the standards of Family life.

The Family was evolving and maturing, and so was the target pool of new disciples. Dropped-out, counterculture youth littering the beaches of California or the pop festivals of Europe were no longer the source for new members. In addition, almost all homes now included small children. Given their strong communal understanding, all adults are responsible for the care and direction of all children; parents were therefore becoming increasingly wary of inviting total strangers into their communities. As a result of these factors, Family homes began requiring a probationary period for prospective members. Six months was eventually established as a uniform policy. This probationary period allowed the potential new recruit to understand the nature of life in The Family, and also allowed the disciples to assess the quality and commitment of the new member. The probation period has gone a long way toward stabilizing community life and eliminating short-term, "flash in the pan" disciples.[9]

9. The Family, like most New Religious Movements, has not been successful in retaining members. Of the over forty thousand persons who joined from the outside, only about three thousand remain as full-time disciples.

Most of the disciples had responded to the call to go south and east. The only disciples remaining in Western Europe and North America were those unwilling or unable to go to the mission field. Most lived in small, scattered homes and had little oversight or direct communication with the leadership. In February of 1986, Father David commissioned several ambassadors to go to North America and Europe as "Searchers." After some success in Europe, the Searchers went to North America to recover the lost sheep. The quest was a success. According to Family sources, some two hundred former members rejoined, and many homes were rejuvenated. However, Father David still viewed North America as alien territory. The mission emphasis remained south and east. Between 1986 and 1987, over three hundred disciples left North America for Asia and Latin America.

Many of the returning disciples were teenagers who were considered in need of spiritual direction and training. In response, The Family established a Teen Training Camp (TTC) in Mexico, initially designed to run for June and July of 1986. The camp was so successful that it continued. Similar Teen Camps were established in South America and Asia.

In the early stages of the Teen Training Camps, several teenage girls related experiences of inappropriate and uninvited sexual contact with adult males. This problem was reported to World Services, and Maria responded. In August of 1986 she instructed the woman responsible for child care literature to write an official internal memorandum titled "Liberty or Stumblingblock." "Liberty or Stumblingblock" clearly defined the policy regarding sexual relationships between adults and minors:

> For the record, we want to say that we do not agree to adults having sexual contact with children. The Family should just not do it. Even though teen sex with adults may be tolerated in some countries, we are against it, as its fruit is more bad than good. Adults should refrain from any sexual involvement with all underage children and minors . . . it should be emphasized to our teens and children that they need do nothing against their will. They can always say, "No!"

However, this memorandum was not a MO Letter and did not come directly from Father David or Maria. The Prophet had repeatedly affirmed sex to be enjoyed as fully as possible. Pulling back from that total affirmation proved difficult. A short time later, adult sexual contact with minors was made an excommunicable offense, but as late as 1989 the problem still existed in some locations. In the fall of 1989, Maria issued "Flirty Little Teens, Beware!" Again, adult men and women were warned sternly that any sexual involvement with minors was not tolerated and would result in immediate excommunication. However the tension between the strong affirmation of sexuality and the necessity of restraint is evident:

There is nothing wrong with fighting against giving in to sexual desires if in some particular situation they're wrong. *Let's face it, sex is not something that's* always *good, clear across the board. Just because we promote sex & we believe God made it & that it's his wonderful creation doesn't mean that it's* always *good under* every *circumstance!* "All things are lawful, but all things are not expedient or edifying!"

I Cor. 10:23. *There are times when sex is not good!* . . . *one time when it's* definitely not *good is when it involves a* minor! . . . *you are going to have to be convinced that it's absolutely* not worth it *to get involved with these teen girls. The rules & penalties we've established should certainly help you! ("Flirty Little Teens, Beware!" ML #2590, Oct. 1989)*

The Family continued to place further limits on sexual expression. By the end of the decade, sexual activity among children or young teens was increasingly discouraged. Current policy forbids sexual intercourse between children under age sixteen. As might be expected, the policy is not uniformly obeyed by all teens, and sanctions are not severe. However, any adult sexual contact with a minor is now the most serious breach of Family rules. There are no excuses or mitigating circumstances. Any adult found to engage in such conduct is automatically excommunicated.

The year 1987 saw another major shift. Flirty Fishing had become central to the life of many disciples. In mid-1986 a former *Music with*

Meaning home located near a Philippine military installation was converted to a regular witnessing home. The disciples began witnessing to the men on the base. The women realized that FFing an entire military base would be an overwhelming task. With Maria's strong encouragement, they pulled back from Flirty Fishing and began normal personal witnessing and follow-up. They had remarkable success among the Philippine military, not only in the numbers converted, but also in follow-up ministries of spiritual training and Bible studies. "Daily Food" books were produced by the thousands for converts who could not commit to full-time discipleship. Great things were happening, without FFing. In March of 1987 Maria issued "The FFing / DFing Revolution" (ML #2313). This letter did not end FFing, but it did encourage the disciples to follow the example of the home in the Philippines.

By this point, Flirty Fishing had become problematic. Many homes were dependent on it, primarily by means of influential supporters developed through long-term relationships. Homes with quality FFers fared very well. Other homes struggled to get by, creating a class system that was inconsistent with communal values. However, the AIDS epidemic was the primary reason for stopping FFing. In the fall of 1987, a policy memo banned sexual contact with outsiders, except "close and well-known" friends who had long-term relationships with Family women. This policy is in force today. Any sexual contact with outsiders is now an excommunicable offense.

Flirty Fishing was halted, but it was never repudiated. On the contrary, most loyal adult disciples look back on that era with warm nostalgia. They still view Flirty Fishing as a proper and fruitful ministry for that time. They claim more than 113,000 persons were led to faith in Jesus through FFing witness, most of whom would not have been open to any other approach.

It is evident that the Children of God / The Family of Love / The Family exists in a state of almost constant change and evolution, if not revolution. The years of 1988 and 1989 were to witness even greater changes. In early 1988 Father David proclaimed the "School Vision." Education emerged as a top priority. Large school homes were established in all areas, with close to one-third of the Young Adult (YAs) and adult disciples involved in full-time teaching as their primary task.[10] The number of homes continued to drop and the average size increased sharply. By the end of 1989 there were almost a hundred school homes, serving over three thousand children. The Family poured resources and energy into developing curriculum and instructional tools. These efforts spawned a whole new ministry and means of support. Today The Family produces scores of very popular children's videos for the general public.

As the teens continued to gather in larger numbers, disruptive and destructive conduct increased. The Family responded with "Victor Programs," periods of intense discipline, Word study, work, and spiritual oversight. They defend the Victor Programs as mild compared to "System delinquent teen rehabilitation programs." Victor Programs became common, and in some places involved harsh and even abusive treatment of young people. Teens and Young Adults who stuck it out look back with mixed feelings on "Victors." Many older teens rebelled and left. By 1991, the program was expanded into the Discipleship Training Revolution (DTR), aimed at preparing the teens to be ready to take over the task of Family ministry in the future. After a few years, Maria found certain aspects of the program far too harsh, and she ended it. She apologized to the teens hurt most, and ordered the key adult leadership in the program to apologize personally to teens they had mistreated. Several of these adults were demoted and sanctioned.

Political change in India precipitated an even more dramatic shift. By 1987 India was the most fruitful mission field, with two thousand disciples. Most were North Americans or Europeans. Virtually all were on tourist visas or in the country illegally. In 1988, the Indian govern-

---

10. Through the 1970s and early 1980s, disciples were classified as children up to age 11 and adults at age 12. In the mid 1980s The Family developed closely defined age sets with clear distinctions in rights, responsibilities, and behavioral expectations. Today these categories are Infants, Toddlers, Young Children (YCs: ages 3–5), Middle Children (MCs: ages 6–8), Older Children (OCs: ages 9–11), Junior End Time Teens (JETTS: ages 12–13), Junior Teens (ages 14–15), Senior Teens (ages 16–17), Young Adults (YAs: ages 18–20), and Adults. With the coming of age of the older members of the second generation, a further distinction has been introduced: First Generation Adult (FGA) and Second Generation Adult (SGA).

ment clamped down, and many disciples were forced to leave. Father David had earlier predicted that the Great Tribulation would begin in 1989 and Jesus would return in 1993.[11] Knowing The End was near and persecution would greatly increase, he ordered the disciples in India to go home. By the end of 1989, over eight hundred disciples had returned from the East.

In anticipation of enhanced persecution, Father David ordered one other change, a change that ran counter to the very heart of discipleship since the earliest days of "Teens for Christ." Toward the end of 1987, the Prophet ordered a halt to street evangelism.

Things are really tightening up in many of our foreign fields today. . . . I suggest they (disciples) get off the streets and go strictly into inside witnessing . . . in fact I'm insisting, that you stop this wholesale street litnessing and witnessing! As far as I am concerned, the day of street witnessing and litnessing is past! Including busking. From now on my advice to you people worldwide is stay out of sight! ("Inside, Out of Sight! Get Off the Streets!—The No-More Sudden-Discipleship Revolution," ML #2385, Dec. 1987)

This letter had some impact on the style of evangelism, and also reflected a general tendency to look inward in order to get God's End Time Army ready for the final days.[12] The return of hundreds of battle-hardened missionaries from the East also pointed up again the disparity in the "standard" of Family life.[13] World Services found that a number of disciples in North America and Europe were:

very weak folks who continue to receive D.O. mailings simply because they tithe and supposedly remained reasonably loyal. However,

11. When this prediction was disconfirmed in 1993, Father David reminded his disciples that he had only predicted these events on the basis of his own interpretation of world events. He had not prophesied. All disciples who remain accept this explanation, but the distinction was lost on all but a few up to 1993.

12. Among the disciples, Father David's authority as God's End Time Prophet is absolute. To question Father David's authority is to leave The Family. Personal witness did drop substantially in 1988, but much of this attrition was due to massive relocation from "mission" fields and the growing emphasis on child care and schooling. Nonetheless, The Family reported over 9.5 million personal witnessing events in 1988. That is 826 for every man, woman, and child.

13. The term "standard" refers to the full range of expectations on a disciple including spiritual life, Word study, personal conduct, home cleanliness, separation from the System, and witnessing.

it has been reported that a number of these weak people spend much of their time sitting around drinking beer, smoking, criticizing the Family and murmuring, and in reality are only in the Family in name only! (WS Advisory, "Tightening up our Family," July 1989)

In an effort to create an End Time Army ready for the final tumult, World Services suspended all homes in North America and Europe until a visiting official could interview all adults and recertify the home. A new category of membership was established, TRF Supporter (TSer). These were persons who wished to remain connected to The Family, but were unable or unwilling to maintain the new standard of disciple life. "DO" (Disciples Only) was the term for fully committed disciples and homes. In 1989 almost fourteen hundred were "TSed." These people were invited to remain loyal by tithing and receiving general public literature. However, at this time, to be "TSed" was essentially to be kicked out. TSers could not receive DO literature and had no access to guidance or direction from Family leadership. Regular disciples were prohibited from direct contact with them. Many were TSed as family units, but there were a number of situations where husbands and wives were separated and parents were separated from their children. From 1989 to 1994, the total number of disciples remained at approximately twelve thousand. The percentage of those on TS status increased from approximately 10 to 25 percent. After 1993, the attitude toward TSers softened considerably. Currently termed "Fellow Members," they enjoy fellowship with DO homes and take a much more active role in support of Family objectives. It is not uncommon for disciples to move to Fellow Member status temporarily to handle personal issues, or simply to take a break from the rigors of DO life.[14]

With respect to the overriding mission, the most significant shift came in late 1989. A number of disciples had already begun to infiltrate China and Eastern Europe as short-term "tourists" or English-language teachers. Father David's New Year's Eve message "In Tune with the Times!" (ML #2602, January 1990) established Eastern Europe as the major mission field for the near future. The Family responded with typical enthusiasm. Hundreds of disciples now work in Eastern Europe, al-

14. In mid-1997, the nomenclature was changed. TS became Fellow Member (FM), and DO became Charter Member (CM).

1 as underground, unregistered missionaries. The young people
en most eager to respond to this challenge. In 1995 almost two
1 YAs left North America for the former Soviet Union and the
number continued to grow in 1996 and 1997.

Eastern Europe is fruitful territory. The Family has discovered a land that is similar to the initial environment of the 1960s COG. It is filled with disillusioned young people who have rejected their political, economic, and religious "system." The former Soviet Union is a harvest ground for new disciples. And the enthusiasm and willingness of the young people to take on the hardships and sacrifices of missionary life have rekindled the spirit of The Family.

Although all of these changes had long-term consequences, the most significant change was also the most subtle. By the end of the 1980s, Father David was nearing age seventy. His health and energy level were failing. Throughout the 1980s Maria was emerging as a more prominent figure, taking on ever greater roles and producing an increasing percentage of the MO Letters. The Prophet essentially retired at the end of 1988. For all practical purposes, Maria assumed the role of spiritual leader and guide for the movement. Apollos, a highly trusted and long-term member of the inner circle, had become the primary theologian. Peter Amsterdam took over administrative control of The Family. This new situation was never formalized or announced. Few disciples were conscious of the change, though all knew that Father David was developing Maria, allowing her greater latitude and authority.

In October of 1994, David Brandt Berg passed away. He had predicted that he would die before the Great Tribulation and the Second Coming of Jesus. Shortly after his death, Peter and Maria were "mated."[15] They now lead as a married team. However, consistent with the belief in the active relationship between the earthly realm and the spirit world, Father David still speaks regularly and guides The Family from heaven.

While these various internal changes worked together to reconfigure the community once again, forces from the outside fostered a signifi-

15. Shortly after Peter arrived at Father David's home in the late 1970s he began working closely with Maria. In time, they developed a romantic relationship. Father David was "generous" regarding the relationship between Peter and Maria, and both Father David and Peter enjoyed a wide range of sexual partners.

cant shift in the late 1980s and early 1990s. From the earliest days of the COG, the disciples had faced strong and often hostile opposition. Attacks came from parents, religious leaders, police and political authorities, the media, and most of all from the professional anticult industry. Given their insular nature and millennial ideology, The Famiy interpreted virtually all opposition as religious persecution. The disciples have been vilified in the media. They have been harassed, kidnapped, assaulted, and even bombed by religious opponents. They have been followed, intimidated, arrested, and imprisoned by law enforcement authorities. For the most part, the persecution related to their radical commitment, unconventional sexual ethics, opposition to the System, and ever present public witness. In general, they maintained a nonconfrontational response to these attacks. When persecution came, they suffered the immediate consequences, sought the assistance of "friends," went underground where possible, or moved on to more safe and receptive fields. But everything changed in 1988 when the media, the anticult network, a disgruntled ex-member, and the U.S. State Department combined to take opposition to a new and far more dangerous level. The target shifted from the disciples to their children.

Richard and Vivian Shillander were American disciples serving in Thailand. Vivian Shillander voluntarily left The Family and took the youngest of their five children with her. According to Family sources, she signed a power of attorney at the U.S. Embassy in Bangkok that gave custody of the four children who remained in Thailand to her husband. In 1988, Vivian Shillander came into contact with the anticult movement. Assisted by two "private detectives" and financed by the ABC television network program 20/20, she returned to Thailand. With the assistance of the U.S. Embassy, she forcibly abducted her four older children. Cameras for 20/20 recorded the whole event as a *Mission Impossible* style rescue, even while the terrified children, ages seven to thirteen, tearfully begged to remain with their father.[16]

The Shillander affair was an omen of things to come. Over the next

16. The event was aired on ABC's news program 20/20 in 1988. Shillander left The Family in Thailand and, with his Thai wife, went to South Dakota to be near his children. He got a job and a lawyer. After seven years of struggle, he won custody of his three older children. He remains loyal to The Family. These events were not reported by ABC News.

six years persons associated with the anticult movement, supported by testimony from a number of ex-members, laid charges of child abuse and sexual molestation against The Family in Europe, Australia, and South America. The incident in Spain reflects the general nature of these events. According to Family sources, several ex-members, in co-operation with Spanish anticult groups and the Barcelona Bishops Conference, laid charges of child sexual abuse with the Catalonian police. After several months of intense surveillance, but no investigation by appropriate social services authorities, the Barcelona Family home was raided in July of 1990. The adults were arrested, then released. However, 22 children, ages 1 to 14 years, were held in institutions for 11 months. According to Family sources, during their incarceration, Dr. José M. Jansa, a dermatologist with close ties to the Spanish anti-cult group ProJuventud, posed as a psychiatrist and was allowed frequent access to the children. Rather than determine the extent of abuse, Dr. Jansa attempted to "deprogram" the children. When that failed, he submitted false psychiatric reports to the court. All the children were eventually returned to their parents, and all adults were cleared of all charges. The presiding judge described the actions of the government as "reminiscent of the Inquisitions."[17]

In the fall of 1992 there unfolded a most remarkable series of events that demonstrates the hostility of some former disciples, and the extent to which the secular anticult movement will go to destroy unconventional religious groups. According to Family sources, two ex-members, Edward Priebe and Daniel Welsh, attempted to infiltrate and take over the only remaining Family home in the Philippine Islands. Mr. Priebe and Mr. Welsh were aided and financed by anticult groups in the United States and assisted by persons with the Manila office of the evangelical Christian group "Youth With a Mission" (YWAM). Mr. Welsh called the home, impersonating Father David and advising the

17. The sometimes humorous, most often terrifying and traumatic experiences of adults and children who have suffered harassment, assaults, arrests, and even torture in England, France, China, India, Mexico, Argentina, and the United States are presented in later chapters. For a fuller account of the legal cases brought against The Family in the past 6 years, see Moorman Oliver, Jr. (Santa Barbara County Sheriff's Department, retired), "The Inquisition Revisited," in Lewis and Melton 1994, 137–52. For a short but penetrating analysis of the anticult industry and the use of child abuse charges as a tool of antireligious repression, see George Robertson, "Island Pond Raids Begins New Pattern," 153–58 in the same volume.

home that he would be sending a special representative. Priebe and Welsh persuaded the shepherds to attend a special meeting in the United States. Then, according to Priebe's own journal, he planned to dethrone Father David and convert the disciples to his interpretation of Scripture and vision for The Family. Priebe apparently anticipated that the Philippine government would establish camps where disciples from all over Asia could be brought and held while he reprogrammed them. Family leadership in Asia got wind of this situation, came to the Philippines, and confronted Priebe and Welsh. Then they called the police. Taken into custody for questioning, then released pending further investigation, Priebe and Welsh fled the country.

This episode would have passed as just one among hundreds of bizarre events in the history of a most extraordinary people. However, Ed Priebe located a storage facility that contained numerous video and audio master recordings. Mr. Priebe stole several trunks of these tapes and shipped them to a fellow anticult activist in California, Sam Ajimian. After an investigation by Philippine authorities, arrest warrants were issued for Priebe and Welsh on charges of fraud and grand theft. Those warrants are still active.

Several locally produced "Love Videos" were among the items stolen. These were home videos of Family women and young girls dancing semi-nude. All "Love Videos" had been ordered erased, but these had been tucked away in the archives and escaped detection until discovered by Mr. Priebe. These tapes were edited, then reproduced and offered to authorities and anticult activists for use against The Family. In 1993 Priebe took a copy of one "Love Video" to Argentina, where it was used to justify police raids and long-term incarceration of Family adults and children.[18] The dance video was planted in one home, then made public by the Argentine authorities as evidence of child abuse. The tape was released to the international media, and portions were shown on television all across South America, Europe, the United States, and Canada.[19]

18. Details of this most repressive attack on The Family are given later in this work in the life experiences of adults and children who went through it.

19. In a later chapter, one of the women who danced on videos made in the Philippines, and whose young daughter also participated, describes the impact that broad public exposure of these old, private videos had on her family.

The various attempts to take away the children dramatically changed the way The Family related to the outside world. Shortly after the Shillander affair, Father David instructed the disciples to stand and fight for their children. Disciples all over the world began active protests against the governments that were attacking their communities. Forthright public relations campaigns were undertaken. In several areas of potential concern, The Family took preemptive measures, inviting in law enforcement and social services agencies to conduct investigations of the care, welfare, and education of the children. In addition, World Services made a conscious decision to open their communities to legitimate scholarly inquiry, confident they had nothing to hide.

However, the event that most rocked The Family was far less sensational or dramatic. In 1993 a wealthy English widow, whose adult daughter had found Jesus and joined while on a religious quest in Nepal, filed suit in British High Court, seeking custody of the daughter's infant son. Child welfare agencies had determined that the child had not been abused and was in a safe environment. But, the judge determined that his decision would not be based on the actual circumstances of the child in question. Rather, he began a thorough and comprehensive judicial evaluation of Family history, ideology, and moral conduct in order to determine if the child faced any potential danger as a member of this particular religious community. The anticult establishment came full force into the proceedings, and the woman pursuing custody of her grandson had substantial resources to invest. The case lasted almost three years.

In the end, the judge granted care and control of the child to his mother; the boy remains in The Family. Yet through the long proceedings, Family leadership was repeatedly required to come to terms with the past; to explain a number of passages in their literature that did seem to condone sexual contact with minors; to respond to the testimony of numerous former members who had been mistreated and abused. In essence, this case forced open the closet doors. And in the midst of the whole painful process, Father David died.

In late 1995, as part of the requirements to close out the case, Peter Amsterdam wrote a letter to the judge. The letter openly admitted the policies and practices of The Family had, in some instances, been harmful. The letter went on to identify some writings of Father David as a root cause of some of this destructive behavior. To that extent, Father David had been wrong.

However, The Family has resolutely and successfully defended itself against all charges of current sexual misconduct with minors or any form of child abuse or neglect. Worldwide, over six hundred children have been removed from their homes and examined by court-appointed experts. These experts have detected no abused children, and not one child has been legally removed from the custody of his or her parents. Of the hundreds of adults accused, arrested, and put through judicial proceedings, not one has been found guilty of any misconduct.

Still, at the very time when persecution by the System was most severe and the internal focus on discipline and winnowing out of marginal disciples most intense, many of the harder edges in The Family's stance toward the outside softened. In the 1980s, the movement went through a rough-and-tumble process of maturation. In the 1990s, The Family has begun to mellow.

From the beginning of the movement, Father David set himself and his followers against the church, "the god damned, hypocritical, idol worshipping, churchianity of the System." In November of 1991, he published "Go to the Churches" (ML #2867), encouraging disciples to visit and perhaps even fellowship with open-minded congregations.[20] More significantly, he encouraged the disciples to direct their many converts to Jesus toward local churches for care and training in the Christian life.

Father David had always fostered a very negative view of disciples who deserted the movement and went back into the System, "like dogs returning to their vomit." But in the late 1980s and early 1990s, more and more teens were leaving. In most cases their parents wished to maintain a good relationship with these departing children. Maria helped The Family see that leaving might well be the appropriate ac-

20. By and large, the disciples have not found this an easy task. Most churches that are "open-minded" enough to accept the peculiarities of the Children have no interest in their enthusiastic evangelism or spirited worship style. Those more evangelical churches that do resonate with The Family mission and witness react strongly against the prophethood of Father David and Maria, their view of the spirit world, and most adamantly against their unconventional sexual ethic.

tion. In addition, testimony by a number of ex-members in various trials and hearings forced Family leadership to face the fact that many people left the movement for very good reasons.

From 1994 on, The Family has committed to a "Ministry of Reconciliation." As Peter Amsterdam sees it: "We know that many people were mistreated and hurt by things The Family did, particularly the leadership. That was never Father David's intent, but it happened. We cannot undo those things. But we can try to find as many as we can and to let them know we are deeply sorry. And also that we have changed. We have learned from our mistakes." Over the past several years, Family leaders have attempted to reach out to ex-members around the world in an effort to heal old wounds and establish friendly relationships where possible.

Another significant shift came with Father David's 1991 New Year's message, "Consider the Poor" (ML #2755). He directed the disciples to begin helping the poor and the helpless, "like Jesus did." Almost immediately, the disciples responded by providing aid and comfort to the homeless in the United States and responding in disaster relief all over the world, particularly to refugees in Eastern Europe and Southeast Asia. Disciples started ministries to prisons, street gangs, illegal aliens, unwed mothers, drug addicts, and abused children all over the world. "Consider the Poor" has taken root very quickly. It is now one of the central ministries, but always tied as closely as possible with a direct, personal witness for Jesus.

In keeping with Family theology, Father David now resides in the Spirit World with Jesus. He communicates directly through prophetic experiences of Maria, Peter, and other World Services leaders. The transition of earthly authority had been ongoing for a number of years, and his mantle fell easily on Maria and her consort, Peter Amsterdam. Father David predicted he would die before the Great Tribulation; his death stands as one more sign that The End is near. It is still too early to evaluate the full impact of Father David's passing. In the short term, his "kids" have not skipped a beat. Membership remained stable. In terms of ministry, witness, and souls saved, 1995 through 1997 were the most successful years in Family history.

Although the transition from Father David to Maria went quite smoothly, The Family changed dramatically in 1995. World Services published and implemented the "Charter of Rights and Responsibilities," known as "The Love Charter," or simply "The Charter." The Charter contains the basic beliefs and details the fundamental rights and responsibilities of the disciples, as well as the rules and guidelines for communal life. World Services retains overall authority, but day-to-day life is far more democratic. The disciples are strongly encouraged to live "according to their own faith" with a minimum of supervision and direction from the leadership structure. Smaller home size is mandated, and most significantly, disciples have the absolute right of mobility.

The Charter is the latest cycle in the ongoing revolution that is The Children of God. But what is this revolution really about? Asked that question, the disciples invariably point to the numbers. In the years since David Berg first took his Teens for Christ to the streets and beaches of Southern California, the Children claim to have distributed almost 850 million pieces of literature, personally witnessed to over 250 million people in 167 different countries, and personally led over 23 million people to pray and receive Jesus as their personal Savior. That is approximately one person every forty-five seconds, for thirty years.

But the heart of this unique religious movement does not lie in the numbers. Nor is it located in a chronicle of events or set of theological and ideological formulations. The play is the thing. And to know The Family we must turn to the players. Who are these people? Who were they and what transformed them into Children of God? What are the core beliefs that guide and sustain their lives? How have they lived and loved and suffered together these thirty years? What do they pray for, hope for? How do they understand God to be at work in their daily lives? What does it mean to be one of Father David's disciples? No historian or social scientist can really answer those questions. The Children alone can tell us. They have decided to do so.

2. Becoming a Child of God

We open their story at the point at which individuals enter into the community. Over the last thirty years, millions of persons encountered the Children of God, hearing their warning of the End Time and their petition to receive Jesus as Savior. Hundreds of thousands have been challenged to "forsake all," abandon the "System," and commit fully to life in The Family. Many thousands from all over the world took the challenge. Only a small percentage have sustained that initial commitment over the high peaks and dark valleys that mark The Family journey.

Who are these people, Father David's loyal disciples? Who were they? What made them so willing to turn their backs on their former lives, their education, careers, friends and families? What did they leave behind, and what were they seeking? And above all, why the Children of God? What transformed them into Father David's Children?

One popular assumption about New Religious Movements, or "cults," is that persons drawn to these groups are easily manipulated, lack intelligence, or suffer some form of character disorder. It is widely assumed that anyone who would submit to the direction or control of a person like Father David must have some basic personality defect. These assumptions do not mesh with my experience. The wide range of personalities, backgrounds, and life experiences of members rightly discourage any attempt to formulate a description of a "typical" disciple.

Disciples are not weak-minded or simple people. Though less broadly educated than the general population of North America, they are thoughtful persons who have made, and continue to make, conscious choices about their lives. They do tend to filter information and experience through a uniform and well-defined interpretive grid, but hardly more so than persons deeply committed to other religious traditions, or for that matter to the labor movement or to the Republican Party. A limited number of interviews with the parents of long-term members, most of whom were less than enthusiastic about Father David or The Family, were conducted. In each case, these parents described the member as their most capable and strongest child, the one they most expected to succeed in life.[1]

One approach to the questions of who would join such a movement and why, and I think an invaluable approach, is to seek out the disciples' own self-understanding. Of course, this approach requires some caution. There is the well-established tendency for all people to value positively the choices made, and value negatively choices rejected. Furthermore, the telling and retelling of one's conversion experience and decision to join is common parlance. Certainly time and ideology have shaped and reshaped the memory and the recounting of the testimony. But in most cases, with patience and persistence, I was able to find my way behind the stock formulations. Over six hundred disciples offered a distinct experience, his or her own story. Yet several predominant themes do mark off a general pattern.

The first aspect of this broad profile is a shallowness in meaningful personal relationships. Most potential recruits were not particularly close to family or friends. The disciples generally recall themselves as lonely people. Most recounted feelings of disconnectedness. They almost always coupled this sense of otherness with disappointment in the present and a lack of hope for the future. Virtually all disciples viewed their prior lives as marginal and filled with discontent. But they were not passive in their discontent. The most common term of self-reference was "searching." It may be that we all search to some extent, but most potential disciples were active searchers. They recall either ardently reading and researching religious or philosophical literature, or literally being on the road, looking for someone or something to give their lives meaning and direction.

Second, but of first priority to the disciples, they joined to follow Jesus. The Children of God began as Jesus People, and they have remained firmly and self-consciously committed to that original vision. Every person linked his or her movement into The Family directly to a

1. This finding is consistent with other research. See David Millikan, "The Children of God, Family of Love, The Family," in Lewis and Melton 1994, 190.

call of God to serve Jesus as fully and completely as possible. The Children often cited the biblical model of the early church as a basis for their decision to join. Most have vivid memories of a religious experience or clear spiritual guidance that influenced or confirmed that decision.

The third generally viable observation about the joining experience concerns the immediate context of the decision. Neither Father David nor ideology appears to have been a primary factor. Most people knew little of Father David at the beginning, and a few joined in spite of him. By and large, new disciples did not decide to follow a guru or spiritual leader. Most were aware of the wider community and its rejection of the conventional church. This lack of identity with socially accepted religion was often an attractive feature. However, only a very few persons made any effort to research the history or basic beliefs of the group prior to joining. Clearly, the primary motivation was not to affiliate with a movement or an organization. Rather, new disciples committed to an immediate community of people with whom they experienced love, acceptance, excitement, a sense of worth, and a challenge to pursue what they perceived to be God's highest calling.

I have selected nine stories that broadly represent the wide spectrum of life in The Family. The experiences of those whose stories are recounted span five continents and represent a broad cultural and ethnic diversity. The stories fall into two categories, those of people with significant Christian background before joining, and those of people whose commitment to Jesus and The Family were virtually a unified experience.

We pick up our story once again in 1966, several years before the birth of the Children of God. David Berg and his family are traveling the American South. He has yet to break fully with conventional Christianity. The small band sustains itself by presenting musical programs to various churches and Christian organizations. And a teenage Southern Baptist girl in Florida is waiting for them. Lydia was raised in a solidly Christian home and up to age fifteen had fit in fully with the "church crowd." Then things began to change.

I began to have real questions of what Christianity was. The only thing I knew was my church.[2] I was confused and searching. I made a

decision to switch over and join the "bad crowd." My attitude and
behavior seemed to cause more problems between my folks. My
mother threatened to send me to a girls' home. So, I tried suicide,
drug overdose. Almost did it.[2]

When I tried to kill myself, I apologized to God. I prayed, "God, if
you are really real, I'll give you my whole life, I'll dedicate everything.
But I have to know that you're real." Then my mom told me she was
going to take me to hear a group called The Bergs. It's funny now. I
thought she said "The Birds." You know, the rock group. So I say,
"sure."

At the meeting they tell everyone how they are going out into the
streets, beaches, and reaching teenagers for Jesus. Caleb had been in
a gang and on drugs. I had just read Cross and the Switchblade. *It*
was like that book had come alive. *I met with Faith after the meeting*
(Father David was not even there) and told her about a friend in
Texas they should see. She looked straight at me and said, "What
about you?" I said that I had no talents, couldn't sing or play guitar,
or anything. She replied, "The best ability is availability. You make
yourself available and God will use you." She prayed with me and I
went home. I really wanted to see them again, but there was no ad-
dress, no phone number.

Anyway, the next day is Sunday and they show up in my Sunday
school class. I invited them home and three of them stayed with our

2. It is impossible to capture these oral statements on paper. Tone, volume, facial
expressions, and physical gestures all add to or qualify the meaning of what is said. I
will use a few stylistic forms in an effort to recapture the "feel" of the conversations.
Informants' statements quoting themselves or other sources will be in double quotation
marks. Statements that come across as asides, or explanatory interjections will be
placed in parentheses. Words or statements given with considerable emphasis or emotion will be in roman type. Statements made in jest or with humorous intent will be so
indicated by my observation. At times I will make an observation regarding the context
of the testimony. I will place these observations in brackets, for instance [at this point
she began to cry] or [said in jest]. When required, my part of the conversations will also
be in brackets. Additionally, I will attempt to punctuate in a way that will give the
proper flow and tempo to these oral statements. Family literature often employs underlining or bold print for emphasis, which will appear in roman. Father David also developed his own distinctive grammar and spelling, which is retained in the quoted texts.
Disciples normally take a different name when entering the movement. They are also
free to change their Family name and many do. Informants will be identified by placing
a Family name in parenthesis after their statement. These names will be drawn from
typical Family names. With the exception of Peter Amsterdam, they will not be the actual names of the informants.

family for several weeks. The more I was with them, the more real they were. And no one had to tell them what to do. Faith was fifteen, Caleb and Hosea seventeen, and they organized everything themselves.

Soon I just started going out with them. They took their guitars, sang on the street, just talked to people. I wanted to do what they were doing. I had four months left to finish high school, but I asked my parents if I could go with them. No Way! I told the kids I wanted to join them. They were OK with it for the summer, kind of give it a try, but only with my parents' permission. I had met Dad [Father David] prior to this, but not had much contact with him. It was the kids I wanted to join with.

My mother really understood. So they were leaving. That morning my mother comes to my room and says, "You're not going to school. The group is leaving and you're going with them." Now I'm on the spot. I prayed and opened my Bible again. I looked down and read this verse, "Blessed is he that readeth and they that hear the word of this prophecy and keep those things which are written therein, for the time is at hand." I knew that verse was for me, and I needed to go. So I left with them. I joined them on February 15, 1967.

I was the first female disciple to join. But that's how it is looking back now, "the first female disciple." [laughs] At the time, I wasn't joining anything. When we would go out and meet people, there was no idea at all that we were starting any kind of movement. We were just witnessing. Because we saw that kids were coming off drugs and were finding the Lord, we wanted to continue to do it.

Lydia reflects tendencies among certain Christian young people who found The Children of God an attractive alternative to conventional church life. As the 1960s came to a close, waves of social discontent, shifting values, youthful idealism, and radical opposition to "the establishment" began to lap at the doors of the church. The institutional church responded with a wide range of strategies and programs aimed at retaining the loyalty of the youth. This attempt at accommodation with the 1960s generation went across the full denominational spectrum in America. However, conservative, evangelical and fundamentalist churches struggled deeply, particularly over the challenge to "American values."

Throughout the late 1960s and early 1970s, large numbers of Christian young people turned their backs on the established church and sought fulfillment of their hopes and dreams elsewhere. Some found The Children of God. Miriam is one of those. She was raised a Baptist and considered herself to be a "good church girl."

In 1969 my husband was in the Air Force in Florida. It was the time of the Flower Children. We were into that in a lot of ways. I mean, I carried my Bible everywhere. But we were also very much getting into the back-to-nature, back-to-our-Creator kind of thing. We were really against materialism, you know, the American Dream and all that. So I guess you could say we sort of got into the hippie movement, as much as you can when your husband is still in the military and you work for an insurance company! [laughs] At church we were not accepted very well. We dressed different, dressed funny for them. You know, long hair, no makeup, bare feet.

John had a friend he did drugs with. He got out of the Air Force and left Florida, just wandering, hitchhiking somewhere. He met some kids from The Family, got saved, and joined. He wrote to John and told him all about it. He said they were not like other Christians he knew anything about.

John went to visit. When he came back, he was so excited. He had prayed to receive the Holy Spirit, and now he was saying, "This is it, this is what I want to dedicate my life to." I really had trouble relating to it all at first. He could hardly explain it to me himself. That was our first contact with The Family.

Then a road team came down to visit us. They moved in and we became a home together. I guess you could say that is when I "joined," but I honestly don't remember thinking anything like that. We just banded together, and started witnessing together. Then I quit my job. I started taking Bible classes every day, and witnessing every day. That was 1971. Maybe that was when I actually joined. Honestly, there was not a clear point that I can recall thinking, "I'm joining the Children of God." It was gradual. It just happened. (Actually, the more I think about it, that road team joined us—they moved in with us.) We felt for us personally, this is it! In twenty-five years I have never doubted that. Not once!

The factors that predisposed young Christians to join are as varied as the persons themselves. However, one consistent theme runs through the memory of almost everyone. The total commitment required of new disciples caused much of the early animosity and hostility. But it was this requirement of a radical commitment that most attracted many of the disciples. Andrew, an early Asian disciple, is an excellent case in point. He was born into a good family and attended university. He became a communist, then a "born again Christian."

An Indonesian girl who was with Campus Crusade for Christ, she witnessed to me. I prayed with her and got saved. I became involved with Campus Crusade in a big way. But it just wasn't enough. I wanted something that was a little more action packed. I wanted more expected of me. And I wanted to see other people putting out their whole hearts, whole lives. I guess I was just comparing the commitment of the Christians I knew then with communists that I worked with before. A few of my communist friends even got shot, one died. I guess I was just expecting more from the Campus Crusade folks. Maybe it wasn't fair.

Then I attended a training session for all the Campus Crusade leaders in the Philippines. On our way home, a couple of Children of God members got on our bus. That's when it started for me. They passed out this MO Letter, "Mountain Men." It talked about the Jesus revolution and that like turned my key. It seemed like they were very dedicated and totally committed. They gave me an invitation to visit.

So I went to visit the colony. This was October of 1974. Even today I can shut my eyes and still see this great big banner across the dining room. It had the verse: "And all that believed together held all things in common and sold their possessions and goods and parted them to all men as everyone had need." And somehow, I could tell they meant it.

It was such excitement, like electricity in the air. They made me feel very welcome. But I don't recall anyone trying to get me to join. But I knew they were it. This was what I had been longing for since I first found the Lord. Next day, I went back at 7:30 in the morning. I just said to them, "I have to join, right now." But they wanted me to wait two weeks, to be sure I really knew what I was getting into, that I really meant it. I did. *I went back and forth every day for my two weeks, then I was in. Quit university, forsook all for Jesus. And I never looked back.*

The Children of God were not the only group to espouse a radical approach to the Christian life. In the late 1960s and early 1970s, the COG was only one aspect of a much larger Christian counterculture youth movement known as the Jesus Revolution or the Jesus People Movement. The young people in the Jesus Revolution tended to be highly evangelistic, held a high view of the Bible, were attuned to religious experience, and generally were alienated from conventional institutions, including churches. Populated by a mix of former drug addicts and street people, with a large number of refugees from mainstream churches, the Jesus People Movement was self-consciously unorganized and consisted of widely diverse subgroups (Enroth 1990, 592–93).

On a few occasions, the Children of God were able to win over an entire subgroup within the Jesus People. These were the only occasions of a mass joining. The experience of these persons helps to clarify the place of the COG in the broader Christian counterculture movement and adds further clarity to a primary appeal. Rose came into The Family in one of these mass conversions.

I ended up living in a Christian commune called the Jesus People Army. It was OK to be a Christian and still be a hippie, a revolutionary. But it was sponsored by a regular evangelical church. After a while it became clear they thought we Christian hippies were OK, for a while. *But they basically viewed us as a stage, something we would pass through. Then we would become like them. Most of us didn't think that way.*

Well, we heard about the Children of God. They were really hot, *on fire for Jesus. So, we invited a few of them to come up to our commune for a couple of weeks to help us get going for the Lord. From the moment they arrived, the whole thing was wild,* electric. *A few had some real reservations about all the End Time stuff and the absolutely radical commitment to Jesus. But most really were glad they had come. It was clear to me right away.* These guys had it.

It was a smooth sort of takeover. But after a few months, the lead-ers of our commune began to have real trials about Father David and the MO Letters. But by then, we were all 100 percent into the whole thing and those leaders just left. Father David was very radical, revo-lutionary. *He showed us that being revolutionary was what Jesus was and what Jesus wanted. It was not just a* stage. *Father David didn't want us to stop being revolutionaries for Jesus,* ever. *It hasn't always been easy, but I have no doubt I did the right thing. I did what* Jesus *wanted me to do.*

It is not possible to ascertain the percentage of disciples who have had prior Christian commitment. Most of the disciples in this study claimed that they became Christians as a direct result of the witness and influence of The Children. The majority of these young people had little or no religious training or affiliation, though a good number re-called some interest in spiritual issues before their initial encounter. Virtually all of these disciples viewed their prior lives as empty, painful, unrewarding, and without direction.

Active opponents of New Religious Movements tend to portray groups like The Family as predators, seeking out the weak and vulner-able to snare into their trap. Richard Delgado argues for governmental regulation that would require "extremist groups" to provide an oppor-tunity of "informed consent" to prospective members. In that argu-ment, he lays out the stereotypical model of the "cult joining process." He begins with the assumption that cults employ "powerful tech-niques of coercive persuasion (brainwashing) to produce obedient fol-lowers." According to Delgado, the typical recruit is a youth who is "just above the age of majority and is physically and psychologically normal. The home life is ordinary: there is no apparent pathology of any sort. The youth is often a college student, or at some other 'in-be-tween' period of his or her life—uncertain, at loose ends, anxious (all normal experiences)."

The process is almost scripted. The youth is invited to a meeting and free meal where the "target person finds himself or herself sur-rounded by other smiling young people of about the same age who demonstrate great interest in his or her clothes, ideas, experiences. He or she is showered with flattery, smiles, hand-holding, and feigned affection. . . . The group does not identify itself." At the end of this meeting, the youth is invited to a retreat "held in an isolated setting" where the recruit has "little time for rest, privacy, and reflection; a more experienced cult member accompanies the recruit at all times."

The key component in Delgado's scenario is the "cult's maintenance of an inverse relationship between capacity and knowledge, the two key ingredients of informed consent." Information about the nature and identity of the group, its leader, its unconventional lifestyle and ideology, all are given out in carefully orchestrated stages, so that the recruit gradually loses the capacity "to respond according to his or her ordinary frame of reference. Knowledge and capacity are thus maintained in inverse proportion." The end result, according to Delgado, is truly tragic: "When the process has continued for a number of weeks or months, the recruit may be deemed ready for the duties of a full-time member: fundraising on the streets, work in a cult-operated business, or scavenging for edible garbage. The new member appears simplistic in his or her thinking patterns, stereotyped in his or her responses, unresponsive to relatives and former friends, and indifferent to events in the outside world. He or she has become a cultist" (Robbins, Shepherd and McBride 1985, 111–18).

The Children are aware that many outsiders view them as just such an extremist cult that attempts to lure innocent and unsuspecting young people into its evil fold. They find the notion both offensive and ludicrous. The concepts of "deliberate deception" and "coercive persuasion" are foreign to their experience. Many disciples readily admit that they knew little about The Family or Father David when they joined. Noah, the public relations officer for North America, points to simple logistics as the main reason that potential disciples lacked substantive knowledge about the group.

Most folks want to join then and there. We delay that now, but even so people do join without knowing everything about us. It was more like that in the beginning. But how could they know everything? If we sat down and gave a basic "Babes Course" to everyone who expressed an interest in joining, why that is all we would be doing. And that is not our main task. Our main job is to reach people for Jesus. Besides, does everyone who wants to join the Baptist

*Church or the Lutheran Church know everything, even the things
Baptists or Lutherans regret having done or said? I doubt it.*

* * * * *

*As far as not having everything we do and believe out in the
open—well, we have good reason. In the beginning everything was
right out there in public. And what happened? We were hounded,
made fun of, attacked, arrested, beaten. And over again the anticult
people tried to kidnap us and "deprogram" us. Is it any wonder we
began to be more cautious? Any reasonable person would. But that
too is behind us now.*

*Our main purpose has always been to draw people to Jesus, not to
draw people to us. In all my time with The Family, I can only recall
one instance where a fellow was really pushed, really browbeaten.
Like, "Brother, you better join us or you will be failing God." Things
like that did happen in the early days, when we had quotas for new
disciples. But even then it was rare. It did happen. Occasionally some
one would drag a guy back who obviously wasn't disciple material,
had not really made the commitment himself. Those kind would always be gone in a day or two. But that never happens any more.*

The disciples simply will not allow interpretations of their initial experiences that include deception or coercion. As we will demonstrate in
later chapters, these same people openly acknowledge that they were
manipulated and coerced by Family leadership during their lives as disciples. But they all insist that neither coercion, nor deception, nor ma-
nipulation played any role in their decision to join.

While often minimizing the significance, many disciples readily acknowledge that they joined at difficult or stressful times in their lives.
From the earliest days, most disciples encountered The Family when
they were young, discontented, disconnected from family, generally
adrift, and above all, "searching." The experience of Nathan, an
American youth who joined in 1972, is a model of this most typical
searcher.

*I was eighteen. Just completed my first year of college. I wanted to
get away. Away from everything really, but mostly away from
America. I was extremely disillusioned at the time—with college, my*

parents. I am from a Jewish background, but very secular. Most things in life really bothered me—the Viet Nam War, materialism all around me, the whole American mindset.

So I took off, hitchhiking across Europe. I was searching for some kind of answer to the questions of existence. But it was not as easy as I thought. I had absolutely no idea what I was looking for. I had no contact with spiritual things at all. We Christians talk about people being lost. Well, I was really lost!

I end up in Amsterdam. I kept a diary, still have it. In Amsterdam I wrote: "I will never find the Truth, because I have come to see that there is no real Truth. Everyone has to fictionalize the Truth for themselves." I figured the best way to do that was drugs. So, I started doing heavy drugs.

It was the summer of 1972. There must have been a million hippies and dropouts in Amsterdam. There was no place to stay. Some street person found me a bed in a hostel. I think you could say that was my wake-up call to reality. When I arrived, a kid on a top bunk was using a needle to do heroin. And then he got sick, real sick. It really hit me. Is this what you want for your life? Well, obviously not! But what? I was really confused, even a little frightened. But I didn't know where to turn. I just started wandering the city.

I got to Dam Square. There was a team from the Children of God, out witnessing. They looked like everybody else. I wandered over and started listening. I found myself in the conversation. I was trying to argue philosophy with these guys. But they were very sweet to me, very kind. And every time I raised a question, this guy, who was also Jewish, he would always answer from the Bible.

Anyway, it started to rain. Everyone was packing up and heading out, going home. They told me I should pray about all this. But they didn't tell me what to pray. In my heart I was desperately longing for God to show me the Truth. But I didn't know what to do. They said "good-bye." I never felt so alone, so absolutely alone. I sure didn't want to go back to that hostel. So I asked them if they would take me home with them.

When I got to the home, it was time for dinner. What a scene. Most lived out in the park. But it was raining that night and everyone was

*going to sleep in the house. It was wall-to-wall people. I can't begin
to describe what it felt like. They had no money, that was obvious.
The dinner was these big pots of boiled potatoes and boiled cabbage.
Believe me, I was used to better. Anyway, they didn't charge for the
meal. You had to quote a Bible verse to get your food.* I didn't know
any Bible verses. *I had never even read the Bible. But this guy taught
me John 3:16 in the line. By the time I got to the food, I could say it.*

*When I got to the serving area, the brother dishing out the food
must have seen something in my face. He looked at me and said, "I
know what you are thinking, and you're wrong. This is the best food
in the world. Because it is made with love."* And he was right! *There
was so much love in that room. I was deeply impressed. With them
and with the* Bible.

*At the end of the evening, they asked all the visitors to leave. They
had this big guy to bounce out the visitors. I begged them to stay.* I
had no place to go! *They let me stay the night.*

*So I slept on the floor. When I woke up, this guy next to me was
praying in tongues.* That was interesting! *[laughs] I stayed and we
had Bible classes the whole day. That night, they put me on dishes. I
had never washed dishes in my life. But it was OK. I prayed the
prayer to receive Jesus. Actually, I think I did it* several *times.
[laughs] Then I prayed to receive the Holy Spirit.*

*There were real temptations to leave. The first six-week period, I
was a Babe. I took Bible classes, went to the park witnessing. There
were other Christians there too. I met several who begged me to
leave. They said the COG were way too extreme. They told me to "go
back to college and be a good Christian there." But The Family was
saying something else. If you* really *love Jesus, then drop out and
serve Him full-time.*

*I really thought long and hard about it. Suddenly, all my rebellion
against the System, against the American dream, my family, all that
turned around once I was given the chance to be a* real *rebel. I mean
this wasn't marching in some silly protest, or heading out to Europe
for the summer. This was really doing it. The college thing pulled at
me, and my family too. But I knew. I had never been happy in the
System. I was always disappointed, disillusioned with it all. I also
knew I was weak. I could easily say that I would serve God, live my*

life only for Jesus. But I didn't think I could really stick it out, without The Family. So I did it. Sold my return ticket to the U.S., gave up all that I had. It's not that I haven't had doubts or questions over the years. Everybody has doubts. But, I am still here. And I still know *it was the right thing.*

Several aspects of Nathan's story match up with the classic cult-recruitment scenario. Yet Nathan adamantly rejects any such interpretation of his experience.

[You are aware of accusations that The Family tricks or forces people to join.]

Have I ever thought I was tricked into joining a cult? *[laughs]* By who? *Every person I met was just like me, eighteen, nineteen years old. Most had only been in the Children of God a few weeks or months themselves. When did they get transformed into these sinister cultists, so they could then get me?* And for what? *It's silly, really. I was in real trouble and they really helped me. But even that misses the real point. Anybody who believes the "tricked by the cult" stuff just doesn't understand, or can't, or refuses to understand. It was Jesus who changed me. It was God. I had a choice to stay or go. And I followed God!*

This study revealed another factor that tends, at least in some cases, to negate the validity of Delgado's insidious-cult-recruiter stereotype. Although many disciples found The Family through the chance encounters of street evangelism, a significant percentage were introduced to the group by close friends or family members. Their "recruiter" was often a person who knew them well, cared for them, and shared with them a positive and trusting relationship. In many cases, they had shared extensively about the nature of their Family experience. Jonathan, a Canadian disciple who has lived in South America since joining in the early 1980s, came into the movement through the influence of a younger sister.

My sister and I were very close. She had been a high school exchange student in Brazil and met The Family there. She came back to Canada, but was very unhappy. She returned to Brazil and got saved and joined. I thought she was crazy. A year or two later, I found my-

self in real trouble. I was a confirmed atheist, but I was desperate to find some meaning in life. I never gave it a thought to go to a church. I decided to visit my sister in Brazil. I was twenty-six at the time. I spent several weeks there, living in a Family home. I remember being very impressed by them, the overwhelming level of support they gave each other, the caring, the love. I had never even known that kind of thing existed. I was also impressed by their self-confidence. Though I thought a lot of what they believed was just ridiculous.

I returned to Canada and went back to university. My sister kept in touch with me, but I didn't take a lot of stock in what she tried to tell me. Part of my problem was that I was a homosexual. And it made me miserable. The last two years or so [before joining] I had become desperate to escape that lifestyle. I knew it was selfish, and superficial, and lustful. I felt the degradation of it constantly, but I could not stop. I could not escape. Finally I became suicidal. I gave up any hope for my life. I was committed to a psychiatric hospital for two weeks. At that point I was sure I would either die or end up insane.

Then, for some reason, I remembered my little sister. And I re-membered the love those people had. As soon as I was released from the hospital, I caught a plane to visit her. She and the others were very caring, very understanding. I was invited to a large fellowship meeting. People started giving their testimonies of how Jesus had changed them, saved them. And I could see it, the beauty and truth in their faces, in their lives. And the love they had for each other was simply overwhelming. But I couldn't let go. I was trying to under-stand it all intellectually, which of course you can't.

Finally a brother came to me and said he had a special burden to help me, that he would pray for me to find the truth. I finally allowed myself to face it all. So I prayed with him. Up to that very moment, I had never considered the possibility that God was real. But I prayed, and something began to happen to me. (What you people call a reli-gious experience.) I felt this change, this energy within me. Then I opened my eyes. I could see little threads of light linking all the peo-ple together. To this day, I do not think that was either a hallucina-tion or a vision. Those threads of light were real. God put those threads of light there to help me see.

I prayed to receive Jesus. I asked the Lord to save me and change me. And He did. It was absolutely real, and I am changed. That was in 1980. And I am as convinced now as I was on that day of the truth of redemption in Jesus Christ, that the End Times are upon us, and that God has a plan for my life. So I joined The Family, there in Argentina. I have been in South America ever since, never went back. This is where my life is now. And it is truly a good life.

Jonathan is representative of a good number of disciples who joined as mature young adults. These people came into the movement with considerable life experience, and virtually all of them carry difficult and painful memories. An inability to cope with the uncertainties and tenuous nature of life "in the System" is the most consistent attribute among this class of disciples. Their stories make clear the degree to which The Family functions as a place of refuge. In many instances The Family remains a sheltering environment of comfort and security for a good number of persons who, for a wide variety of reasons, found life in the outside world either unmanageable or unbearable.

Interestingly, many disciples in this general category recall themselves as the aggressive agent. They were the ones doing the seeking, initiating contact, often at considerable effort. Sometimes they met with little encouragement. Faith is just such a person. She joined at age twenty-seven.

When I think back about my life before The Family, I guess it appeared to be pretty normal to people who didn't really know me. I was raised in the Roman Catholic Church. But I quit going very young. I had a good education, and I was a teacher. My husband had a good job and he did his best with me. He loved me and treated me with care and respect. He just didn't know what to do with me.

My life never was right. For years I suffered. I was always, constantly depressed in the System. Friends, my family, everyone tried to help me. It just kept getting worse. I was in psychological therapy for years. I can't remember all the details. To be honest I have tried to forget. I know my husband tried. In the end he just couldn't handle it anymore. I blamed him then; I think I blamed everyone. But it was not his fault. My life was miserable and I made his life miserable. Finally, he left.

I guess that was the low point. I was so desperately unhappy. Then I began hearing from God. I know that will sound strange to most people. It certainly was strange to me, then. It sure sounded strange to my family and friends. It was not an audible voice. I just began to hear from God, *to know that He wanted me, somehow, to do* something *for Him. So what does a Catholic woman in Quebec do with that? I went to see a priest.* He was a lot of help! *[said in jest] He told me I was crazy. (He wasn't the only one who thought that.) He told me I should forget all this, get back together with my husband, have children, and live a normal life. I tried.*

But I kept hearing from God. I began to look into different missionary groups, Catholic orders, things like that. But I had no peace in my heart. By this point I was becoming very desperate. Then I began to have visions, mostly in my dreams. They were visions of young people with little kids who traveled around the world telling people about Jesus. Now I was really ignorant. *I did not even know what that meant. I did not know anything about salvation or having a relationship with Jesus. But I had these visions.*

I told one friend. She had seen a picture in the newspaper of a group that sounded like that. I got the paper, and there was a picture of young adults and kids singing in a hospital. I just looked and looked at that picture. It really clicked *inside me. I knew I had to find these people.*

I found a phone number. When they answered, the first thing I said was, "How can I join?" I can imagine now what they must have thought. [laughs] They were pretty cautious, made me wait three days. Then they came and got me and took me to the home. As I went through the door, the little kids rushed up to give me a welcome hug. I guess I must have froze for a moment, then had tears of joy. These children were the very same *kids that I had seen in my vision.*

They explained salvation to me and I prayed to receive Jesus. It was the most wonderful *experience. They read some MO Letters to me, told me they were the Children of God. That meant nothing to me. But I recognized the love, the spirit.* And I recognized those kids. *I knew I was* home.

But they wouldn't take me in right away. I don't think they thought I was all that stable of a person. They made me wait two weeks. Made me really consider the decision, pray about it. I asked the Lord to show me. Early one morning, the Lord woke me twice and He spoke to me. I could hear His voice: "Yes, this is where you should be; you will be my instrument and I will use you there!" Twice I heard it. Same voice, same words. I heard God speak to me.

So I know God wants me in The Family. I do not think there was one moment in my life that I was happy. I'm not sure I even knew what happy was. But since that day, I have known real joy. I belong here! I have true peace that God spoke to me, that He leads me, and that The Family is where He wants me for the rest of my life.

* * * * *

[At this point I asked Faith to imagine what her life might be like if she had not joined The Family. After a lengthy pause in which she unsuccessfully struggled to contain her emotions, she began to weep. Through the tears, she managed this reply.]

* * * * *

I know God has always loved me and He always had a plan for my life. . . . So I don't think about what my life would be, had I not found the Lord and The Family. . . . I used to, the first few years, but not any more. . . . I don't want to. . . . I can't.

Many disciples carry a deep sense of having been rescued. They have warm and joyful memories of their initial encounters with the disciples, as well as the experience of joining the group. However, many others had much more difficult and traumatic transitions. These difficulties almost always centered around disputes with parents and other relatives. The decision to abandon the "System" inevitably implied some level of renunciation of those left behind. Dramatic and highly traumatic events often surrounded younger disciples who came out of cultures with strong family traditions. None is more illustrative than Priscilla, a thirty-year-old Greek disciple who first encountered The Family in 1982.

I was very desperate, desperate to find God, or find some meaning in my life. A few times I tried to ask my questions in church. But the priest put me down. He didn't want those kind of questions, I guess. I became very suicidal.

One day, I noticed this new shop, a religious book store. I began to talk to the lady about life after death, how confused I was. She said she knew someone who might help me, and she invited me to her house the next day. The people I met there were Children of God. They explained salvation to me, that Jesus loved me, and asked me to pray and receive Jesus. Some were praying and speaking in tongues. It was all very strange to me, but I prayed and received Jesus as my Savior, and also prayed and received the Holy Spirit of Love.

I felt so light, so elevated. *I just knew Jesus was in my life. All my burdens and pain were gone. For a week I had beautiful dreams about Jesus. They gave me a Bible and verses to read and learn. I got some MO Letters. I began to go to the home once a week for classes, but I did not drop out. I was only sixteen, and Greece is a very traditional society. They had me take a low profile, tested my commitment for three months. And they wanted to know about my family.*

My parents were very opposed. They did not know the people were Children of God, but they were very opposed anyway. I wanted to drop out and join. But The Family told me I must finish school, obey my parents and the law. I became a secret member, not living in the colony. It was very hard. My heart was with The Family, but my life was at home and in school. I witnessed a lot about the End Time and Jesus, but I longed for more closeness to The Family.

This went on for over a year. My parents were very insistent that I do well in school, become a doctor. Then one night my mom caught me reading the Bible, when I was supposed to be studying for exams. They got worse toward me. They stopped trusting me, started following me, doubting me. So, I started really witnessing hard to them. (As you can see, I wasn't the wisest teenager who ever lived.)

At age eighteen I could get my own passport. That was about the time of the MO Letter calling everyone to go to the East as a missionary. The shepherds took me aside and said they were now willing to take me in when I turned eighteen, if I was willing to go to India as a missionary. After two years, now I really had the chance to do it.

The shepherds told me I must be honest and open with my parents. So I told them everything. That is when they found out I was with the Children of God. Things really got wild then. *They were out-*

raged. *They got all the bad press: "Hookers for Jesus," "Whores." They had all the FFing pictures. It was shocking!*

I replied, "What is this? *These are not the people I know!" I was a Babe, and not living in the colony. I was not allowed to read the FFing letters, and I didn't know much about it.*

Next, they brought this rich guy from Australia and arranged for me to marry him. They offered me a trip to Europe to get me away. I was not interested. So they packed me off to my father's old family village, very remote in the mountains. Basically they tried to put me away. But I refused, started walking back home.

So, I told my parents I wanted to join. They absolutely freaked out. *It really turned into a* **very** ugly *scene. They got physical with me, and they locked me in my room. I was eighteen by now. I began to pray, and the Lord told me to trust Him. I loved my parents and it was very hard for me. Then I decided if I was not in the home by midnight, that night, well then it was finished. I would not join.*

I said to my dad, "The Family members are very nice, very sweet. They don't kill people, they don't eat people." *I asked him to please take me to The Family home. He says, "OK, get your stuff, I will take you."* I was shocked. *But I knew I could not take my dad to the home, it was underground. But The Family had a close friend who lived nearby, and I hoped I could stay with him. I prayed to Jesus that He would help me find this place. I was upset, confused, shaking. About* 10 P.M. *we found the building, a high-rise, secure apartment building. I went up to the security guard, then pressed the friend's number. No answer. So I pressed the next button down. A person answered and I said, "Hello, it's me. Please open the door." And he did.*

I went straight to the roof, afraid the security guard would catch me. I hid behind the water tank, and I began to pray and read the Word. I was very, very *scared. But the Lord was speaking to me, telling me to trust Him. I went down the stairs, rushed out the front door, and just started running to the bus stop. But it was* 10:45 *by now. The last bus had gone. I was becoming very sad. It seemed clear that I was not going to make it by midnight. That I was not going to be in The Family. Then, just as I was about to give up, a taxi comes*

*by and stops. It was the girls from the home, coming back from
FFing. They gave me a ride. And as I walked through the front door of
the colony, the clock struck twelve. I just cried. I knew it was from
the Lord.* And I knew I was home.

*I am not proud of this story. It makes me sad. I was immature,
self-centered, and very self-righteous. It must have been very hard for
my parents. Their only daughter at eighteen, joining the Children of
God, and going off alone to Bangladesh. If I had it to do over again, I
would do a lot differently. But I would not change my decision to
join.*

*I still loved my parents. I wrote them constantly. In time, both my
father and mother prayed to receive Jesus. Things are good now. I get
home as often as I can, a couple of weeks every summer. I was officially married in Greece, in the Orthodox Church. That made them
very happy. They love my husband and my children. We make sure
they see the kids as often as we can. Of course, they still don't like
The Family, don't agree with our doctrines and practices. But they
see I am happy. They know the kids are happy and well cared for.
They know there is love in our home.*

And so it began for thousands of young people all over the world.
Few, if any, had even the slightest inkling of what lay ahead. But how
could they? "I'm not sure I've ever known what was coming next.
None of us have. That is part of what makes it such a great life. We do
know that Jesus loves us, and that Father David loves us, and that we
love each other. We really do walk by faith, not by sight. And that is
the *only* way to truly live." (Noah).

One story remains that captures in vivid fashion the fundamental
motivation that moved many persons to join. From the earliest days in
Southern California down to the present, The Family has drawn persons who, for a host of reasons, could no longer find their place in the
world. Sometimes it was a shattering in personal relationships. Most
often it was profound disillusionment with life and a radical rejection
of the religious, family, and social structures that sustained the world
around them. They found love, acceptance, and a new way of life. They
also found a New Nation, an alternative society in which their ongoing
rejection of the worldly "System" not only made sense, but aligned

them with spiritual forces that would ultimately prevail in the universe. These disciples rejected the world and found life in The Family an ultimate expression of that rejection. But many others had an almost opposite experience. They had been rejected by the world. They were alone, fearful, often hopeless, and with little sense of control over their own lives. They were the perishing. For some of these young people, The Family was the last grasp on life itself. As much as any other disciple, June captures this sense of raw survival. She was raised in a small farming community in South Australia. By age eighteen she had quit school, joined a "biker" gang, and had abused alcohol and drugs for years.

At age eighteen, I left Australia and went to New Zealand. I just had to get away. I had to try and find some reason to live. I got a job as a waitress, but soon I was back into the drug scene. I began drinking heavily, mixing it with a lot of pills. I did not do heroin, but just about everything else. My life was just slipping away. I had no friends, no one to talk with. I became more and more depressed and lonely.

One night, it all came crashing down on me. I was out, alone in the streets. I finally realized that there was no hope. My life meant nothing and would never mean anything. I was high on drugs, but I still remember it all very clearly. I stood alone in the street for a very long time. Then, I decided that I simply could not go on any longer. So, I started walking back to my apartment to take a huge overdose of drugs. I had decided to kill myself. No note. No cry for help. I would have done it.

Walking back, I began to cry. I kept thinking "I'm going to die now, and no one has ever loved me!" There I was, stumbling along, eyes filled with tears. I was thinking "no one loves me and now no one ever will," when this young guy comes out of nowhere. He just steps in front of me and says, "Hi, I really love you." It just really stopped me cold. I said, "What?" And he said it again, "I really love you, and Jesus loves you."

I was very cynical, very hardened against religion. So when he mentioned Jesus, I just told him to "f— —off!" But he knew I was in trouble, and he just wouldn't leave me. I don't remember exactly all that we talked about that night. He began showing me things from the Bible. Every question I had, he turned to the Bible. I was amazed, the Bible did seem to have a lot of answers. I was desperate to find anything, some truth, some peace, or my life was over.

He didn't convince me. But at least I didn't kill myself. For the next week, he talked to me every day. He kept telling me that my only hope was Jesus. But I was at such a very low point in my life, I found it impossible to believe anyone or anything.

Finally, after about a week, he came to me and got down on his knees. He began to cry. He said, "I don't know what else to do. If you don't receive Jesus, I just don't know what is going to happen to you." I didn't want to let him down. I knew he really cared about me. I wanted to do it, for him. I just couldn't.

But that night, for the first time in my life, I prayed. "Jesus, I've tried everything else and nothing has worked in my life. You are the only hope I have left. If you don't work, then there is nothing else left for me." Then, I prayed to receive Jesus in my heart. And He came! I *felt this beautiful feeling of peace, like this huge weight was lifted off me. I just cried and cried. I was so happy. I said to Jesus, "You gave me the Truth. Now what do I do?" And He showed me. I got this vision of all those lonely, sorrowful people I met biking and hitchhiking. And I knew Jesus wanted me to tell them about His Truth.*

The next day, I got up and threw all my cigarettes and drugs and alcohol in the garbage. I was laughing. I called this fellow and said, "I prayed to receive Jesus in my heart. Now what can I do?" He said, "Come live with us and serve the Lord." So, I quit my job. I gathered up what few things I owned, moved in, and began telling others about Jesus.

They were the Children of God, but I didn't know anything about that or about Father David, never heard his name before I joined. But I knew they loved me. And I knew they loved Jesus and wanted to serve Him.

So that was the beginning of my serving the Lord, the beginning of my life in The Family. That was over twenty years ago. There have been a lot of good times. And a lot of hard times, very hard times. *But there is no doubt in my mind at all. I owe* every minute *of those twenty years to Jesus, and to The Family.*

So they came. So they continue to come. In the following chapters we will examine the various factors that formed this gathering of diverse people into The Family. We will begin by exploring the belief system that shapes and sustains their life.

3. We Hold These Truths

T he Family is a remarkably diverse community. Its membership spans a wide range of economic, educational, religious, cultural, ethnic, and national backgrounds. There is no such thing as a "typical" Child of God. Yet, in the midst of this diversity, the disciples are guided by a common vision. Although life in The Family is not uniform, it is coherent. Since the earliest days of the group, new disciples have normally engaged in a rigorous program of study during their first six months. Beyond this initial period of instruction and indoctrination, everyone is expected to spend at least an hour a day in the study of the Bible, MO Letters, and other Family literature. The Family is established and maintained as members learn, adopt, and internalize a clear set of theological and ideological commitments.[1]

The Family is definitely not a static entity; change is endemic. At the start of the movement, the Bible was the sole source of religious authority. However, in matters of doctrine and ethics, Father David soon adopted a position of "progressive revelation."

We need the Word of God in every form possible, treasures both new & old! The Bible *is the one to begin with. . . . But we also need to have His present Word—dreams, visions, spirit trips, as well as direct answers to prayer, direct revelations, messages, prophecy,*

---

1. The study of New Religious Movements has been entrusted primarily to social scientists. Perhaps due to training and disciplinary focus, they have not given significant attention to theology or the doctrinal teachings of New Religions. However, theology is often at the core of these movements. In The Family, doctrinal belief is often the primary motivating factor in the lives of the disciples. The failure to understand and give proper attention to theological content not only limits our understanding of cults or New Religions, it also can have significant consequences. The tragedy of Waco is the most recent example: "The single most damaging mistake on the part of federal officials was their failure to take the Branch Davidians' religious beliefs seriously" (Barkun 1994, 41). The study of The Family awaits a careful and complete analysis of their theology. See Hubbard 1998, 59–62.

*tongues & interpretations — information straight from Heaven to
show us exactly what He wants us to do right now!*

*The original recorded Word as found in the Bible is a wonderful,
wonderful book. . . . Of course, a lot of things have changed since the
Bible days, so if you want & need some later information, for today,
then you need to faithfully read & study the MO Letters! In fact, you
will learn a lot more about the present as well as even about the past
& certainly about the future, by reading the Letters! ("The Word, The
Word, The Word!" ML #2484, Nov. 1988)*

This approach to revelation keeps open the possibility for refinement,
revision, or substantive change of any and all beliefs and practices. In
one sense, such developments are primary characteristics of the group.
However, most of the essential theological positions that shape and
guide the life of the disciples were fully developed by 1975 and have
not changed greatly since that time.

An exhaustive analysis of Family doctrine is beyond the scope of
this work. My primary focus is the life experience of the disciples. The
aim here is to identify and flesh out the core beliefs that are central to
that life experience. These core beliefs center on Jesus, Salvation, and
Discipleship; Father David as God's Prophet; the Spirit World; the End
Times; the System; and God's End Time Army. The nature of human
sexuality is the most distinctive and controversial component of theology and practice. Sexuality will be considered more fully in the following chapter.

It is difficult to conceive of a person sustaining a life in The Family
without affirming, at some level, the core values. However, the disciples are not programmed robots. Differences in knowledge, interest,
and theological sophistication are clearly evident. Some latitude of interpretation is permissible in most areas. More significantly, the intensity with which the disciples hold certain convictions and doctrines
varies considerably.

Personal salvation through faith in Jesus Christ as Savior is the
linchpin of Family theology. The teaching of Father David on the nature of the Trinity and certain aspects of the life of Jesus are far outside
the orthodox tradition. However, all disciples share an understanding
of Jesus Christ that is generally consistent with the view held broadly

within Evangelical Protestant Christianity. Jesus was born of Mary, lived a sinless life, died on the cross for the sins of the world, rose from the grave, and is returning soon to this earth. All people who do not "know Jesus" are lost and without hope in this world. However, eternal salvation is not hard to come by. All that is required is that a person repeat a short prayer inviting Jesus to come into his or her life as personal Savior. Virtually every piece of literature distributed to the general public closes with a petition to "receive Jesus," like the following quotation taken from the "Our Heavenly Home" poster of 1985:

Are you *ready for heaven? If you're not* sure, *all you have to do is receive* Jesus *into your heart, then you'll* know *that the Heavenly City is* your *Eternal Home too! Just pray this simple prayer & Jesus will come into your heart right now: "Lord Jesus, please forgive me for all my sins. I believe that You are the Son of God & that You died for me. I now open the door of my heart & I ask You, Jesus, to please come in & give me Your free gift of eternal life. Help me to love You & to love others by telling them about You & Your Love. In Jesus' Name I pray, Amen."*

The disciples have an almost mechanical understanding of salvation. Once an individual repeats this prayer, that person is saved and has secured an eternal place with Jesus in heaven. Such salvation through faith in Jesus Christ as Savior does not require any particular outward evidence of significant change. The disciples are generally resigned to the fact that most people they lead to Jesus "will not go much farther with the Lord." However, no one has the slightest question regarding the eternal sufficiency of this simple act of faith.

Whereas salvation carries minimal requirements, discipleship is an entirely different matter. The people who make up The Family have not just received Jesus in their hearts. They accept fully the fundamental division of humanity between the Kingdom of Darkness and the Kingdom of Heaven, and they have committed their lives, their fortunes, and their honor to bringing as many people as possible into heaven. No one captured the centrality of that mission better than Matthew, a Canadian disciple who has served since the early 1970s.

I was born into the Covenant Church and raised in a good Christian home. I prayed to receive Jesus as my Savior, the same sim-

ple prayer of faith we use now. But somehow, I felt the Spirit leaving the churches in the late 1960s. So I began searching for a group of people who wanted to witness for Jesus like I did, to serve Jesus like the early Christians in the New Testament. Then I met the Children of God. They were absolutely committed. I knew I had found the group that would live and die for Jesus, the people who would do any-thing *to win souls for* Him.

There have been a great number of changes over the years. We have made a lot of mistakes. But this has never changed. Our main goal was and always will be to reach souls for Jesus. And we forsake all else in life to do it. I have led over ten thousand souls to the Lord. [responding to my slight smile] I know that sounds like an exaggeration, but it isn't. God has used me. *You want to know who we really are, well* this is it. *We have broken all our idols, left everything behind us to win people for Jesus. Most people view us as extremists.* They're right. *But this is the real* extremism *of The Family, the extremism to win souls for Jesus.*

My dedication, my absolute commitment has never been to Father David, and has never been to The Family. It has always been to Jesus, *and to the task of winning as many souls as I can before the End Time comes. I have said this to others many times before, and I will say it to you now. If you can show me another group of Christians that is more committed, more dedicated to Jesus, does more and sacrifices more to witness for the Lord and win souls for Jesus, you show them to me. I will leave today and join that group, if they will have me.*

Witnessing has been the defining task of discipleship since the earliest days of the Children of God. In those early years, it seemed to border on obsession. Yet, no one looks back to that era with any sense of bitterness or loss. It is quite the contrary. Sarah, a long-term British disciple, recalls her first years with the Children:

I joined in 1971, and I hit the streets witnessing that very same night. It was what really excited me; I saw what was possible with God's Spirit. On my first night out in London, six people got saved. One was a Muslim and two were drug addicts. It was absolutely thrilling *to see those people willing to receive the Lord.*

It was tough at that time, especially for girls. We used to go out until two or three in the morning on one of these big, double-decker buses with "Jesus Revolution" written on the side. The shepherds did not want us to look out the window. They didn't want the "whore of Babylon" to tempt us. [laughs heartily] We weren't supposed to look out the window, but then we would spend the whole rest of the night in Babylon witnessing. I would say that qualifies as youthful idealism, wouldn't you? What days those were! Life was very intense. We would come home, sleep eight hours, then up for breakfast and out on the streets again.

I never saw it as a hardship. Witnessing was the music of my life. There were strict quotas then: on the number of people to witness to, new disciples won, getting out the lit. I haven't thought about those years for a while now. But I loved it, never been happier. There is nothing I loved more than being out witnessing, telling people about the love of Jesus. I never felt used, never felt I was being asked to do something I did not want to do. I never resented it. I was very happy in those years. I saw a great number of souls come to know Jesus. Later, I did develop some resentment towards the leaders. The week my second child was born, I was asked why I didn't get my quota. I was OK about that then. But later I found out leadership women got six weeks off duty when they had a child. That I resented.

The Family has matured. The era of twelve-hour days on the streets is gone. Sarah has a host of other ministries and responsibilities, and she has eleven children. In many ways, long-term disciples now look to the second generation to carry the torch. Yet, witnessing is still conceived of as the central task of life. The week I visited Sarah's home was a hectic one. My visit was surely part of the distraction. At the close of the week, I attended the home leadership meeting. Weekly statistical reports were to be sent out the next day, and the home had not met its required quota of witnessing. Individual quotas on new disciples, souls won, and iterature distribution are in the past, but all Family homes must meet minium requirements of active witnessing. The next day, two of the three adult women in the home got up early, filled their bags with tapes and videos and posters, then set out on a cold and rainy morning for a nearby town. They spent the entire day distributing their "tools" and sharing about Jesus with whoever would listen.

At the close of most interviews, informants were asked for a final thought, usually framed: "If you could say one thing about The Family that would help the outside world understand who you are, what would that be?" No one mentioned Father David, the sexual ethos, or any of the more unusual aspects of the community. Most responded with sentiments that were captured passionately by Sherah, a French Canadian.

I believe The Family is of the Lord's *Spirit, the Lord's leading and guiding. We are* His *instruments to reach out to people and to help them. To help them in any way we can, with food, or comfort, any other way. But* most of all, *to offer them Jesus' free gift of eternal life, so they can go to heaven.*

That is what The Family is really *about. I know we are not perfect, far from it. We have made mistakes in the past, a lot of mistakes. And we won't be perfect in the future either. But we are learning. Learning to really love each other and to reach out and love those outside too. So, I guess it is God's love. To share God's love in every way we can, that is The Family.*

Paradoxically, Father David was a universalist who taught that in the end, all creation would be reconciled to God. In *The Book of the Future,* a compilation of Father David's teachings published in 1984, his universalistic position was unequivocal:

So I believe that eventually, even the rebellious angels will be re-deemed. . . . They're going to be judged severely, some even harshly . . . before the Lord will lay off the rod & finally forgive & restore eternally in Universal Reconciliation!

If God's going to salvage mankind in Universal Reconciliation, why not stretch it a bit further to also include the rebellious spirits? . . . "Even the Devil" *in the end!*

How Good *is God!—How* Kind, *How* Loving, *How* Merciful! *The Bible says there's no end to His mercy. . . . He is not going to lose one of His sheep.—Not one soul! He's going to save them* all! (Book of the Future *1984, 315–17*)

Though universalism is the official theological stance, this doctrine sits very lightly on the disciples. On eight to ten occasions, informants were asked how they held together their driving compulsion to reach as many people as possible for Jesus with the belief that everyone would eventually be saved anyway. Most responded in puzzlement, indicating they had never given any thought to the matter. Noah was the only disciple to give a reasoned response:

I guess it is like if you were out on a ship, and you saw someone floundering out in the ocean, being circled by sharks. Now, suppose you could somehow know that the person in the water was eventually going to make it, that they would eventually be washed up on shore and would survive. Wouldn't you still throw them a life preserver and rescue them now, if you could? But to tell you the truth, I never think about that at all.

Universalism is perhaps the best example of a doctrine that bears little impact on the lives of the disciples. However, there are other theological positions that are profoundly shaping. The identity and role of Father David tops that list.

In the early days, David Berg claimed no special status or rank. In fact, he tended to play down his own status. He was normally referred to as "Uncle Dave" and generally considered himself to be a father figure and spiritual guide to a lost and confused group of American youth. When he first became aware that some of his followers were beginning to memorize his teachings along with the Bible, he was quite concerned. He labeled it "man worship" and was fearful it might take their eyes off Jesus. However, as the movement continued to develop and grow, Father David quickly came to a radically different self-understanding. Though it is difficult to substantiate, it appears that Maria played a significant role in this process.

By the end of 1970, Father David possessed a clear vision of his special role in human history. He was God's Prophet for the End Time. From that point on, he spoke to his young followers as one having the authority of God. In January of 1972 he established this claim to absolute spiritual authority in explicit terms:

I'm Aquarius—I'm the Water Bearer—the Water Bearer of whom all the others were just types. I am Aquarius—this is my age! I'm the

Water Bearer! Jesus told me so, because I'm bringing the Water of Life to this generation. . . . Every sign is a different age, and this is the Last! I bear the Water of God's Word and Jesus sent me for this age.

* * * * *

[What comes next is understood to be the voice of God, speaking of Father David.]

* * * * *

This is the Water Bearer of all ages whom I have ordained to bring forth the Water of Life to the children of this Last Generation. . . . Therefore, if thou wouldst have light and if thou wouldst have meat and if thou wouldst be satisfied, thou shalt hearken unto the words of my David and must kiss his breasts and drink his milk. . . . Heed thou and hearken therefore to My Servant, for this is that David whom I have spoken of for the Last Generation—the Prophet of this Age. ("A Psalm of David!" ML #152, Jan. 1972)

Once Berg had clarified his status as God's unique Prophet for the End Time, all disciples were called upon to submit fully to his absolute spiritual authority. He left no room for ambiguity at all.

God made me your shepherd! And you had better follow, or you're going to miss God and His Will. It was not my idea!—It was God's! If you think you can be a part of God's mighty Movement without following its leadership—His chosen leadership—you are mistaken! If you think you can be a Revolutionary for Jesus and not follow the one God chose to start that Revolution—you're going to be sadly disappointed! I did not choose to be your leader: God chose me!—I merely obeyed! . . . Those who rejected God's leadership through His anointed ones fell by the wayside, or were destroyed! ("The Laws of Moses," ML #155, Feb. 1972)

Father David's developing claims of divine appointment and absolute spiritual authority roughly coincided with his withdrawal from direct contact with the disciples. It was therefore necessary to channel that authority through the MO Letters. He acknowledged his own transition on this crucial issue, while fully affirming that the MO Letters constituted "new Scripture." God's new message was as authoritative as the Bible, in some cases clarified or superseded the Bible, and was more likely to be of immediate value.

*I was shocked when I first heard that certain people were memo-
rizing MO Letters, "Sounds like man worship!—Departing from the
Faith, the Bible, the Scriptures! Ah, that's building a new Scripture!"
Well, let me tell you, there was a time when Moses' and David's writings and the Prophets were new scriptures, and yet today the Church
condemns any new Scriptures, and new messages from God's new
man! . . . There is plenty that's good for you to study and memorize
of what they [biblical writers] said, but much is old hat and out of
date—except what Jesus said. Even some of what Paul said seems no
longer up to date. . . . As long as you've still got Christ and love the
Revolution, may God deliver you from old worn out Bible studies,
and old worn out prophetic interpretations, and old endless Scripture
memorization, if it means you haven't got time to listen to what God
has to say now. ("Old Bottles!" ML #242, July 1973)*

The early disciples accepted the conservative Christian view of the
Bible as inspired and infallible, the perfect Word of God. To accept the
MO Letters as equal to and even surpassing the Bible placed Father
David at the very right hand of God. And the Children did.

At times, Father David's claims to Divine insight and authority
seemed almost limitless. Some descriptions of that authority can, from
the perspective of an outside observer, border on the absurd:

[God speaking of Father David]

* * * * *

*For this is even he of whom I have spoken, and he whom I have
loved from the beginning, and he whom I have promised that I will
give. . . . Even the spittle of David is of more value than the words of
man, wise men of this world. . . . Yet even the excreta of his vomit,
and the tears of his eyes, and the offal of his bowels, and the piss of
his penis, can give life unto them what are athirst. ("The Birthday
Warning!" ML #215, Feb. 1973)*

However, the disciples were not offended by Father David's graphic
metaphors or tendency toward wild exaggeration. They found these en-
dearing qualities and marks of a truly revolutionary personality. And
they believed.

Despite these assertions of divine insight, The Prophet consistently acknowledged his human weaknesses and capacity for error. He freely admitted that he had been wrong in claiming the Jews had special status with God. He openly confessed his bout with alcoholism and his times of doubt and fear. On other occasions, he attempted to deflect responsibility for mistakes and prophecies that did not come to pass. The first major problem came in 1973 when the Comet Kohoutek did not conform to his predictions. In 1983 he wrote to his disciples:

> I was so mad at the Lord after the "40 Days" came to an end & it didn't happen & the comet completely disappeared! Ha! I was one mad Prophet! I was about like dear Jonah! I told Maria I was threatening to quit because the Lord didn't keep His Word.
>
> The Lord repents and changes His mind once in a while. . . . Moses prayed and got Him to change his Mind. PTL He says, "I am the Lord, I change not!" (Mal. 3:6) Sometimes he changes His mind, but basically, fundamentally he doesn't change, He's still love. (The Book of Remembrance 1983, 1:97)

In 1986, Father David wrote "Interpreting Bible Prophecy!" This Letter modified considerably the earlier claims to Divine Truth:

> I have tried not to be dogmatic about things, that it has to be this way, it has to be that way, because sometimes I just don't know, except for the things that are very clearly so in the Bible! . . . You know it's not easy to confess when you've been wrong, but it's a lot easier than staying wrong to try to support a false position! . . . Which is what I had to do regarding the Jews. . . . It was a very hard and trying experience that nearly killed me!
>
> You have got to be careful how you interpret me, Beloved, you've got to be careful when you read my Letters. Sometimes I come flat out with convictions that things are absolutely so. But if I sort of beat around the bush a little bit & say, "Well, I'm not sure but it sounds like so & so, & it looks like so & so," that doesn't mean it has to be so!" . . . My interpretation could be wrong! The only thing you can really count on is what I said that God said, that I know! But my interpretation, my opinion, my theory could be wrong. ("Interpreting Bible Prophecy! Rightly Dividing the Word of Truth!" ML #2210, Aug. 1986)

To an outsider even moderately familiar with the MO Letters, Father David's claim that he "tried not to be dogmatic about things" appears monumentally inconsistent, if not ludicrous. However, the disciples seemed to have accepted and welcomed this redefinition, while retaining their loyalty and affection for The Prophet.

Even with these qualifications, Father David continued to function as the divinely anointed leader and spiritual guide for the Children. But Prophet of the End Time was not his only title; he was also King of God's New Nation. He claimed not only absolute spiritual authority over his disciples, but also political authority and the homage due their rightful king. Old Testament passages referring to King David were appropriated for God's new King David. From the very beginning of the movement, he established himself as sole commander of the faithful. These claims were made explicit and grounded in biblical authority in 1984.

The following Bible verses were written years after the death of King David of old, & are fulfilled today in David and his children, in the Latter Days!

"For thus saith the Lord God; Behold, I, even I will both search my sheep, & seek them out. And I will set up One Shepherd over them, & He shall Feed them, even my servant David; he shall feed them & he shall be their shepherd. And I the Lord will be their God, & My servant David a prince among them; I the Lord have spoken it. And ye My flock, the flock of My pasture, are men & I am your God" (Ezek. 34) "Afterward shall the Children of Israel return & seek the Lord their God, & David their King & shall fear the Lord & His goodness in the latter days. — Believe in the Lord your God, so shall ye be established; believe his prophets, so shall ye prosper!" (Hos. 3:5; 2 Chron. 20:20) ("I Will Set Up One Shepherd!" ML #1962, Jan. 1984)

The Book of Remembrance was published in 1983 as an internal document. The main goal was to inform the disciples about the history of the movement and about Father David. One chapter is titled "Our Beloved King—In Person! The First Impressions, Effects & Blessings of Meeting Dad!" It is a collection of disciples' memories on first meeting Father David. It is clearly intended not only to be historical, but also to

establish a normative approach toward The King. Just a few excerpts
will suffice to demonstrate that approach:

*He was just exactly as his Letters portrayed him—so fatherly, con-
cerned & loving, & kingly, yet 'real!' . . . He put his arm around me
& cuddled me up close, just where I wanted to be! I was 'home' at
last & felt as if all life's search had ended here, in Heaven! Jesus I'd
known all my life, & meeting my shepherd David was so similar to a
born-again experience!* (Book of Remembrance 1982, 1:351)

* * * * *

*My first meeting with Dad also helped me understand better how
we're to reverence, respect & fear the Lord; because to be honest I
was 'shaking in my boots!' Ha! But seeing his sincere concern & care
for us made me know that Dad did love me in spite of all my naugh-
tiness in the past. Later I compared meeting Dad to a life-after-death
experience where one goes to be with the Lord, standing before Him
while being shown a review of their past lives, the good & bad I'd
done, then finding out that there would be another chance! Having
met Dad was a life changing experience for me in every way!* (Book of
Remembrance 1983, 1:356)

Consistent with the ideology of the time, both of these testimonies end
with the female disciple having sexual intercourse with Father David.

After the necessity to win souls for Jesus, Father David's claim as
Prophet and King is the most consistent theme in Family literature.
With one exception, every disciple I spoke with professed loyalty to
Father David and confidence in his role as God's End Time Prophet.
However, the life experience of the disciples is far more diverse and
complex than might be expected from a simple analysis of the literature. The process by which individuals came to understand these roles,
the range of meaning they invest in "King" and "Prophet," and the intensity of conviction and devotion varies considerably.

The vast majority of people who joined did so with little or no
knowledge of The King. Not a single person claims to have joined
because of The Prophet, and a few entered with strong reservations
regarding him. Noah has a very high view of The Prophet. That was
hardly the case at the beginning.

After praying to receive the Holy Spirit and beginning to witness on my own, I decided to join. But I wanted no part of Father David at all. I didn't see the point. I didn't like some things I knew of him. I told my sister I would join, if I didn't have to buy into all this Father David stuff. She said it would be fine.

Well, I went with them to join a home. The young guy who answers the door looks at me and says, "Do you believe that Moses David is God's End Time Prophet?" I was really angry. I thought I had been set up. I actually reached back to hit the guy, but my brother-in-law grabbed my arm and took me to another section of the house.

Most of the disciples came to an affirming view of Father David as part of their overall incorporation into Family life. Acceptance of The Prophet's role and status was a central component of the socialization process. John, an American disciple from a Roman Catholic background, presented a typical scenario.

I was an eighteen-year-old hippie drug dealer when I was picked up by some Children of God while hitchhiking. I was in before I ever even heard of Father David. It wasn't presented directly, like "you must believe in this guy!" We mostly studied the Bible, and I read a few milky Letters. It was clear after a while that he was the founder and leader of the group. But nothing came out directly that he was Prophet of the End Time. I certainly didn't join because of Father David.

After a few months, the Shepherd explained to me who Uncle Dave was, that he was Prophet of the End Time. I wasn't asked to make any kind of commitment to that, it was just stated. Gradually, as I read further in the Letters, it just unfolded to me. I related very easily to the Letters. As I became closer to people in the home, gradually, I just accepted it. I loved The Family and knew it was right for me. If Father David was right for them, he was right for me.

A good number of disciples express a profound attachment to The Prophet. Ruth, a well-educated woman who joined in 1975, spoke of Father David with passion and deep conviction.

It is hard for me to express how deeply I loved Dad. When he died,
it was very, very hard for me. We all anticipated it. But I was really
shaken. I cried, almost uncontrollably. I never personally met Dad,
but he was my life. For the last twenty years I have been living what
he got from the Lord. I know this is heavy, that it may sound super
radical to you. But there is no other way to say it. He was my life!

I still have him. I miss him greatly, yet I still have him. I have his
Words. And I have his spirit.

Father David made a point of consistently reminding his disciples
that he was a sinful man who was fully capable of making mistakes.
Everyone I encountered views Father David as fully human. However,
some disciples expressed such an intense love and regard for "Dad"
that their devotion to him is virtually fused with their devotion to
God. Joyful, a European who joined in the mid-1980s, gives evidence of
this deep devotion.

Father David knows exactly how I feel, what I am thinking.
[Despite her use of the present tense, the Prophet had already died at
the time of this interview] He puts my dreams into words. He makes
Jesus so real, so simple for me. When I stop and pray and listen for
God, Jesus speaks to me. Father David makes the way for me to find
that, to find real life in Jesus.

When he died, I asked myself, "Have I followed the Bible and the
MO Letters as I should have? Is Father David proud of me in heav-
en?" When I read his Letters, they are still so beautiful for me. [At
this point she began to weep softly.] I never met him. Now that he is
gone, I can see his picture. I can look in his eyes and see how loving
he was, see how the Spirit of God was with him. The Spirit of David
is like Aquarius, flowing down to us. He was faithful to say the
Truth, not caring what others think. The Spirit of David is powerful
and alive in my life, and in The Family. We lift up the banner of
David, we believe it. We are giving our life for it.

All affirmed that Father David was human and capable of making
mistakes. But disciples who hold an extremely high view of The
Prophet have no real expectation that he could ever be wrong or mis-
guide them. Though they accept the formula of Father David's human-

ity, they live their lives with no doubts that he spoke for God and
would always lead them in the right path.

However, this rather simple approach is not the whole story. Some
view him in a very different light. Not a few people related serious
doubts and struggles over the authenticity, role, and authority of Father
David. Some disciples had difficulties early in their tenure, usually
over a specific teaching or attitude of The Prophet. Jeth, who joined in
1980, recalled his early difficulties:

> I was in several weeks before I knew anything about Father David
> at all. No one had even mentioned him. I was not very receptive to
> the whole idea of Father David, at first. Later, at a Family meeting,
> someone read the MO Letter "Keep on Believing." I found it interest-
> ing and encouraging. I think that is my first memory of a positive re-
> action to Father David. After a while, a sister gave me a volume of
> basic MO Letters. I read them and generally liked them. I found they
> made sense. But there was very little emphasis on having to accept
> the Letters as true. They were just there.
>
> I really cannot remember a specific moment when someone said to
> me: "Father David is the End Time Prophet." I just gradually began to
> see it. I had the experience of the people I was with. For me, it was
> seeing people put into practice the teachings of Father David, seeing
> how well they worked. That is what validated the Letters and Father
> David, at least for me. His advice and spiritual direction worked.
>
> I was very troubled by the apocalyptic letters. What appealed to
> me was the love, the forgiveness in their lives. When I read the
> Letters all about the Tribulation, destruction, God's retribution, I
> didn't handle it very well. In fact, I rejected it. But I loved The
> Family. So, I just put all that aside for a time. In a few years, when I
> was more grounded, I was able to deal with them better.
>
> When I think back on those early days, Father David doesn't play
> into them much at all. It was my connection to The Family, to the
> people there, and also their support in reading and understanding the
> MO Letters. That is how I came to see him as a prophet.

While some disciples like Jeth were able to put aside their difficulties; others struggled for years trying to come to terms with the full im-

plications of the Prophet's claims to authority and special access to God. As might be expected, many were reluctant to express specifics about their doubts or negative feelings toward The Prophet. Simeon, a long-term European disciple, was the most open.

When I first joined, I knew nothing of Father David. I had the Lord, and I knew The Family was for me and others. Then it began to dawn on me. There was this person, this "prophet!" I did not like it at all. It did not appeal to my sense of equality. I couldn't swallow it, not for a long time. Mostly, it was the principle of it. But also some of the MO Letters, I had a hard time with them too.

I do remember a brother joking with me about my lack of acceptance of Father David and some Letters, saying "you really choked on that one." I was in India, and all I had was a New Testament. I cried out to God to show me the truth. It was tough. I was a very weak disciple when it came to this. It took a long time for me to accept Father David. I remember waking up many mornings asking myself, "What are you doing with these crazy people?" But, I stuck around. I gave it all up: alcohol, smoking, drugs, sex, gave it all up. But not for Father David. For the Lord.

I always said what was on my mind, my doubts of Father David. But somehow, God kept me in. I recall one morning, I was really struggling with doubts about Father David. I had this huge old Bible. I opened it and the first verse I read was 1 John 5:1. "By this we know that we love the children of God." The actual words "children of God," there in the first sentence. That was confirmation for me, kept me going for years. But some things were still hard to swallow. But I always asked myself about the fruits. I and the rest of the brothers and sisters were out witnessing for Jesus, winning lots of souls to the Lord. We were never going out and telling people about Moses David, only about Jesus.

I have lived with a pattern of doubt for most of my life in The Family. But I am sure this happens to some church Christians the same way. In the end, I always came to the same conclusion. The movement is of God. We are bearing good fruit. I am supposed to be in The Family.

Now it is simple for me. Things I do not understand, or am not

*sure of, or don't believe something that is taught by The Family; I
just don't let that bother me anymore. I believe the things that really
matter. I believe in Jesus. I believe that He died to save me, and that
He will come again. I don't need much more than that. My favorite
line through the years has been, "Lord, if I am on the wrong track, get
me out!" The Lord never got me out.*

Virtually all disciples accept Father David as God's End Time
Prophet. Some did so immediately. Others struggled with the concept
for years. Furthermore, the depth and intensity of belief is quite varied.
Some view him as right next to Jesus. Others are far more cognizant of
his human frailty, viewing him as both a prophet and "a weird old
man."

Generalizations are inherently risky for such a diverse group of
people. However, some patterns do emerge. First, every disciple was
questioned about his or her relationship to Father David. Female disciples were more affirming and far more passionate in their expression
of affection and appreciation. Male disciples were more likely to
express reservations, questions, or doubts. With few exceptions, males
were much less likely to speak in terms of affection and personal
relationship.

Second, there appears to be an ongoing evolution in the de facto role
of The Prophet. His claims to authority and his impact on the disciples'
lives seems to have reached an apex in the late 1970s and early 1980s.
After this point, Maria and other members of the inner circle began to
play a more central role in directing the movement. For many, there
was also a maturing with respect to Father David. Seth, a long-term
American member, gave thoughtful reflection here.

*There are certainly levels of anointing, and Dad's level was high.
Back in the '70s he taught us, "Right now you are dependent on me,
on my channel." But he looked for a time when we would hear more
from the Lord ourselves and be less dependent on him. And that
came.*

*Father David was not perfect, far from it. I never thought he was. I
liked that about him. He told us about his problems and I respected
that. It gave me confidence that it was the Lord in control. Dad has*

died now, but it has gone very smooth. My personal family, who are not very positive about us, wondered what was going to happen now that our "guru" was dead. I said, "I don't think anything is going to happen. If this has been the work of a man, it will come to naught."

I never met Dad. I think it is best I never did. I honestly don't think Dad is or was so essential to The Family. He was just a man that God used. He made us unique. What The Family is today is because of his training and all that. But he was just part of what God was doing. And we were never just one man.

Simeon articulated this shift in more practical terms, particularly with respect to the nature and authority of the MO Letters.

Father David often said his prophecies and predictions and teachings were only his theories. That we could take them or leave them. But other times he was pretty strong we should take them. And that is the way it was. In theory, we had some choice. But in practice, it was never like that. And we all had very, very high confidence in what he said, and in the MO Letters.

It is different now. When we read an old Letter, we can say: "OK, this says such and such here, but in other places the Bible or the Letters say something different or qualifies it. So we need to think it through, put it all together." In the old days, when those MO Letters were fresh, nobody did that. We were not able to do that. At the time they came out, the Letters were the Word from God. We believed them as they were.

I struggled with this, far more than most. When I did understand the Letter was strictly Dad's opinion, I took the latitude he gave. But many people did not. They took every word Dad said as gospel. That has pretty much changed now.

Peter Amsterdam stated that "Father David's health had been failing for a number of years and he essentially retired from active life at the end of 1988. He continued to counsel with Maria, write an occasional letter, and offer his advice." From 1989 on, Father David played little direct role in the operation of The Family. Peter indicated that all disciples were aware he was transferring authority to Maria, but few knew of the extent of his retirement. Noah, a very well informed disciple, was present for these statements, and he was clearly surprised.

A popular view of religious communities like The Family holds that the charismatic leader manipulates, controls, and somehow binds his or her followers to the group. A survey of Family literature might well support such an assessment of Father David and his disciples. And there are certainly disciples with a passionate loyalty to King David. They virtually fuse their commitment to The Prophet with their commitment to God. However, for the most part, my observations led to a different conclusion. For most disciples, primary devotion and loyalty is to The Family itself, to the community of people with whom they share their lives. Loyalty and devotion to Father David is a necessary corollary of that primary commitment. He did not draw and does not hold disciples in The Family. The Family draws and holds the disciples to Father David.

In October of 1994, David Brandt Berg died. His Children were deeply saddened but not surprised. He had often predicted his own passing before the End Time. A few people have struggled. Angela, a long-term American disciple, shared her experience:

When Father David died, I cried. I cried a lot. We depended on him so much. And his death has changed The Family. I guess it has affected me personally. I always have had a lot of faith in Dad. He was so real, so loving, so down-to-earth. Now he is gone. Moma [Maria] is wonderful. But it has taken some adjusting for me.

How am I doing now? Well, I guess I am just holding on. It does take some adjusting to the new letters, prophecies, new situations. I mean, I really miss Dad. I always had faith he would tell us where we were, what was happening, what to do. When Dad wrote, it was right, really from the Lord. I still go back to Dad's Letters. I still love Dad very much, and I look forward to seeing him. And I know he speaks and leads The Family from the Spirit World.

Angela's deep sense of personal loss is not generally shared by the larger community. Many expressed satisfaction that "Dad" was no longer suffering and that he is now safe from his many enemies. Additionally, the disciples are uniformly certain that he has not left them alone. There is absolute confidence that The Prophet is alive and well in the Spirit World, working hard on behalf of his Children.

When we first received the letter that Dad had died, it was a shock. But not like some terrible loss. I actually felt happy for him; it was a celebration really. And it was an easy transition to make. In fact, the media in the United Kingdom claimed he was not dead, because we were not grieving enough.

I know he is still with us, that he speaks to us from heaven. He is still God's Prophet. And I know that if it were necessary, he could speak to me too. I have really felt his presence a few times, as if he were speaking to me. I sense words of encouragement, and I just know it is Father David speaking to me. He still guides The Family, and speaks to us from heaven. And his special job is to guide Maria.
* * * * *

[Can he speak or minister to more than one person at the same time?]
* * * * *

That is a very good question. I haven't thought about that. [thoughtful pause] No, I don't think so. Dad is not the same as the Lord. I think he would not be able to do that. (Heaven)

The continued role of Father David in the Spirit World is fully consistent with long-established Family theology. In early 1970 the spirit of Abrahim, a martyred fourteenth-century gypsy Christian, entered Father David's body and began to speak through him in a broken and heavily accented English. This experience was a watershed event for the Children of God. In April of 1970 Father David published "Abrahim The Gypsy King: The True Story of Our Spirit Guide" (ML #296). From that point on, Family literature consistently addressed issues related to the Spirit World. The reality and immediacy of angels, spirit helpers, and dark spirits became an ever-increasing dynamic of religious discourse. Peter Amsterdam offered a brief exposition of this transition.

Dad had met some gypsies. Abrahim, who was a Christian that had passed on hundreds of years ago, was like a spirit helper or guardian angel to these gypsies. Abrahim transferred over to Dad. Our theology is that heaven is not just sitting around. We believe the

spirit life after death is very similar to this one. Part of that activity is
to help from the Spirit World, in a limited way.

Some people say, "You communicate with the dead!" Well, we
don't look at it that way. We just look at it as a vehicle of the Spirit.
Some people have certain responsibilities and some spirits actually
try to help. The same with the gift of prophecy. We believe in the gift
of prophecy. These messages can actually come through, or come
from these various passed-on spirits.

In the case of Abrahim and Father David, I only saw it a few
times. The English was pretty lousy. Abrahim took over and spoke
through Father David. It was quite wild stuff, different than a normal
prophecy that came from another spirit or another channel.

Interaction with spiritual forces and the direct guidance of God
through the Holy Spirit and other spiritual entities is an ever present
and powerful dynamic of life in The Family. Virtually every disciple
regularly prays for and receives comfort, assurance, and guidance from
God. Such guidance and comfort occasionally comes in the form of
dreams or visions. Most often it occurs in the experiences of "prophecy," usually in a context of communal prayer. These messages from
God through the Holy Spirit or spirit guides are often the decisive factor in both individual and community decision making.

In the summer of 1995, a van full of young people on a mission trip
to Austin, Texas, was involved in a serious accident. The young man
driving and several others were injured very seriously. Five teenage
girls were killed. Very soon after the accident, Father David and Jesus
spoke in prophecy through several members of Maria's personal household. Then the apostle Peter and the apostle Paul spoke in prophecy,
primarily to encourage the young man who had driven the van. Soon,
the spirits of the five young women began to communicate from the
Spirit World, offering forgiveness to the young driver and expressions of
joy and ecstasy at being in heaven with Jesus and Father David, and
generally affirming that this tragedy did not mean that God was not
watching over The Family.

Joel is father to both the young man driving and one of the young
women who died.

The Austin accident, yes. This will be hard. My son was the driver of the van. He was legally at fault. My daughter, Joy, she died. It was the worst experience of my life, very hard for me. I can't put it into words; the pain, the sorrow. But, I know the Lord was always there with me. So I have come through it.

It was a very dark time for me. Hard to understand. But then we got the prophecies. Joy spoke in prophecy from the Spirit World to someone in Moma Maria's house. We don't know who for sure. And when I read the prophecy, I knew it was my Joy speaking. It was ex-actly what she would have said, and how she would say it. It was her way of phrasing things, even down to a pet name for her brother that only she used. It was her.

I know she speaks. I have heard from her. I prayed and asked the Lord to let her speak to me. She spoke in my mind, but it was her voice I heard. It has been a great comfort. I know she is with the Lord, is truly happy now. And I know that all this happened for a rea-son, a reason that we will someday understand.

I know there are some who have problems with all this. But I know it is true.

A few of Maria's letters respond to skepticism regarding the extent and nature of the prophecy surrounding the Austin incident. However, only one or two disciples were open about any reservations. In general, the disciples have accepted this enhanced Spirit World communication, and it has placed the incident within a meaningful framework.

A good number of people recounted personally moving and pro-foundly shaping experiences of visions, dreams, and encounters with the Spirit World. Often these came in the midst of great personal loss or need, and clearly worked to hold their world together and affirm the hand of God on the lives of individuals and the community.

We are people of faith, and God has honored that. In those early years, we had no money at all. Sometimes we had no food. Somehow, God always supplied our need. I know God takes care of me. Sometimes from this world, sometimes from the Spirit World.

* * * * *

[Can you give an example of God providing from the Spirit World?]

* * * * *

Sure. Several years ago I went to the doctor, five months into a pregnancy. He told me my baby had died. But I had to go through the whole labor process to get my dead baby from my womb. How can I explain what that was like? There are no words. It was a very hard time for me, very traumatic. It is the kind of time when doubts can come. I love my children. My baby was dead. And still inside me.

I knew if my water would break, it would be easier. I asked God to be with me, to break my water and help me through this terrible time. That is when the vision of my baby came. I could see this beautiful baby girl floating above me, a girl with golden hair. She said that I should not feel bad for her. She was in heaven with Jesus, and would be much happier. She told me to just let go and let it happen. It was so moving. So beautiful.

* * * * *

[Tears welled up in her eyes, and she paused for a moment.]

* * * * *

I told her that if she was real, she should reach down and touch my stomach, and have my water break. And that is what happened. And then it all happened. But it was so good. So pure, peaceful.

And I knew that she was my baby, and that she would come back to me. I had a baby girl next. She was just like the vision, golden curly hair. My child now is the same spirit as my baby that died. I know that is true. From the beginning, she has been very, very mature for her age, ask anyone. And that is why. (Conchi)

Communication with Jesus, the Holy Spirit, and other spiritual entities is a vital and sustaining force in the lives of most disciples. But, the Spirit World also has a dark side. The Devil and his demons are not only "real" in a theological sense, they are ever present and actively at work in the world. And the Devil's primary target is God's own special End Time People. Dark spiritual forces are almost always postulated as the primary source for negative experiences. The breadth of this understanding can easily be seen in a quick survey of Family literature. Opposition and persecution, physical illness, community discord, lack of disciplined behavior on the part of children, and personal failures of all types are primarily conceptualized as the result of Satan's attacks.

Informants repeatedly affirmed this overall orientation. However, it was in the "down times" when I observed the depth and intensity of these beliefs: playing basketball, washing dishes, watching videos. Even in the most casual conversation, disciples of all ages spoke freely of the Devil and evil spirits at work in the world and in their personal and community lives.

Family members are a joyful and often humorous people, with a wonderful capacity to laugh at themselves. But I never observed a disciple joking or in any way making light of evil spiritual forces. There is no flippant "the devil made me do it" attitude among these people. However, Father David clearly taught that though Satan was very powerful and deceptive, ever ready to attack and even oppress at times, he could not "possess" the Children. Satan has no ultimate power over them. The disciples appear to have fully internalized this teaching. They are confident that God is with them and that adequate spiritual power is accessible to eventually thwart any attack from the Dark Side.

Physical illness is one area of spiritual vulnerability. Disciples believe and practice a form of spiritual healing common to the Pentecostal wing of Protestant Evangelicalism. The appropriateness of conventional medical care is uniformly supported. Doctors and hospitals are appreciated for their ability to treat illness and injury, and disciples who pursue conventional treatment for medical problems are not viewed as spiritually problematic. However, the fundamental cause of illness or physical affliction is most often understood to be spiritual. It is reasonable and prudent to seek a spiritual cure as a first response. There are many stories of God's healing power. The following incident illustrates the practical theology of the Spirit World. Solomon is a Canadian disciple who has spent most of his Family life in the Orient.

I was in Tokyo street witnessing. I met this wandering, hippie-type guy from the States. He was quite sad and depressed. He came out and told me his main problem. His family was very critical of his sexual relationships with women. I was a babe, just new in The Family. I didn't know any better at the time. So I tell him of Dad's teaching that sex is free and wonderful, if done in love.

Later, I received a letter from his sister. It was very rebuking. Now, Dad taught us to pray over letters we receive. I failed to pray. Father

David teaches that there is a talisman, spirits can travel on objects. So this letter came. I opened it, and it was very negative toward me and The Family, quite a curse. I just put it away. Two days later, I wake up with this affliction, genital sores like herpes. I never had anything like that before. The shepherds prayed over me and gave me some cream. But it wouldn't go away.

One night I was in bed, almost asleep, and I just woke up. It came to me. It is the letter! I got that letter and went to the shepherd right then. I said, "We must pray over this letter and rebuke it right now." We prayed and rebuked it. We cleansed the evil spirits by God's power. And I burned the letter. Next morning, I woke up and the affliction was totally gone. It never came back. It was a miracle. The Lord showed me the curse from the spirit of this letter, and then He delivered me. It was very *real.*

Disciples generally conceptualize and verbalize problems, difficulties, and human weakness in distinctly spiritual terms. They are much more likely to say "I had the spirit of pridefulness" rather than to say "I was proud." A significant number of young adults still carry unresolved resentment related to the practice of labeling and dealing with typical childhood misbehavior as spiritual problems. However, most disciples are strengthened and empowered, knowing that spiritual resources are available to meet and overcome any challenge, difficulty, or tragedy that life may bring their way. Jonathan, of Brazil, offers a most clear example of how this access to spiritual power operates.

I was an active homosexual. Then I was saved, and entered The Family. For the first year or two, it was a constant battle. I had no further homosexual contacts. But the past kept pulling me back. I was saved; I knew that. I had the Lord's Spirit. And the sisters were always there to help me as much as they could. But it was still a very difficult struggle.

Then this MO Letter came out. It really helped me see why I was still struggling so much. I had assumed all along it was just me, that I was the problem. But I saw there was something else involved. I needed deliverance.

So, I asked four people who I trusted to come and pray over me. It was not some big, elaborate exorcism ceremony, or anything like

*that. They just laid their hands on me, and prayed that God would
release me from the power of the homosexual spirit.*

*I am not sure I can describe in words what went on inside me,
what I felt and experienced. In fact, I know I cannot explain it. But
when it was over, I knew. God had delivered me. And I have been free
of that spirit from then on. Before, it was something I had no control
over. But now I am free from the spirit of homosexuality. I am free in
Jesus.*

The Spirit World is an ever present, powerful, and tangible reality. The
disciples interpret life as a profoundly spiritual adventure. This adventure is both personal and cosmic in scope.

From the earliest days, millennial expectation has been a central focus of theology. David Berg developed his essential understandings of
the End Times well before the formation of the COG. He taught that
human history will climax in a worldwide political, economic, and
moral meltdown. The Antichrist will arise to save the world and for
three and one-half years will establish his reign as a wise and benevo-
lent leader. Then, his true nature will be revealed. He will declare his
divinity and require the world to worship and obey him, persecuting
unto death all those who refuse. Satan, acting through the Antichrist,
will have almost total control of the earth. All people will be required
to carry the "Mark of the Beast" as a control mechanism. The Great
Tribulation will last for three and one-half years; then Christ will return for his church. The Antichrist will be defeated in the Battle of
Armageddon, Satan will be bound, and Christ will establish His
Millennial Reign on earth. At the end of a thousand years, Satan will be
released for one final confrontation. At Satan's ultimate defeat, the
Kingdom of Heaven will be established forever, and God's Children
will live with Him in the Heavenly City.

This overall construct is consistent with beliefs that are held in substantial sections of the Christian church. Most other schemes place the
Rapture of the Church before the onset of the Great Tribulation, freeing Christians from the horror of those years. Aside from this detail,
the basic content of Family End Time theology is not particularly unusual. What does distinguish The Family is the special role they will
play in this grand drama, and the intensity of their conviction that the
End Time is upon us.

The disciples do not simply believe The End is fast approaching. They know it. And they live out their lives accordingly. In the early years, the immediate expectation of the coming Tribulation was so intense that even Father David felt it necessary to dampen the fire. In early 1972 he offered the following directive to community leaders:

Why do some of you leaders try to scare your people to death with such horrible stories and skits of what you think their tortures are going to be like in the Tribulation; or even conduct surprise scare drills in which some of you pretend to be officers invading their premises in the middle of the night to yank them out of a sound sleep pretending to arrest them? I realize you may think this is good practice to prepare them for the future, but I think it's too hard on them and apt to scare somebody to death or literally make them ill from fright. You could give somebody a heart attack! Jesus has promised to give us power for the hour and grace for the Great Event when it comes, but not before it comes.

So let's please stop these extreme tactics! We're going to suffer enough in the future without dwelling on it now! ("The Law of Moses!" ML #155, Feb. 1972)

Not long after this Letter, Father David began speaking as if The End would not come before 1993. Peter Amsterdam remembers the impact of that new teaching.

In the early years, late 1960s and early 1970s, most believed the End Time was right around the corner. I did. But in about 1973, Dad came out with a letter indicating it probably would not occur before 1993. He thought it would happen in 1993, based on his reading of history and the Scripture. But he was not absolutely dogmatic about that. I can not speak for the whole Family, but I think most were looking for 1993. It did not happen. I don't necessarily believe The End will come next week, or even next year. We are not into a set date. But we are all pretty much in agreement that we are now in the End Time. I fully expect everything to unfold in my lifetime.

The coming and going of 1993, with no "End" in sight, was a major disappointment for many. Well into 1995, this issue was quite sensitive and was one of the situations where I had to overcome defensiveness and evasive responses. Recently, some have adopted a reinterpretation of Father David's prophecy on 1993. Bethany, an American who has spent her last twenty years in South America, made it very simple.

We misunderstood Dad at the time. When he spoke of The End coming in 1993, he was talking about America. He was not talking about the whole world or the real End. And he was right. America did start to die in 1993. It is like in Genesis, where God says that Adam will die the day he eats the fruit. He didn't actually die on that day, but he started to die. That is what Dad meant, that America would start to die in 1993. And it is very clear that has happened. Dad was right.

However, others are not so sure and are still troubled.

* * * * *

I was very disappointed when The End did not come in 1993. And I wasn't alone. We just knew from what Dad had said, that 1993 would be it. But it didn't happen.

* * * * *

[How did you handle your disappointment?]

* * * * *

Well, you just hang on. So much has been just like Dad said. I am just hanging on. (Ashnah)

Regardless of the 1993 disappointment, the knowledge that each day is lived in the shadow of The End remains a powerful dynamic and informs life at all levels. Perhaps the best evidence of the strength of these convictions comes in the observation of casual interchanges. While I was visiting a home in Europe, a discussion developed over the appropriateness of the evening's video for younger teenagers. Family communities are generally protective of their children and seek to prevent them from being exposed to immoral or violent influences. The video that night was approved for adults and older teenagers, but one thirteen-year-old girl wanted to be included. She offered the following argument: "Mom, you know we are going to see a lot worse violence than this in the End Time. Watching a movie like this will help us be ready, so it all won't be such a big shock when it happens for real." No one laughed.

Radical belief in the imminent End has shaped the life experience of most disciples. It continues to serve as the primary motivation and justification for the life of sacrifice and hardship.

We live a very, very difficult *life. It is not that we* like *to suffer. We do it because God has chosen it for us, to prepare us for the End Time. I honestly never thought I would be here at age forty-three. I never thought about the future a lot at all, at least not a future in this world. Even if we are wrong on the End Time, I have still lived a good life. I have won thousands to the Lord. It will not reflect badly on what I have done with my life. But, we are* not *wrong. (Anna)*

In the early 1970s an associate of mine received a promotional mailing from a well-known fundamentalist Christian college that shares the same general millennial theology with The Family. The packet contained an abstract of a recent chapel message by the college president, in which he had interpreted the "signs of the times" and the Bible, leading him to the inescapable conclusion that Jesus would return within the next two or three years. Also included in the package was a request seeking contributions toward the college's ten-year development fund.

The Family has no ten-year development fund. Disciples do not plan for a future in this world. The decisions they make are profoundly informed by the imminence of The End. This orientation toward the future came through most clearly in the testimony of Isaac, a South American disciple.

My wife left some years ago. She took our three children with her. I still loved her. She left with some real negative feelings, so we haven't had much contact. I really miss my kids, but my End Time vision—living in the expectation of Christ's soon return—helps me through the pain of not having my kids and my wife. If I did not truly believe that the Lord was coming, and coming soon, I might well have made a different decision regarding my kids and my wife. I would have gone to much greater lengths to keep my family together.

See, the End Time Vision is central to who we are. We do not even face questions like pensions, retirement plans, how or where we will live when we all get old. I have built absolutely nothing for any future here on this earth. But I don't worry about that. The End Time

Vision also gives us a real sense of urgency about life. We don't have the luxury of a lot of time.

The depth and intensity by which the Children are shaped and influenced by the immediacy of the End Time Vision clearly sets them apart. There is also a firm conviction that their separation from the world, absolute dependence on God, communal lifestyle, suffering, and hardship will uniquely prepare them both to survive the Great Tribulation and lead other faithful Christians through those very dark years.

[What will be the role of The Family during the Tribulation and Millennium?]

* * * * *

We know we are going to be the leaders, at least some of the leaders. Most believing Christians think there will be a pre-Tribulation rapture. So most Christians are going to be in turmoil and confusion when they find out the Tribulation is upon them, and the Antichrist has come, and Jesus did not whisk them away to some heavenly mansion. No group of Christians is as prepared for the Tribulation, or the Millennium, as we are.

It is logical. Who would you send to run the 100-meter dash in the Olympics? People who like to jog and think there might be an Olympics some day? Or would you send people who know, who have worked their whole lives training, and who can run the fastest? The Tribulation will be a terrible time of pain. But we have been through a lot of tribulation already. We have been through the pain of prison, beatings, persecution. We have been maligned and despised by the world. And we have done it all while living by faith, trusting God fully for everything. We will be ready!

We are going to be priests and kings to rule over the peoples here on earth. We have been preparing to survive the Tribulation, and reign with Jesus. We have devoted our whole life: mind, body, spirit, everything. Who else is He going to choose? (Noah)

This sense of special status has been endemic to the movement from the beginning. Family ideology has consistently identified conventional society with the dominance of Satan in the world. Biblical passages such as 2 Corinthians 4:3–4, which identifies Satan as "the god of this world," are used to validate the stance toward the outside. This theological understanding of the "true Church" is common to any number of Christian traditions from the first century down to the Amish settlements of modern America. Like many who have come before them, Family members take their view of "the world" with radical seriousness.

This is the "System" which forms the fundamental "other." The System is evil, dangerous, and corrupt to the core. It will soon be the object of God's uncontrolled wrath. Disciples hold passports, obtain drivers licenses, and get legally married when necessary. But they operate on the fringe of society, with as little interface with government or any other System institution as possible. They do not vote, unless required by law, or participate in civic life at any level. They educate their own children. They intentionally insulate themselves as much as possible. To paraphrase an old gospel tune: "This world is not their home. They're just passing through."

Although the System is evil by nature, all who live in it are not necessarily "Systemites." Well over 99 percent of persons led to receive Jesus by the disciples have remained in the System. All who express faith in Jesus have found salvation. However, Father David was adamant from the very beginning that conventional churches of all stripes are part and parcel of the System. In the first MO Letter, "The Old Church and The New Church!" he makes it very clear that conventional churches, by rejecting his prophetic ministry, had ceased to be the church.

[God speaking]

* * * * *

They claim to be mine—My Wife—My Church—but the relationship is in name only. . . . Therefore is this hypocrisy and not a marriage. This is pretense and not love . . . their temples are as the temples of men and of devils—an abomination unto Me. . . . [t]heir holy days do horrify me. . . . She hath cast forth My children, and her that was dear unto Me and she hath beaten My prophets. She hath harmed Mine anointed. Therefore shall I beat and harm her with great wrath. ("The Old Church and the New Church!" ML #A, August 1969)

"Churchianity," the term for mainstream Christianity, was a "damnable deception and an accursed counterfeit." This position has moderated over the last five years, and the disciples are much more open to working in cooperation with Christians outside their community. But the basic view of the church as part of the System remains.

However, Father David also taught that the resources of the System could and should be appropriated for the work of the Kingdom. In accessing those resources, it was sometimes appropriate and necessary for disciples to conceal their identity. It was not unusual for disciples to establish relationships with outside Christians in this way. Zeb, an American disciple who has spent much of the last decade in the Orient, is a good example of both the connection and the tension that exists with the broader context of the Church.

In 1982 my wife and I and our four kids went to Mexico to join up with a threesome we had known before. We weren't there long till we got rocked by persecution from a Baptist missionary named Van Wood. He was a good fellow, and enthusiastic for the Lord. But he found out about the brother and his two wives. He had a hard time with it. So he went around trying to discredit us with all our provisioning contacts. It became his mission to get us out. So, we left.

We landed in California. We were on the road, living in a trailer most of that time. We made some good contacts with churches. We met a Baptist pastor from Texas who got involved with us. He even supported us in Thailand. We operated without the Children of God label. We were just independent Christian missionaries. We did a little with churches, not a lot. They tended to ask a lot of questions. We did get connected with Calvary Chapel in Los Angeles. They supported us in Thailand.

When we got to Thailand, we had some contact with other Christians, but we never developed any relationship. As we got stronger there—more homes, and more ministry to the poor—then the churches became more active in opposition to us. We did disaster relief, worked with refugees, prisons, orphanages. That is when the persecution really got going. Most was instigated from the churches. We had only tourist visas, no official registration. The churches would try and find our weaknesses and attack us. Try to get the government after us.

It was mostly the American and European missionaries that caused the trouble for us.

The disciples appreciate that there are many Christians out in the System. But there is little or no sense of identity with outsiders. Their special status with God sets them apart from all other religious communities. Some moderation has developed recently, but disciples do not "fellowship" with anyone outside the ranks. I encountered more than twenty disciples who had departed, spent significant time out in the System, and then returned to the fold. None reported attending any church or establishing any relationships with outsiders during these periods of separation.

Their special status with God carries a high price. The demonic nature of the System, the total impotency of the conventional church, and the impending End all work together to create a continual crisis environment. To survive and complete the assigned mission in such an environment requires absolute dedication and commitment. It also requires a level of unity and discipline that can be achieved only through a structure of authority similar to that of a military establishment.

Through most of their history, the choice placed before the disciples was clear. The Lord calls for absolute commitment and obedience. In these last and desperate days of battle against the Devil, drastic measures are necessary. Participation in God's elite End Time Army requires total obedience to God, and to the structures of authority God has ordained in Father David and the leadership of that Army.

No matter how much the Lord tells you, or what the written Word in the Bible and the Letters say to do, you're bound to eventually get off the track in some way if you don't have some kind of direct physical oversight! I am sure that is why the Lord has always given His people leaders . . . some person in human form to instruct them & advise them & counsel them & command them to do His Will. (Daily Bread, 1984, 8:268–69)

The authoritarianism has softened over the past few years, particularly under the recently adopted Love Charter. But the disciples have lived most of their lives under the direct control of their leaders. Father David's Letters are filled with instructions that leadership personnel are to be kind and loving, and with clear instruction to all disciples that they must obey leadership under any and all circumstances. The degree of control varied with time and place, but in general most every aspect of their lives was subject to the advice and consent of those in authority over them. Sudden change and dislocation were commonplace, particularly in the early years. "I was a singer and dancer in an off-Broadway show when I got saved and joined The Family. Deborah, Father David's daughter, found out about me and in two weeks I was shipped off to Paris to join the show group there. I was not given any choice, she simply ordered me to go. That was the way it was back then. You did what you were told (Amptha)."

Most disciples are surprisingly open about difficulties, trauma, and pain they have suffered at the hands of insensitive, authoritarian, or abusive leaders. More than a few were willing to speak of their own culpability in the abuse of power that plagued the movement in the first decade.

Our biggest problems as a whole have been bad leadership. We have had leaders who have not stayed close to the Lord, and have not followed the spirit of the MO Letters. I was one of them.

I was a shepherd in the years before the RNR, by far the worst time for bad leadership. I was really caught up in the "Chain" [the leadership organization]. I was really into the power of it. And I was guilty of many of the abuses that went on then. Financial abuses of the other disciples. I pushed people much too hard. I pushed them to get unreasonable quotas of literature out, to get funds. And I used that money to live a much better lifestyle. At the time, I thought I was going about it the proper way. But I wasn't. I was very authoritarian toward others. I pushed them around. I was certainly not as loving and caring toward the people under my authority as I should have been. I was like most of our leaders. I was caught up in the status, the power thing. I hurt people. And it hurt me. (Thomas)

Several themes consistently emerged in discussions about the nature of authority and leadership. The RNR, when Father David fired the entire leadership, is universally seen as a watershed event. The era prior to 1978 is the Dark Age of the abuse of power. Many of the top-level leaders left or were ejected from the movement. The disciples believe that changes in policy and spirit have worked to minimize the potential for mistreatment and abuse. However, as crucial as the RNR was, it did not alter the basic orientation that requires an authoritarian system of community organization and control. There are numerous stories of tension, stress, and mistreatment received at the hands of appointed leaders, both before and after the RNR.

I was a leader. At that time it was suggested leaders be married. So I was asked "to pray about" a wife. Now, when a leader asked you to "pray about" something back then, that pretty much meant that you should do it. I got direction from my shepherd toward a certain girl. So, I asked her to marry me. She said yes. We had never even held hands. She was quite attractive, and I was the only one not chasing her. I guess I was the lesser of evils. [laughs] We had a huge meeting. Thirty-two couples got married at once. Family style, not legal marriages. [Laughing. He found some of these memories amusing.]

It is not that all *the leaders were dictator types. But to be honest, most were. People really abused their authority and position. But then again, we were just kids. We didn't know what we were doing. Things got better as we all matured, but problems still remained. It is much better now, but it still happens. (Nathan)*

Generally, the disciples hold a complex and somewhat ambivalent appreciation of the authoritarian nature of their movement. They fully accept the necessity of discipline and clear lines of authority. They are aware of trials, trauma, and abuse. Yet, even in the face of serious abuse and profound personal loss, disciples consistently attribute these difficulties to the character flaws of individuals. They do not find fault with the nature of the community, and especially not with the leadership of Father David.

I have had some very wonderful Shepherds. Before I tell you this story, I want that very clear. The shepherds in Mexico were an unusual thing for me. You must remember as I tell you this, that these people were sent back, kicked out of The Family later on.

There was jealousy in the home. I was sharing [having sexual intercourse] with the male shepherd. His mate was having a hard time with it. About this time, we had an outbreak of measles in the home. My infant girl got very sick. I asked for special prayer from my shep-

herd. She refused to come. Finally, I insisted that she come. When she saw my little girl, she said we should take my baby to a hospital. But, she refused to give me a ride, and she refused to contact the doctor friend that she had. She insisted that I take my little girl to the poor people's hospital instead. I had no choice. There was only one oxygen mask and another child was using it. So, my little girl couldn't get the oxygen that she needed. I was trying to get it to her with a tube. But I couldn't get her enough. My little baby girl died.

* * * * *

[At this point, she was completely overcome with emotion. She sat for several minutes, crying over her loss. Eventually, she was able to recover enough emotional control to continue.]

* * * * *

My little girl was born in Mexico, and she died in Mexico. . . . I have never spoken with anyone about this. It is so contrary to the rest of my experience in The Family. . . . I love The Family, and for the most part my shepherds have been very good to me. There is no better place. I see individuals with their weaknesses, but I have mine too. There are things people need to forgive me of. (Alice)

Alice lost her baby girl. Still she hangs on, faithful to The Family. The communal spirit and the various components of Family ideology create a network of meaning that sustains the disciples through life's darkest hours.

Radical commitment to Jesus, the Prophethood of Father David, communion with the Spirit World, and the End Time Vision inform every facet of Family life. Father David's Children have also retained their early vision of "Revolution for Jesus." It is very important that disciples see themselves as "revolutionary." And no aspect of their shared experience has been more "revolutionary" than the total restructuring of the sexual ethic. We now turn to this most complex and controversial dimension of life in The Family.

4. The Law of Love

While attending the 1996 annual meeting of the American Academy of Religion, a colleague and I had breakfast with several religious scholars. We all spoke of our work. One among us was a well-known theology professor at an equally well known evangelical seminary. When I disclosed my interest in The Family / Children of God, I thought we might lose him. Upon recovering, he responded to me: "That's the pornography bunch. Why, that is the most pernicious cult there is! How could you be interested in a thing like that?"

Their rejection of the world, communal lifestyle, communion with the spirit world, the prophetic role of Father David, and their authoritarian leadership structure have all alienated The Family from the church and the "System." But the radical and "revolutionary" teaching and practice of human sexuality has marked these people off, in the minds of many, as a "pernicious cult," a "thing." Nowhere is The Family more "revolutionary" than in their unique doctrine of sex, the Law of Love. It is the single most distinguishing mark of this most unusual community. And this troubles them.

Peter Amsterdam shares a general concern about the relationship of his community with the world of evangelical Christianity. Peter realizes that they will never be fully accepted by the wider church, but he hopes for toleration and, at a minimum, to be left alone.

I know our views on sex are a real problem; I just don't understand why it is such a big deal. It is all we ever hear. We are mostly about Jesus, telling people about Jesus. Sex is only 2 percent of what we are. I just don't think it is fair to make that much of it.

* * * * *

[Peter, that is like the bull saying, "Why is everyone so concerned about my horns? They are only 2 percent of what I am."]

* * * * *

[Laughter all around.]

The Christian church has struggled for two thousand years with human sexuality. The Family is certainly not the first community within the broad Christian tradition to revolt against well-established sexual mores. The Church of Jesus Christ of Latter Day Saints adopted polygamy. This construction of sexual relationships was first developed among the leadership, and then adopted as a principle of the church in 1852. In 1848, the Congregationalist John Humphry Noyes founded the Oneida Community. This Christian communal society was based on an open and affirming understanding of sexual relationships and the institution of "complex marriage." Noyes held that persons could achieve spiritual perfection in this life and could live out that perfection just as they would later live in heaven. He believed that heaven would be a true commune, with no private property and no monogamous marriage. Complex marriage was envisioned as an earthly expression of this later heavenly state, where sexual relations between adults would no longer be considered adultery.

In the mid-twentieth century, the Jamaa movement in Central Africa developed other themes that would also appear in Family doctrine, including the concept that ideal Christian unity could best be achieved through sexual union of the brothers and sisters, and particularly of the sisters with the priest. But I have discovered no community that has attempted to stretch the boundaries of sexual freedom as Father David's Children.[1]

When I began this journey, they asked only for accuracy and fairness. In exchange for that assurance, they granted wide access to their literature, much of it intended solely for use within the community. Some of the early literature dealing with the more extreme sexual activity has been repudiated and withdrawn from all homes. Most young people and new disciples have never seen the bulk of it. In addition to this access to highly restricted written material, Moma Maria and Peter Amsterdam personally approved this study. They encouraged the

1. For a brief but well-informed overview of the development of the Family sexual ethos, see J. Gordon Melton, "Sexuality and the Maturation of the Family," in Lewis and Melton 1994, 71–95.

disciples to cooperate fully.[2] Hundreds of disciples, from young teenagers to seasoned adults, shared the most intimate details of their personal lives. For most, this was the first time they ever spoke with an outsider about their life in The Family. For some, it was the first time they openly recounted memories of some dark and difficult times. Such trust requires responsibility, a responsibility to be both accurate and genuinely sympathetic.

I intend neither an apology nor a tabloid exposé. Some readers will undoubtedly consider much of what follows disturbing. The intention is not to offend or to shock. However, the story of the Children of God is best told in their own words. In this chapter, we will focus on three central aspects of Family sexuality: sexual relationships among adult members, the Flirty Fishing ministry, and the sexuality of children. The chapter will close with a consideration of sexuality as spiritual metaphor and heavenly reward.

In the early years, the COG came under widespread criticism for their Spartan and Puritan lifestyle. The colonies were sexually segregated. Virtually all of the first wave of disciples entered the movement as unmarried young adults. Complete sexual abstinence was required of all single members, and this policy was uniformly enforced. When these young people abandoned the System, they consciously turned their backs on the "world." This was the world of drugs, alcohol, greed, and materialism. It was also the world of promiscuous sexual activity. Jerusha described herself as a "dropout, hippie drug dealer, living on the beaches in Hawaii with my drug-dealing boyfriend." In 1972, she was dramatically converted to faith in Jesus. And she joined the Children of God.

When I first joined, there was no sex at all. I mean none! *The boys and girls were kept very separate. They didn't even like us to hold hands. I had been in a lifestyle where "anything goes." I tell you, it was* rough *those first few years. I liked sex, and I missed it. But it was good for me. I guess. [laughs]*

I accepted this completely. It was who the Children of God were. It was not easy for me, but I was chaste for my first few years. To be

2. Though The Family is less authoritarian than in the past, "encouragement" from leaders like Maria and Peter carries a great deal of weight.

honest, I was not all that happy about it. I mean, I kept busy, but there were times, "like how much longer does this go on?" So, what would happen is that you would start looking for a husband, because you were needy. You know.

Sexual purity was a key element of the early COG lifestyle. However, a shift was in the wind, even at the very start. "Scriptural, Revolutionary Love-Making!" was one of the earliest MO Letters. Subtitled "Your right to enjoy married love," it specifically targeted married couples and was supported throughout with scriptural quotations, particularly from the Song of Songs. The Letter is marked by direct and explicit language, and by a remarkably casual tone. Subtopics include: Where, When, Positions of Love-Making, How to Embrace, How to Make Love, Petting, and Entry. A few short quotations will suffice.

Where: In bed—Heb. 13:4. On the grass, under the trees—SoS 1:16–7. In the field, the village or the vineyard—SoS 7:11–2. In a chariot—SoS3:9–10. Variety is the spice of life!

Entry: SoS 4:16–5:6; 6:2, 1–12—Open to me . . . I am come in . . . Make haste . . . like the chariots . . . like the roe—8:14 (He enters, they pump and try to climax together, wait for each other, try to help each other finish, taper off, and, if needed, he finishes her with his fingers—which may also be needed to help open her hole for the first time if a virgin, gently with lubricant. He withdraws, eats, sleeps.) SoS 2:5—I am sick of love . . . stir not my love till he pleases.

("Scriptural, Revolutionary Love-Making!" ML #N, Aug. 1969)

Father David began to reconsider sexual ethics in the very early stages of the movement. His personal relationship with Maria broke the bonds. By 1971, he was engaging in sexual intercourse with female disciples within his personal household. These activities were known only to his immediate family and close associates. He was reaching some startling new conclusions on the relationship between sex and religion. Soon he began sharing these with his disciples.

Though overt sexual imagery begins earlier, 1973 is the year of the new sexual ethic. It is marked by the publication of "Revolutionary Women" (ML #250, June 1973), "Revolutionary Sex" (ML #259, Mar. 1973), and "Come On Ma!—Burn Your Bra," (ML #286, Dec. 1973). In

"Revolutionary Sex," Father David spells out the emerging ethic. Sex is not sin.

Although nudity and sexual activity are perfectly normal, lawful activities as far as God is concerned and as far as humanity is concerned, . . . in the Western culture, it has been made taboo. . . . It all starts with the false doctrine that sex is sin. . . . whereas the normal, healthful, natural, God-created, God-given and God-permitted attitude toward sex should be absolutely no different from our attitude toward any other normal physical activity, such as eating, exercising or even sleeping. . . . It is just as wrong for you to starve your body of its normal sexual needs and satisfactions as it is for you to starve yourself to death by not eating. ("Revolutionary Sex!" ML #259, Mar. 1973)

Father David went on to affirm the naturalness and moral acceptability of nudity and masturbation. The cover drawing for "Revolutionary Sex" features a nude young woman lying on her back on a grassy hill, stroking her breast with one hand and masturbating with the other. In this Letter, The Prophet offered his interpretation of the biblical teachings on sex. The only sexual activities proscribed by the Bible were fornication, adultery, incest, and sodomy. He understood the Bible to offer exceptions for the first three. Only male homosexuality was completely forbidden. The full implications of these "exceptions" would unfold in short order.

However, Father David did not simply wish to affirm sexual freedom and sexual fulfillment as natural and good. He went on to link sexual liberation with spiritual well-being, and to the very character of God.

From personal experience I can tell you that I have accomplished much more and done greater things and achieved greater success in God's work since I have become more sexually liberated and enjoyed greater sexual activity than ever before.

It was not until I kicked over the traces, thumbed my nose at old-fogey churchianity and all of its old-bogey inhibited sexual superstitions and really let myself go and enjoy sex to the full, wild and free, to the absolute utmost, it was only then that God also helped me to

achieve this spiritual and mental and physical freedom that I have
since had, to completely explode in a total orgasm of psychological,
social, economic, political, religious and sexual freedom and liberty
and worldwide accomplishments.

From my personal revelations and Bible study, I am convinced
that Jesus Himself could have enjoyed His Father's own creation of
sexual activity with some of the women He lived with, particularly
Mary and Martha, "yet without sin."

Sex is no sin and if sex is no sin, then why would it have been sin-
ful for Jesus! . . . Even the angels of God enjoyed union with the
daughters of men. . . . God Himself had to have had intercourse with
Mother Mary in order to have Jesus. ("Revoutionary Sex!" ML #259,
Mar. 1973)[3]

Early in 1974, Father David began developing what he termed the
Law of Love. The initial position was laid out in "The Law of Love!"
Letter and more fully developed with the publication of three MO
Letters at the end of 1977 and in early 1978.[4] His essential premise was
that God had granted the Children a special dispensation: complete
freedom from the restrictions and limitations of the law. "We are the
last Church! We are God's last Church, the last step in God's progress
toward total freedom for His Church and the last chance to prove that
the ultimate Church can be trusted with total freedom in this last gen-

3. This text offers an excellent example of the various ways the disciples have dealt
with some of the more provocative statements from Father David. All disciples I questioned about this issue affirmed their belief that Jesus more than likely had sexual relationships with several of his female disciples. According to Family theology, this sexual
activity was consistent with Jesus' sinless life. All affirm the "virgin birth" of Jesus.
Some of the disciples I encountered did not believe God physically had sex with Mother
Mary. When pointed to this passage, a few would respond like Joshua, a long-term
American disciple: "Oh, Dad could really say some wild things, couldn't he? It's like
Jesus saying to pluck out your eye, he didn't mean it actually, just an exaggeration to
make a point. See, often we are way off course, looking way too far to the left, and Dad
wants us to look straight ahead. So what he does is say or do something really extreme,
jerk our heads all the way to the right. Then, when we settle down, we are looking
straight ahead, like Dad wants." Others responded like Noah: "We believe in the virgin
birth, in that Jesus was conceived in an immaculate, a miraculous way. But we also believe that God probably sent one of his angels to implant the seed and the spirit of Jesus
in Mary. We believe that all beings in the Spirit World have a body, and have a form of
sex. So, that is not inconsistent, to think that Mary had intercourse with a spiritual being, and still that Jesus had a virgin birth."
4. "Love vs. Law!" (ML #647, July 1977); "Our Declaration of Love" (ML #607, Oct.
1977); and "Is Love Against the Law?" (ML #648, Jan. 1978).

eration!" ("The Law of Love!" ML #302, Mar. 1974). The Law of Love simply stated that all decisions and behavior must be motivated solely by love for others and for God. Resting on his interpretation of Jesus' great commandment in Matthew 22, Father David freed his Children from all legal restrictions in the Bible. This was no license to act without restraint. The disciples continued to live under very close supervision, with clear lines of authority and clear regulations of community life. Any action taken out of self interest, lust, or greed was sin.

Can you be trusted with total life, love, liberty and the freedom of the Spirit, or do you have to be kept in the cage of the law for the transgressors who are ruled only by their own carnal lusts and lack of love? The answer depends on you and whether you can keep the rules of love to enjoy such liberty that brings such life!

As in marriage and all other social relationships with each other, God's Laws of Love are still the same: 1. Is it good for God's work? 2. Is it good for His Body? 3. Is it good for you? Does it glorify God, His Body and edify your own soul? Does it help someone and harm no one?

All variation from the norm of personal relationships, any substantial change in marital relationships, any projected sexual associations should have the willing consent of all parties concerned or affected, including the approval of leadership and permission of the Body. If this is lacking in any quarter and anyone is going to be harmed or unduly offended, then your actions are not in love nor according to God's law of love! ("The Law of Love!" ML #302, Mar. 1974)

The Children were now free from specific biblical regulations, most particularly the law against adultery. "As far as the Bible says, for us there is no such thing as adultery! There is no such thing anymore as a Biblical law against adultery, as long as it is done in Love, because the 'Law of Love' supersedes all other laws" ("Love vs. Law!" ML #647, July 1977). In 1980, Father David issued "The Devil Hates Sex! But God Loves It!" He was very clear.

The Devil hates sex, & yet he's got the world deceived into thinking that he loves it, . . . The only reason God had to make any prohi-

bitions about sex was because of their perversions & their perverted attitude toward it. But as far as God's now concerned, there are no more sexual prohibitions hardly of any kind. — Except He sure seemed to hate sodomy *& I don't see where He withdrew that.*

The only way you can possibly regain the freedom and liberty that Adam and Eve had in the Garden, total freedom from any guilt complexes about sex, is to find God & the Truth *of God & have the Lord & be led of His* Spirit *& know the Truth of the* Word! *— That all those Mosaic Laws & prohibitive laws & strict regulations are gone & totally superseded by the Love of Christ, the* Law of Love. . . . *As far as God's concerned, there are no more sexual prohibitions hardly of any kind. . . . God's Only Law is Love! ("The Devil Hates Sex! But God Loves It!" ML #999, May 1980)*[5]

The Law of Love validated sexual "sharing" among both married and single disciples. This practice continues as an integral dimension of communal life. However, like other aspects of The Family experience, sexual liberation was far from uniform. Many disciples greeted the new sexual ethic with great anticipation. Others were hesitant and reluctant. Still others rejected it completely. The full impact hit at about the same time as the RNR, when the leadership was fired and the organization essentially was disbanded. Hundreds left the movement, many unable to live with the new moral direction. Those who remained loyal were willing and able to accept this radical new lifestyle. Though the essential ethical norms were established by 1978, the sexual ethos of the Children has changed and matured through the years. It is to their experience we now turn.

5. In this Letter, Father David specifically included incest and age limitations under the category of laws that are now superseded by the Law of Love. However, beginning in 1988, Father David and Maria conducted what was termed the "lit purge." According to Noah: "Father David and Maria realized that some Family literature contained statements that if acted on, would not be in accord with the true meaning of The Law of Love. They eliminated certain statements by Dad that people within The Family might use for their own selfish purposes. This purge went from 1988 through 1990. Certain portions of various Letters were whited out, or cut out, of all Family copies. This was required, and checked on by over shepherds. Some lit was pulled completely from the homes, such as the *Story of Davidito* and other material. In 1988 Father David specifically renounced any and all Family literature that might in any way be interpreted to allow for the possibility of sexual contact with minors." Since 1988, The Family has had very explicit regulations against incest and any sexual contact between adults and minors.

Sexual revolution was a "top-down" phenomenon. It began with Father David and his immediate circle, then spread down through the leadership structure. The process was uneven, at best. Communities were scattered around the world. After the RNR, many disciples had little personal direction, and many were left on their own to interpret and implement the new ethic. The awareness and acceptance of the new sexual code was not at all uniform. One reason for the RNR was that some leaders did not accept Father David's vision. They filtered the message of those Letters, or kept the information from disciples under their care. Prior to 1978, the MO Letters were normally sent to the colony leaders, who then relayed their message to the ordinary disciple. The shift to the new sexual practices was sometimes rocky.

I joined in early 1975. Actually I didn't really join a colony. My brother was in the COG. He and three others were traveling, not associated with any home. I did not understand then. Some of them had somehow gotten to see an advanced copy of one of the MO Letters about sharing. This couple decided to put it into practice, so the girl shared with my brother. They got caught, and the leadership of the home did not see it the same way. They got kicked out of the home, and were on the road. They didn't tell me about this till years later. (Ruth)

Peter Amsterdam offered some clear insight into how sexual sharing only gradually became a norm.

In 1971, Dad got a revelation about "all things are pure and all things are lawful." He allowed it with some of the top leadership. But apparently it got a little out of hand, and Dad said, "forget it." As far as I understand, no one outside of the very top level of leadership was aware of this at the time. I sure didn't know about it.

Then, in 1974, the "Law of Love" came out. It basically stated that you could have a sexual experience with somebody else as long as it was loving and it had certain criteria—consent of everybody involved, and it didn't hurt anyone. There was a list of things.

I was a district shepherd in Europe, and this boy had won a prize for getting out lit, a trip to London. He asked for some extra money:

"So I can go to a prostitute. I've been in The Family for years and I've never had sex, before I joined or after."

I thought, "That's not illogical." I talked to my wife. I said: "Honey, this Letter [Law of Love] says this boy can have sex within The Family, and I think maybe you ought to do it." She says, "No Way!" I showed her the Letter. But, we hadn't heard that any leadership was doing it.

Some time later, I was attracted to this woman in our home. One night, after a dance, we went off and did some petting. Although you could justify it from the Letters, it just wasn't widely done and certainly not widely expected. Her husband was not too happy, and neither was my pregnant wife. We called in the regional shepherd. He reprimanded me. He said: "Look, don't do this again." I was put on probation by an even higher up leader. Now, both of these guys were already into sharing. But I didn't know that at the time.

I know there were a lot of homes where people weren't sharing. Dad wasn't that explicit about it. After the RNR, Dad brought a lot of grassroots-type people to stay in his home. . . . Dad was surprised to learn that so many were not sharing. That is when we started sharing in our home.

It appears that the actual practice of sexual sharing increased gradually through the mid-1970s. It spread as leaders decided to avail themselves of a wider selection of partners. Veronica recalled her first experience:

I was single in Hawaii, and very celibate. But things changed at the top. Most of us were not aware of it. This was about 1976 or 1977. There was a group of top-level leadership in the main office there. One day, one of the leaders talks to me about having a date with one of the other men, a top leader.

That was my first time to share. I was very happy about the change. It had been so long! It was for me like, "This is too good to be true!"

But that one time was it. There wasn't much going on down at the lower levels. We weren't even hearing about it much. I guess there were MO Letters about this, but I didn't know about them. I don't re-

call now if I was instructed not to tell anyone about this date with the leader. But, I didn't tell anyone.

Veronica found the introduction of sexual sharing to be a liberating experience. This was not the case with many others. An undetermined number of people left the movement in reaction to this moral shift. But even among some who remained loyal, the introduction of sexual openness was a stressful time. This was particularly the case when individuals, mostly leaders, did not follow the guidelines of the Law of Love.

The Family is not an easy life. We don't expect it to be. But by far my worst experience was when sharing started. FFing was already going. That wasn't easy, but I had worked through that. But then I found out that some of the men in leadership were sharing with my wife, without my knowledge. They would take her out FFing. Then, when they got back late to the house, while I was sleeping, they would have sex with her. And they told her not to tell me. So she didn't. I woke up one night, and found them. I was extremely *upset. This was* very, very hard *for me. It was right before we got thrown in prison. But this experience was worse than going to prison. It was the* worst *experience of my life. (Isaac)*

Few disciples had this sort of traumatic introduction to sharing. But there are a number of people who struggled deeply with the transition to such a radically new lifestyle.

When I first joined, things were very strict, I couldn't even kiss my wife before we were married. There was no sharing, far *from it. Then the RNR came in '78. Before, there had been some Letters: "Come On Ma—Burn Your Bra" and "Law of Love." I read them, but I had* no *idea they could be taken so far. When the whole sharing thing came out, I was like: "Whoa! What is going on here?" Now, we were about revolution. But, I had pretty conventional ideas of what marriage should be. We were Visiting Servants. So we would visit the homes. I guess there were circumstances where we had to share with others, to achieve closeness with the people.*

*****

[I sense that this was not an easy change for you.]

* * * * *

I really struggled. I am from a very conservative culture. I had real trials with jealousy. I understood the sacrifice, the principle of it. But it was very hard.

A fair number left, but I never gave leaving a thought. I just had to adjust. I could accept the principle. I had more trouble with some who took things to excess. Some of these folks were out of the hippie culture, right off the streets. They really took advantage of the freedoms Father David gave us. Now it was always in his Letters, not to act selfishly. But some people did act selfishly. This had a real negative effect, on us and on our reputation. They hurt some people. And they hurt some marriages. (Andrew)

After the breakup of the leadership structure in early 1978, Father David's explicit edicts regarding sexual practices became directly available to all disciples. He offered specific instructions regarding the positive value of nudity and frequent sexual sharing. He also provided the disciples insight into sexual practices in his own home, which virtually all disciples viewed as the model of righteousness.

One night after a real good dinner talk by Dad on the importance of sharing & how timidity is really just pride, Dad suggested we have a "come-union." He set up a place for Maria & Timothy on the floor, we [Father David and the female writer] had the couch, & a sister took care of sweet Alfred upstairs. Of course it was really good for everybody to just love one another, & was especially new and humbling for dear Timothy, God bless him.

Directly beneath this statement, there is a photograph of a male and female member of the household, nude and fully engaged in sexual intercourse. The caption under the photograph: "A 'love-demo'—what a way to go!—(so this is DO, y'know!)."[6]

Father David coined the term "come-union" to describe the practice of randomly pairing off and engaging in sexual intercourse in a group. He used the term on a regular basis through the 1980s. The play on words was obvious. He was elevating open sexuality to a near sacra-

6. "Return to Madrid!" chap. 61, D. O. (Mar. 1978). Later published in *The Story of Davidito,* 1982, 457.

mental status. In "Sinless Sex!—God's Sex Position!" he provided the biblical basis for the new sexual ethic.

God's first commandment to man in the first book of the Bible, first chapter, the 28th verse, is "Be fruitful & multiply & replenish the Earth!"—or, "Thou Shalt Have Sex!" Think of that! Sex was God's first commandment to man!—And to have sex was man's first obedience to God!

God was so sexy that He put those two most gorgeous people who ever lived in that beautiful Garden of Eden stark naked, totally nude . . . commanded them to immediately participate in sex! . . . And it wasn't a sin! . . . If it's a sin, then God's a sinner, because He made it!

So sex is not evil after all, but a wonderful gift from God to be freely and fully enjoyed in the right relationships! . . . Not only to enable you to have children, . . . but also to have fellowship with the ones you love.

Now try it!—You'll like it!—And thank God for It!—Amen! Wow! Here we go again! Hallelujah! Are you comin'?—I've already gone!

Be a sex revolutionist for Jesus! *("Sinless Sex!—God's Sex Position!" ML #1969, Nov. 1984)*[7]

In general, those who remained loyal joined in the sexual revolution with enthusiasm. Nudity and indiscriminate sex were common in most homes until the mid to late 1980s. These were the wild years. Today, most disciples look back to those days with considerable ambivalence. For the most part, they view their self-described "excesses" as evidence of a lack of maturity, an inability to handle properly the freedoms they were granted. The most common refrain: "Mistakes were made." The majority of disciples were understandably reluctant to detail the "excesses" or "mistakes" of their own lives.

Seth, an American who spent most of his life in Latin America, confessed.

I was one of those people that Father David warned about in his Letters. Many times I was just following selfish pleasure, since there was this freedom. I used people. I'm not proud of it.

7. This letter was republished as the closing section of *Daily Bread*, vol. 8, and redistributed to the disciples in 1988. The *Daily Bread Series* is a compilation of portions of selected MO Letters, intended for personal devotion and community instruction.

I haven't used the freedoms we have as Father David intended them. I realize that, and I think that is sin. The Law of Love is not freedom to share, it is freedom to love. I realize that now, but not so back then. So, I have a lot to learn. It has been a learning process for me and still is, an individual learning process. It is also collective.

Seth reflects a number of themes found consistently among older disciples. The excesses, the mistakes, and the damage done to fellow disciples were the result of individual failures to live up to the highest ideals of the Law of Love. The principles of the Law of Love are sound. If the disciples had simply followed the full counsel of Father David, all would have been well. This appears to be inconsistent with the fact that Father David taught and modeled much of the activity now rejected. They simply do not see it that way.

Living out the Law of Love was not without cost. It is not difficult to imagine the stress on marriages and family relationships. Most adult disciples are no longer together with their original mates. Even in those marriages that did survive, living out the Law of Love brought wounds that were often hard to heal. Angela is a thirty-nine-year-old American disciple who joined in 1974, at age sixteen. She has been married to the same man since 1977.

I have one child, from a Japanese brother. We went to Japan, and my husband was gone a great deal. I met this Japanese brother. I had shared with other brothers before. But this was the first time I really got involved.

I guess we fell in love. It went on for about four months, until my husband returned. But my feelings for this Japanese brother were strong. My husband had real jealousy battles. See, we have this theory about our life together. It is called "One Wife." As The Family, we are all married to one another. It is a good theory. But in practice, it is very hard.

I was not very sensitive toward my husband. I said: "I still love you, but I love this other brother, too." It was very hard for him. Then, down the road a little, he began taking care of the sexual needs of a single sister in our home. They began to get close emotionally. That is how I saw it from the other side. And it wasn't good. Somehow, we made it through and are still together.

A lot of others didn't make it through. I think it was mostly those who would go from one fresh relationship to another, looking for excitement, instead of what Dad taught. I learned from my experience. I still share now, but it is very rare. Not like the old days at all. We still believe in sharing, but it is nothing like it was back in the 1980s.

Everyone was pretty wild back then. Maybe we just grew up. I think it was completely out of control back in the early '80s. Sharing all the time with whoever. Every fellowship, it was "who is having sex with who?" Everyone was doing it with anyone. And doing it everywhere, out in the open. I am glad we are over that.

My child by the Japanese brother, she is getting older now. I haven't talked to her about it yet; I want to wait till I am sure she will understand. My husband has always treated her like his own child, loved and cared for her just like his own flesh and blood. I have known couples where that was not the case, where there were problems. But not with my husband.

I did FFing, and a lot of sharing. Sharing has brought a lot more tension in our marriage than FFing. I guess not sharing per se. Most of the time, we both shared at the same time. So what's to say, right? But when you get involved, have feelings. Then there is tension. That has been real hard on marriages. I have no interest in that anymore. None at all.

Stories like this are common. Yet, all the disciples affirm the principle of the Law of Love. Sexual sharing is considered endemic to the very nature of their life together. For every story of strain, hardship and pain, there are two of care, support, joy, and affirmation of the Law of Love. Jonathan, the Canadian disciple who came out of a gay lifestyle, has extremely positive memories of his first sharing experiences.

When I joined The Family, I confessed my homosexual past. We were at a large fellowship. There was a sister there, married with two kids. (She was a good friend of my biological sister.) She came up to me one evening and asked if we could spend some time together. I thought that was very strange.

We spent almost the whole night together. She was so loving, so caring. She was very, very patient. And eventually, we were able to consummate a sexual relationship. The next night, we did the same thing. When I saw her husband, he was OK about it, very natural and friendly. He said he loved me and he wanted to share his wife with me for my health. He wanted to help me through this difficult time.

I know it was no great sexual experience for her. But she helped me through a very difficult time. It was a sample of love I never imagined possible, on both their parts. This experience really helped me understand the true meaning of the Law of Love.

For many disciples, sexual sharing represents the highest expression of the ideal of mutual love and mutual sacrifice for the good of the community. For some, sexual integration into the community functioned almost as an initiation rite.

I was in about a month before I shared. The shepherds in the home were an American brother and his Japanese wife. I forsook all to join, and I thought that meant sex, too. Then, one night I got this knock on my door. There stood this beautiful Japanese angel, my shepherd's wife. I was real nervous, like "What is going on here?" She said, "God loves you. There is nothing wrong with the feelings and needs God gave us. If you are feeling the need for love, I can help you." I said, "What about your husband?" She replied, "He sent me here." I thought, "Your husband sent you here!" She said, "He wants to share me with you. This is what we do in The Family. We believe in love. I love my husband, my husband loves me. He just felt that maybe I could help you."

We didn't have intercourse, but she satisfied my sexual needs orally. Then she said, "God bless you. Tomorrow I want to read something with you." I slept like a baby, thinking I made it to heaven.

The next day she and her husband sat down and read the Letter "One Wife" with me. That was my introduction to "One Wife." It was beautiful. I thought, "Here I am, sitting with you and your wife. Your wife came to me last night, and you are still my friend. You're feeding me from the Word. And you still love each other. This is perfect. This is love."

She came to me several more times. We made love. Then she said to me, "You should go to my husband and thank him for sharing me *with you."* I'll never forget that day! *All day, I just couldn't. I had this big ball in my throat. It was the most humbling thing I had ever done. Finally I said, "Thanks for sharing your wife with me." He goes, "Oh, that's OK. God bless you. I love you and want you to be happy." I said in my heart, "Is that it? He's OK?"*

That was my introduction to sharing, to the Law of Love. And I was set free. I realized God's love, and that whatever is done in true love is not a sin. And I realized that this Family is wonderful! *(Dan)*

Although "The Law of Love" spelled out the specifics, the disciples most often referred to the Letter "One Wife!" when speaking of the value and meaning of sexual sharing. Written in 1972, "One Wife!" does not address sexual activity. It does lay the foundation for a radical communalism that takes precedence over any personal relationship, including marriage.

God will have no other Gods before Him, not even the sanctity of the marriage god! . . . The Family marriage, the spiritual reality behind so-called group marriage, is that of putting the larger Family, the whole Family, first, even before the last remaining vestige of private property, your husband or your wife!

We do not minimize the marriage ties, as such. We just consider our ties to the Lord and the larger Family greater and more important. —And when the private marriage ties interfere with Our Family and God ties, they can be readily abandoned for the glory of God and the good of The Family! The totality of the Bride and her marriage to the Bridegroom is The Family! We are adopting the larger Family as the family unit: The Family of God and His Bride and Children.

God's in the business of breaking up little selfish private worldly families to make of their yielded broken pieces a larger unit—One Family! He's in the business of destroying the relationship of many wives in order to make them One Wife—God's Wife—The Bride of Christ! . . . The Whole Family—the entire Bride—The One Wife instead of the many wives! ("One Wife!" ML #249, Oct. 1972)

When disciples speak of their sharing experiences, it is frequently in the context of meeting a basic human need. However, they most often defend sharing as the central feature of the "One Wife" theory of communal organization. Sharing is a demonstration that conventional marriage, though still intact, is not the essential or fundamental relationship. Sexual sharing is the most explicit expression of the communal ideal, and the ultimate demonstration of Family unity.

I first shared extensively with child care people assigned to watch over our kids. It wasn't just slam, bam, thank you ma'am. We would talk and fellowship and pray together, read the Word together. I'd often use it as a time to ask them how things were going, and they'd pour out their hearts if they were having spiritual trials. We would talk about it, and then we would have sex.

It really brings a unity, as long as everyone is loving about it. It is when someone is being unloving and selfish, or they're not really doing it properly, then it can be hurtful. And even damaging. In our home, we handled it well. Our single girls were happy because they were getting some sex. To make love with a brother, to pray, it was very precious for them. It was something that brought you closer together, brought you closer to the Lord, and brought a lot of unity to the home. Other people might say that it was pretty rough on them because it wasn't handled so good. But my personal experience is that it has been edifying, strengthening, and unifying. (Peter Amsterdam)

Peter's view of sexual relationships among the brothers and sisters is broadly shared. Although fully aware of the negative consequences, the vast majority still maintain a positive overall assessment of sharing. However, female disciples are particularly more sensitive to the issues of family and marital tensions. Roberta, a French Canadian who has been a disciple since 1975, gave thoughtful reflection on the changing tempo of sexuality.

It started slowly. Then came a very, very quick swing. It went from one extreme to the other. In those days, my mate and I were Visiting Servants. We went to various homes in many places. Usually the Lord led us to share with the couples there, and that was good. I have no problem with having done that. But, of course, today that

would be quite out of place. You barely know the people. I do not be-
lieve that kind of casual sharing goes on today at all.

Then, we moved on from that, moved in another direction. I be-
lieve it really does build unity, helps break down barriers between
people. But to be quite honest, it just is not that important to us any-
more. Most of us have big families now, we are more mature. Our life
is a whole lot calmer now in that regard. But the principle is still very
precious to me. When sharing is done in the Spirit, it really is a won-
derful way to show love and bond people in the home together.

A sexual calm has fallen over The Family in recent years. Disciples
are regularly required to be apart from their mates. On those occasions,
it is both common and fully accepted that a disciple of the opposite sex
should care for a person's sexual needs. Discretion is clearly the order
of the day. Nudity, though still affirmed as pure and godly, is no longer
widely practiced in the homes. "Come-unions" are a thing of the past,
and visiting leaders no longer routinely have sex with their hosts in an
effort "to get to know" other disciples. However, sexual sharing still
functions as a bonding apparatus and a demonstrative act of unity and
mutual submission to the greater Family.

Sexual sharing is a central and distinctive aspect of Family sexual
ideology. However, it is neither the most distinctive nor the most
controversial component. The unique dimension was the extension of
sexual activity outside the community as a tool of evangelism, recruitment, and support.

We have already detailed the development of Flirty Fishing. The program began with Maria's employing her feminine charms, and then establishing a sexual relationship with a man who came to be known as
Arthur. Father David expanded the ministry by recruiting a number of
young, single, female disciples to his household. There he ran a full-
scale field demonstration in relative secrecy, before expanding the
FFing ministry to the entire movement. A series of MO Letters was
sent out to all the homes encouraging wide participation in this new
ministry.[8] The practice became widespread by the end of 1978.

8. These Letters are known as "The King Arthur Series." They are no longer available and cannot be found in any Family home. Noah explained: "We don't do it anymore, so we pulled the King Arthur Letters out of the homes. To be honest, they make
such a strong and compelling case for FFing, Father David was afraid if he left them in

Flirty Fishing was conceived of by Father David and received by the disciples as the most radical and sacrificial method of sharing the love of Jesus with an alienated and lost world. The proposition had been accepted that sex was a pure, God-created, and God-affirmed human need, not unlike eating or sleeping. The meeting of this basic human need as a demonstration of God's unlimited love meshed naturally with the passion to share their message and the urgency of the fast-approaching End. Flirty Fishing was theologically justified as the ultimate sacrificial act of true discipleship.

We found them all the same: Hungry, Lonely, Empty, Unhappy, Dissatisfied and Spiritually Destitute—all longing for Love of all kinds, but especially for a love they had never known before, true love, sincere love, genuine love, the truly great love of their life, the Love of all loves of the Lover of all lovers. . . . He is the power and life of the universe that some people call God but the Bible itself calls Love, for "God is Love." (1 Jn. 4:8)

He is pictured in His Son Christ Jesus, *a Man who loved everybody, even the poorest and the worst of all.* But He has no hands but your hands *and no lips but yours and He has no eyes but your eyes and no body but your own, for you are His* Body, *His Bride for whom He died that you might live and love others as He did with* your hands, your *lips,* your *mouth,* your *tongue,* your *eyes and* your *body broken for them as He was for you.*

Flesh can satisfy flesh, but only spirit can satisfy spirit, *and we soon found that we had to give of both to "satisfy all their needs according to His riches in glory." (Phil. 4:19) . . .* We soon found there was no stopping place, *no limit to which God would go to save a poor lost soul with His infinite love and unlimited mercy!*

There was nowhere to draw the line between the two, flesh and spirit. *It had to be "all or nothing at all" or they could not believe it was real love. . . . The two were inseparable, the one could not go without the other and we had to feed them both together. . . . "Even so faith, if it hath not works is dead!" (Ja. 2:15–17) In other words, if in the faith of God you really love them, they cannot understand it or*

---

the homes, people would have a strong desire to continue or begin the FFing ministry again."

believe it unless you really show them by some visible tangible work or action that puts your words into works and puts your faith into effect and makes it fact and not fiction, a sample. ("The Family of Love—Sin or Salvation?" GP #502R, June 1977)

"There was nowhere to draw the line." Out of the thousands of pages of Family literature, this one phrase captures both the challenge and dilemma facing Father David and his Children.

Flirty Fishing was also justified as a highly sacrificial and extreme measure needed for the crucial times at hand, when the conventional church and ordinary methods would no longer suffice. This method of witnessing could reach persons who, for various reasons, would not be open to any other approach. This is a consistent theme throughout the FFing literature that flowed through the community from the late 1970s to the late 1980s.

We feed their bodies in order to feed their souls. No doubt God is going to the final extreme to save souls by FFing. No doubt that's going to be their last chance, when God goes to that extreme to show them His Love! I really think it's usually their last chance when God has to use such extreme measures to accomplish such extraordinary results.

That was really the kind of love that finally won the hard-hearted Romans, when they saw how much love those Christians had for their God that they would gladly, willingly, walk out to the stake or to face the lions, singing, . . . still witnessing to the crowd. . . . That was the last witness they could possible give: to die for their faith. . . . For a woman to lay down her life, her body, for a total stranger because she loves him & is trying to woo & win him, that's the next thing to death itself. ("Their Last Resort," ML #1085, Oct. 1981)

Almost all adult female disciples were involved in FFing to some degree. Virtually all of them share a positive appreciation of this unique witnessing technique, and feel strongly that their ministry was the work of the Holy Spirit. They are equally convinced that Flirty Fishing afforded them the opportunity to bear witness to persons who would have no other possible chance of hearing about the love of Jesus.

Marsena is a European disciple who spent most of her FFing years in the East.

Mostly I would go to the bar or lounge of a five-star hotel and meet men in that setting. This worked well for me.

* * * * *

[Can you point to one experience that stands out as productive?]

к к к к к

One experience was really productive, *as you say. I had met this Muslim from a place in the Middle East. I met him in the lounge of the hotel, had dinner with him a couple of times, and shared with him about the Lord in a general kind of way. We had become fairly close, but no sex. I think that is one major misconception about FFing. We made friends with a lot of people in our FFing, but we usually didn't have sex unless it was necessary for the witness. Anyway, he was scheduled to leave and go back home when I got a call from one of his associates. He was very ill in his hotel room, and this fellow asked me to come and see if I could help. I found him very sick, in no shape to get on a plane. So, I began to pray for him, and to soothe him and touch him. He became better very quick. Then I completely undressed and got in bed with him. We made love. And then I told him why. I loved him in Jesus and was loving him this way to show him how much Jesus loved him.*

He was completely blown away. He prayed to receive Jesus in his heart right then. I gave him some lit, and he went on his way. But he came back, and I had several other times together with him. We would pray and study and have sex together. One day he invited me and several others to visit his home town. We went for a couple of weeks. We stayed with his family and got to know a lot of wonderful people there. They were all Muslims, and a few people were not all that happy we were sharing about Jesus. But this fellow was very influential, and he told about his miracle healing in the hotel room. That seemed really to impress them. We got to witness to many people in that town those few weeks. And many prayed to receive Jesus.

For some women, the Flirty Fishing era remains the high point of their lives. FFing moved many women into the center of Family life and offered them extraordinary opportunity and status. June recalled those times with obvious nostalgia.

When we first started, we would go to nightclubs and witness, but no sex. Then the King Arthur series started to come out and the full extent of FFing became clear. It was the '70s; people in general were more free sexually. And Father David was saying there was no limit to showing the Love of Jesus. I was really excited about the FF Revolution. I knew it was the answer for the heart cry of so many people. So, I got very involved from the very start.

* * * * *

[How involved?]

* * * * *

Well, I never kept any records. But over a period of eight to ten years, I would say 70, maybe 100 men. And many, many came to know Jesus.

* * * * *

[What is your most memorable FFing experience?]

* * * * *

It is hard to pick out one. I was in India. He was Lebanese, living in a Middle East country. We talked a lot. He had been in the militia and responsible for some of the violence against the Palestinian refugees. I really let him have it. Said how horrible that was, how the Palestinians had as much right to that land as the Jews.

I thought that would be it, never see him again. But he really received it, respected what I said. He wanted to see me again. So, I went over to his hotel. We talked for a long while, then went to his room and I shared sexually with him. Then I explained to him why. And he prayed with me to receive Jesus. He would come over to the house. It was a real testimony to him the way my husband and children received him. He studied with us; he did love the Lord.

This is the key to really understanding FFing. Maybe sometimes the motives weren't always right. I know that. But I really believe with all my heart that the motivation behind FFing was to really show people the love of Jesus. And I know that it really changed people's lives. Sure, there were times when men just used the situation, I know that. But I'd give them the truth and the rest was in the Lord's

*hands. We made a lot of friends through FFing, and a lot of lives were
really changed.*

*When it stopped, it was almost like a culture shock for me. It was
my ministry. I was really being used. I reached a lot of people that
way. The change was really hard to accept at first. How can I say
this? I'm not doubting Father David's wisdom. I can see the Lord's
wisdom here. I don't believe Father David was wrong to have us stop.
But, we could get much closer to people through FFing. That intimacy
of really, really getting close to someone's life isn't there now, like it
used to be at that time. I accept the change, but I do miss those days.*

The Flirty Fishing Revolution did not come without cost. It is not
possible to reconstruct what actually occurred, and the numbers that
are available are difficult to assess. But there is little doubt that many
people left the movement. The majority remained loyal through the
transition. Most of the testimonies regarding the Flirty Fishing ministry are quite positive. However, even those women who were most
affirming admit to complications and difficulties. Sexually transmitted
diseases (STDs) emerged rather quickly as a serious problem. Father
David retained a radical opposition to any form of birth control, so
most of the women operated with little proactive protection against infection. "Sure, we caught things. If fact, it seemed like we got it all. I
sure did. Gonorrhea, herpes, all kinds of things. It was tough. But we
understood it as part of the sacrifice" (Ruth).

Other issues also complicated the lives of many women, including
the development of emotional attachments to their "fish" and children
born of Flirty Fishing. Aliena's experience offers a window into some of
the complexities of a Flirty Fisherwoman.

*I was in New Jersey. The first guy for me, I think he was some kind
of Mafia type. I witnessed to him a lot. I had sex with him, but I witnessed to him a lot, too. He ended up getting married and stopped
seeing me. I had sex with him four or five times. He was my first.*
*****
[How did you process all this when it began?]
*****
I was excited about it. I have to admit it was a bit exciting, some-

thing different. And I was having sex, too. See, I was single when I started, and there was no sharing in my home yet, so it was an opportunity to have sex. After I got married, it was different. I really enjoyed giving. To me, it didn't matter who they were, ugly or handsome. I didn't feel that anything was wrong at all, never questioned it. And like I said, it was a bit exciting.

It wasn't like I was FFing a lot of different men at one time. There were only three or four in the States. One guy got saved. And one was the father of my son. He got saved, too. He was long term. When I first started with him, I was single. Then I got married and didn't see him as often. He was looking for a wife and mother, to have a full-fledged relationship. But, he knew that wasn't what I was going to do. He got saved, but then after a while he just stopped. I think he knew my son was his. He supported a little bit in the beginning, but then he just went away.

Actually, I found FFing much easier after I was married. I was in love with my husband and perfectly happy with him. I wasn't looking for a relationship, so I could pour my heart into it without worrying about an emotional involvement. I actually loved these men more after I got married. See, I wasn't looking to meet my needs anymore. In the beginning, when I was single, you can't help but want to meet your needs, too. It was much more of a ministry after I got married. Two of my nine children are from fish, but my husband has always been very supportive, as if they were his own.

I guess I made my share of mistakes. I should have been much more faithful in my follow-up, with my mail and keeping in touch. There were some precious people, and I regret not faithfully sending prayer letters every month. I would still have some fruit to show for all I did. And there were guys who just took advantage. I think I would be choosier if I had it all to do over again. But, I was young, just learning.

After I was married for a while, started having more kids, I just drifted away from FFing. Even the excitement of it kind of dulled for me. Then the DFing Revolution came and we stopped. I was happy. Had enough. I think most of us were feeling that way, time to change. We were getting older, having a lot of kids. And the world was chang-

ing around us. But it was an adjustment. A lot of witnessing had to change. And that is how we got most of our support.

* * * * *

[You have heard the charge that FFing for support amounts to prostitution.]

* * * * *

Yea. But I never looked at it that way. When you are involved in it, you see that you are not a prostitute. You are not taking, you are giving. You are showing God's love. There was never one moment that I did not feel I was showing God's love, and I always told them. I never had sex with any man without telling him about Jesus and trying to get him saved. So, charges of prostitution never ruffled my feathers too much, except to say how stupid they were. Never did I doubt what I was doing. And never for a moment have I looked back and wish I wouldn't have done FFing. I still feel very strongly that it was a good thing for the time. We have matured, grown in our approach. I wouldn't think of doing it now. It would have to be a direct revelation from God, from leadership or whatever, but I can't imagine that happening now.

Aliena raised two issues that must be addressed in order to comprehend the full scope of Flirty Fishing. The theological justification for FFing consistently defined it as a sacrificial witnessing strategy. However, a substantial percentage of those involved in Flirty Fishing, at one time or another, established a long-term sexual relationship with an outsider. In a number of cases, the disciple did not enter into a sexual relationship until after the man had already prayed to receive Jesus. Most women view Flirty Fishing not only as a witnessing strategy, but as an opportunity to provide care and love for needy persons. Naomi, a Canadian disciple who spent much of her adult life in Latin America, spoke with a great deal of passion about the wider ministry of Flirty Fishing.

The first fish I got close to was Hans, an elderly man. He was missing one arm and one eye. He was very lonely. He lived alone in his apartment, the kind of person who really needed us. I established a friendship with him, going over to his place every week, twice a week for a while. We would read the Word together, spend time together. Because of his age, he was not always able to make it sexually, but he still needed someone to give him affection. He was so sweet. Every month we would meet and he would go out and buy the groceries for the home, and give us donations, too. He loved the Lord, he loved Dad and The Family.

I remember our first time together. When he took off his artificial arm, it was quite shocking for me. I fled into the bathroom. There I just prayed "Lord, this is a little hard!" As I was praying, I had a vision of this man in Heaven, with a whole body. I never had a problem after that. That vision showed me it was the Lord's love. The Lord gave me a real love for him. It was totally unselfish. There was nothing in it for me, certainly no sexual attraction. I didn't care about that. He needed to be loved, cared for. And the more I loved him, the more he loved the Lord.

* * * * *

[Then for you, FFing was not just evangelism. It could be ongoing with someone already converted.]

* * * * *

Sure. That is part of what Dad taught us with FFing, too. A lot of times their need and attachment was ongoing. We couldn't just drop them. If it was real love, we were just going to keep loving and caring for them, as long as the Lord led that way. He was not the only one. There were several I had long-lasting relationships with.

Naomi's relationship with Hans was not an exceptional case. In most cases, the level of support provided by these "fish" exceeded the practice of simply buying the groceries. There is little question Father David envisioned Flirty Fishing not only as an outreach method, but also as a principal avenue for developing financial support and political protection.

I was assigned as a handyman to an FFing home not too long after I joined. This was 1985. I really wanted to do God's work, but here I was getting to enjoy all these beautiful women. And it was their ministry, making men happy.

They were trying to reach people who needed it, men who didn't have faith in God, but were rejected by the churches. This home was particularly trying to establish men who could help The Family. Men who could become Kings. Like Dad said, "go to the rich, because they are the most neglected, the spiritually poor." (Anthony, a Canadian disciple)

Father David made it quite clear on any number of occasions that Flirty Fishing should generate financial support and establish powerful friends who might protect The Family against its many enemies. In "The Seven Fs of FFing," Flirty Fishing is not only cited as a primary Supportive Ministry, but likely the most effective one after the Antichrist assumes power.

As the other doors are closed & you can no longer openly litness anymore, no longer openly busk & cafe & street sing . . . There's three doors closed of the 7 Supporters. Leaving Mail Ministry and FFing as the only two remaining supportive ministries. After the war the mail may be so restricted or so limited that the International Mail Ministry may be cut off completely.

But there will still be one outstanding possible very effucktive, effective, efficient & fruitful supportive ministry left, particularly for you girls! Men will still need women to the very End, so it'll still be an effective & fruitful ministry right up to the end, probably the last of the 7 Supporters when provisioning is gone & you're not even allowed to hold a job anymore because you haven't got the number [mark of the Beast]. But, you'll still be working, girls, as long as they've got your number, your phone number! Hallelujah! ("The Seven Fs of FFing," ML #1083, Jan. 1982)

In a number of circumstances, individual family units and larger homes became dependent on the ability of the women to generate income through Flirty Fishing. Manassas, an American, gave testimony to just how complicated this could become.

I met my most important fish at a hotel in Venezuela. I FFed him and he got saved. He was a Mexican. Quite wealthy and very well connected with the government, though he was in private business.

I established a very wonderful relationship with him. He would

visit me often. Then, I began traveling with him on his many business trips. We went all over Latin America and even to Europe on different trips. We would be together for a few days, or even weeks. I am
sure he really cared for me.

I realize this is hard to understand for others outside. We were
from the free sex, hippie era. Really, this was not that big a deal for
us. When FFing started, there were people who thought it was too
much, too weird. Those people left. And that is fine. But to me, it was
beautiful, wonderful. And there were also times it was not so pleasant, very sacrificial. Sometimes it was not easy to go that far to show
God's love to someone.

During the RNR period, like 1979, my fish moved our entire family
back to Mexico so I could be close to him. I basically became his
mistress. My husband struggled with FFing at first, but he was fine
with this situation. He understood that this was the ministry of The
Family.

I stayed close to this person for several years. I always prayed with
him, and read MO Letters to him. He was Roman Catholic, but he
prayed to be saved. I am sure he loved Jesus, but he didn't understand us. He thought what we were doing was adultery. He couldn't
understand it as good, from God. He put a lot of pressure on us to get
out, abandon Dad and The Family. See, many wealthy Mexican men
had a mistress, and he wanted me for a permanent situation. He justified himself, but really did not like being taught that what we had
was a godly thing.

He bought us a car, a condo, furniture and took good care of the
kids. But then Dad called us back together in the Fellowship
Revolution. We left overnight when my fish was out of the country.
We sold the condo and everything, and just left for Puerto Rico.

In some ways, this whole affair helped me understand how outsiders might see us. I know that we are extremist. And our doctrines,
not just about sex, are very different than most Christians'. But, I
know that The Family is the best way to fully love and serve Jesus.

There is no doubt that Father David and Maria advocated Flirty
Fishing as a means both of witness and for financial support.

I was with the Music with Meaning *team when we got the word
from Dad to disband the whole operation and go off to the mission
field. I was really quite surprised. We were doing well and many were
being saved. But, we were ordered to go. I was advised to go to India.
But we had no money, no support, no way to get there, and no way to
sustain us when we did. I wasn't quite sure this was fair, so I wrote
World Services about it. Maria sent me a message. She was pretty
blunt about it. She told me that she FFed for support of their home.
And if she could do it, I damn well could too. She told me to FF to get
the money and support to go. (Martha)*

The dual function, witness and support, would at times come into tension. This was particularly true when the disciples became involved
in escort services. I encountered only one woman who had generally positive memories of escort-service work. She "kept the focus"
and considered it simply a more efficient and productive approach to
witnessing.

*When I came to the United Kingdom in 1984, a lot of the sisters
were doing escort-service work. At first, I didn't like that idea. But
the more I saw that it could be good, the more I got into it. I was not
into it as intensely as some of the other sisters. I went once or twice a
week. For me, it was an excellent means of witnessing. A Jew was
running the service I worked for. I was quite sure he would hear
about my witnessing, and that would be the end of it.*

*Once, I was with a Libyan diplomat who was quite close to
Gadhafi. He got saved. Another was a former high-ranking minister
from Pakistan. He got saved, too. They prayed with me to receive
Jesus in their hearts. Now, these are people I would have never met
any other way. I don't see how anyone else would have been able to
get through to them.*

*I had always thought escort work was seedy, somehow linked to
crime. I was really surprised by the normality of it all. Most of the
men I met were just lonely and spiritually needy. On two occasions, I
met born-again Christians. I had sex with them. Then I shared Jesus,
and they said they were already saved. One was an American, a minister I think. He was very sweet and thankful. It is funny as I think of*

it. I had sex with him, and he probably belongs to a church some-where in the States. Maybe you know him. *[laughs] (Martha)*

Family leadership is particularly defensive regarding any negative as-sessment of Flirty Fishing. It is still viewed in a most positive light, and the principles underlying it are still strongly affirmed. Escort-service work is downplayed as much as possible. This was one of the few areas where Peter Amsterdam struggled to be completely forthcoming.

[Am I going to discover a lot of disciples who joined through FFing?]

* * * * *

If you happen to be in the right place at the right time. Not a lot of people joined through FFing, but a lot got saved. There are people who, although they didn't join, have become very close and continue to be very close and help us.[9]

* * * * *

[Help you. One of the accusations against you has been prostitu-tion. FFing does seem to have involved relationships that produced material benefit.]

* * * * *

It wasn't like, "If you give me money for our home, we'll have sex."

* * * * *

[That never happened?]

* * * * *

Well, I can't say it never *happened, but it certainly wasn't sup-posed to happen. It was more like, "OK, I'm leading you to the Lord, we're going out on dates, we're having sex. I'm a missionary, I have my home and I have a husband and kids there, and we need help with our rent." These guys understood we lived by donations and they sometimes helped us.*

I can tell you one thing. There was not big money like we've been accused of. If there was, it sure didn't come to World Services. Nobody was into it for that. Later, some girls did get into escort work

---

9. "Help us" is the normal phrase used to describe outside persons who provide fi-nancial, legal, or political support.

where they signed up with an agency. They would call our girls and ask them if they'd like to go. Dad didn't promote that and he didn't say to do that.

It was something that some people tried out. People do that. They try something, and we kind of let it go for a while to see how it works. Then if it doesn't work, we put an end to it.

* * * * *

[Did it work?]

* * * * *

Not really. It probably helped the homes financially. It wasn't a lot, but it did happen. Some girls did that and they arranged it and they got paid. So, under the escort work I think people can say, "That was prostitution." And, I guess, in a sense, it was. But that was rare and it was for a certain little time. And we established that it didn't work so good. It did not bear good fruit in the girls' lives. Spiritually, that wasn't good. So, I guess, to be honest, I'd have to say, yes. In some cases there was what could be labeled prostitution.

Peter's reluctance to discuss this topic is understandable. But, escort-service work began early, had the official sanction of the leadership at the top from the beginning, and continued down to the end of the Flirty Fishing era.[10] The work even received its own Family code name, "ESing." It was affirmed in 1983 by an official publication.[11] However, Peter's assessment that it often "did not bear good fruit in the girls' lives" is certainly accurate. There are any number of women whose memories of ESing were not nearly as positive as Martha's.

There was a sister working at a service. The owner went on a long vacation and that sister took over the service. She was able to get a lot of the sisters signed up. Many of them were trying to raise funds to travel to the mission field.

I had about ten dates through the service. I got 100 pounds each date, plus I would ask for taxi fare. This involved sex every time—

10. "Going Underground!" (ML #750, Dec. 1978). This Letter specifically recommends "Escort Service" as one of the safest "Fronts" to use in the FFing ministry.

11. *The Book of Remembrance*, 1983, 2:225. "ESing" is presented by a photo of an attractive young woman wearing a see-through "French Maid" costume.

that was understood. I always tried to give some kind of witness. It was easier with older men. The younger men only wanted the sex.

London was quite a place for ESing. A lot of the sisters went every night, sometimes two or three clients each night. To be honest, many were getting pretty mechanical about sex. It seemed to me we were all getting a bit hardened.

Some of the sisters were just way too much into the financial end of it. They said they were raising money to go to the mission field. But they were buying TVs and video players, cameras, all kinds of expensive things.

We had meetings of the sisters in London to try and coordinate escort work, to keep from getting too many sisters at one agency. We also shared testimonies. There was one Latin American sister who was confused by this. She had been ESing for years and did not even know you were supposed to witness. She just did it for the money. I am not joking.

Some still had the vision, still witnessing. Others lost sight of our goals of FFing all together. Some never made it to the mission field, just stayed on FFing. I think one or two just drifted off into prostitution. To be honest, we were very close to that already.

I think this is the main reason we stopped FFing. The AIDS thing was a factor for sure. But many people lost sight of the original vision. We were becoming hardened by it. In some ways trapped in it. (Rose)

Most of The Family women strongly affirmed the shifting sexual mores and the Flirty Fishing ministry. Those who could not left the community. But there are some loyal disciples who still carry scars. A few reluctantly shared their memories of the downside in having "nowhere to draw the line."

I joined when I was only fifteen. Life had been hard for me. The Family was a very loving, safe place. But when the sexual freedom hit, it was scary. My first introduction was harsh. (I never talk about this to anyone.) My husband was in leadership. He went off to a meeting that was to explain it all. He came home and explained it all to me. He said, "We don't have husbands and wives anymore. We can have sex with anyone we want to. By the way, I shared with Beloved while I was at the meeting, and it was great. Here, listen to this tape—it explains it all. I have to go to another home to start this there."

* * * * *

[What was your reaction to this?]

* * * * *

My reaction! "Oh my goodness! I am still a teenager. I just had a baby, and now I don't have a husband." I was in total shock. To this day I cannot stand that tape. I cannot tell you how hard this was for me. I mean, how do you do this? But, you adapt, you grow. I made it through. And somehow, we are still together.

When the FFing started, I was twenty and nursing a baby. It was all new to me, I had never even been inside a bar. Now, I must say that you do reach people that you would never get very far with any other way. And because of that, maybe it was worth it. But at first, I was not into FFing very much. Then we moved to Hong Kong. Like the other sisters, I started to work for an escort service to meet men. It was quicker and safer than the bars. That was the reason behind it all, to meet people and tell them about Jesus.

But I got tripped out. I think we all did. And of course there was the money. ESing brought in very good support for the home. We became used to the big money. That is when things really started to go negative. I was used to sharing with the brothers, so sleeping with other men was nothing strange. But it was our motives—we got into wrong motives. I, and many others, even began to hold back our witness. We did not want to lose our jobs with the escort service. We had to keep the money coming in. Our home came to depend on it.

It was not all negative. But mostly it was pretty difficult for me. The ESing was to produce money to support the home. It was that simple—everybody understood. Then, I got pregnant. And it got real tough.

ESing was all over the East. It was very, very common in Hong Kong, Japan, Singapore, Thailand, all over. A lot of homes became very dependent on it.

* * * * *

[I don't mean to be judgmental, but this sounds like prostitution.]
* * * * *

*It was prostitution. That was what we were doing, lots of us. It is
not what Dad had in mind when he started FFing. But it is what we
were doing. The selfish motives really took over. There was a lot of
fighting over money and possessions. We really lost the Spirit. It all
blew up there in Hong Kong. Persecutions came and we all had to
flee. I am sure we brought it on ourselves. The Lord gave it to us for a
cause.*

*I am not proud of this. I have repented of the prostitution I did
while ESing. But that came later. I did not look at it as prostitution at
the time. In my heart, I was trying to FF, to follow the Letters. But
the financial pressures were very strong. Sometimes I would go out on
two or three dates in one night. I just didn't trust God. None of us
did.*

*I have talked to other women who told of horrors, things they were
forced to do by leaders to keep the money coming. I felt a lot of pressure, but I cannot say I was ever forced. I had some bad experiences,
but nothing so horrible that I was scarred for life. I was not maimed
by it. But sometimes it was far from pleasant. And most of all, I know
I did not please the Lord. For me, ESing was a real mistake.*

*I know women who said they were forced to do things that they
did not want to do. [She was most reluctant to go into specifics.] It is
probably how they experienced it at the time. I cannot judge. There is
no doubt that many people got totally tripped out on escort work. It
may have happened. But that certainly was not Dad's vision. And
when he found out about the full extent of it, he put a stop to it. I am
sorry, very sorry that some women were hurt like that. (Cherith)*

The Family continues to affirm the principles underlying Flirty
Fishing, viewing it as appropriate and God-ordained for the time.
However, FFing was halted, for the most part, in 1987. Maria was the
inspiration for this change, and the Letters outlining the new direction
came from her pen. The initial word came in early 1987.

*In a small "test tube" pioneer situation, we have recently discov-
ered how the FFing ministry can be greatly enhanced & made even*

more *effective by placing more emphasis on the Word . . . Although only one man has been* bedded, *literally* tens of thousands *have been* led *to the* Lord.

For some reason or other, a lot of our folks seem to think that the terms are synonymous, that FF means fuck, *but it ain't necessarily so! You can sexually* attract *someone & witness to them, without necessarily going all the way! ("The FFing / DFing Revolution—The Book Is the Hook!" ML #2313, Mar. 1987)*

Maria goes on in this Letter to strongly encourage the disciples to move away from sexual intercourse as a witnessing strategy. She hopes to substitute "The Word" [the Bible and MO Letters] as the primary means of witnessing and developing loyal friends. "The *Word* is the *seed* which brings forth *lasting, remaining* fruit!"

The official change in policy came with "Moma on the New AIDS Rules!—It's Come to That!" This letter clearly marks out the fear of an AIDS epidemic as one of the principal reasons to cease sexual contact as a witnessing strategy. Women who had established relationships with "close friends and long-term fish" were allowed to continue those relationships. However, the fish would be required to use condoms, and the women were strongly encouraged to drop any fish who was promiscuous. There are a very few women who still maintain these types of relationships; most are in Asia. Beyond these exceptions, Flirty Fishing ceased at the end of 1987, and sexual contact with outsiders was banned.

In this Letter, Maria offers further justification for the halt. She seemed particularly sensitive to the degree that FFing had caused spiritual drift in the community, and that financial dependence on FFing had led many away from Father David's original vision.

Our girls will accomplish a lot more with some of their fish by restricting some of their former activities & not just going out nightly on some kind of escort dates with strangers. They can narrow down & concentrate on making real disciples, really feeding their most potential fish the Word! . . . I think this AIDS threat will really shake up a lot of our careless FFers & get them to concentrate more on what they're supposed to be concentrating on, the Word instead of sex!

Another thing some people are going to wonder: "Oh my!—with no more sex with outsiders *whom we've just met, we won't be able to win any more top people or* kings *or* important *friends like these others whom we were able to FF!" But, that's not necessarily so. We Can!*

DFing [moving from a sex-based to a Word-based ministry] is really like depending on the Spirit *instead of depending on the Flesh. Flesh, that's what FFing has become to a lot of our people!—And it's not just the arm of the flesh, it's the whole* body.

Of course, the wrench for a lot of our folks isn't going to be so much, "Oh how are we going to win souls?*"; it's going to be a* financial *problem. And it may be difficult at first. Some may have to tighten the belt a bit & move into a less luxurious house & do this or that, but the Lord's going to bless their faith & obedience—He's got to! ("Moma on the New AIDS Rules!—It's Come to That!" ML #2346, Sept. 1987)*

Maria went on to place this dramatic change in the context of End Time expectations. In doing so, she seemed to invert Father David's earlier prediction that Flirty Fishing would be the only sustainable Support during the Tribulation.

When the Crash really hits, people are not going to be traveling all over & staying in fancy hotels & paying big money for girls, anyway. So we might as well get prepared, *& this is actually an easy way to do it. Our people who are receptive & yielded to this are going to have a big head start. They're going to be already trusting the Lord, not just the flesh.*

So maybe all of this is the Lord's way of getting the entire Family to depend on the Lord *& less on the flesh.—Not just for the sake of not getting AIDS, but to teach us to really launch out & see that we don't have to depend on the flesh. . . . FFing is one thing that a lot of our people have gotten pretty dependent on! It's probably the thing that they get the most reliant on to bring in the most support. So maybe the Lord's just trying to wean us off of some of these things that we put too much trust & dependence on. ("Moma on the New AIDS Rules!—It's Come to That!" ML #2346, Sept. 1987)*

In 1987, the curtain came down on Flirty Fishing. One of the most controversial chapters of life in The Family came to a close. But, we have yet to address the most difficult issue regarding FFing. To what extent were minors involved? Given the terrible hardship Family members have faced over recent allegations of child sexual abuse, this proved to be an extremely delicate one. Hostile former members have laid accusations that young girls were sent to the streets to earn money for the homes. Certainly, that potential was present. The first female infant was born in early 1970. From 1983 to 1987, there would have been a small, but nonetheless significant, number of young teen girls living in Family communities. Until 1986, twelve years old was considered the age of entry into the adult community. And Family literature is replete with references to the purity and God-given nature of human sexuality. But, did it happen?

Noah, our primary informant, was at first quite adamant that minors never participated. In time, as our trust relationship developed, he opened.

I know personally of one difficult situation. There was this girl who joined. She was still a virgin (quite rare at this time) and wanted to do FFing. This was a mistake, but we made mistakes. She had a very bad experience the first time. She was about eighteen, I think. That is the most difficult situation I know of. To tell you the truth, I hear some stories, or hear things reported from the BI Case [child custody case in England], and I feel like I have led a sheltered life in The Family.

* * * * *

[There are reports of really young girls FFing.]

* * * * *

To me, that is the area I am most zealous in defending. As far as my experience and my knowledge, that did not happen. As far as using our teens, like thirteen or fourteen, even sixteen or seventeen, any of our teens, it was completely out of the question. Dad very specifically states that in the Letters, you can read it, he says "No." From my knowledge, I could go on a witness stand and swear, "No, that never happened," with a clear conscience. Now, I cannot say that it never happened anywhere. Maybe somebody didn't obey the Letters.

That happens, people do things that are against the Letters. But then, that is a person doing something, not The Family.

Father David did prohibit underage girls from FFing. However, in the mid-1980s, World Services published a serial short story entitled "Heaven's Girl." It was strictly an internal publication. The story was set in 1993, during the Great Tribulation. Heaven's Girl was the heroine in the encounters with the System of the Antichrist. She is clearly pictured as a minor, perhaps thirteen to fifteen years old. In one episode, on the counsel of Maria, Heaven's Girl "FFs" a government official in hopes of freeing him from the control of the "Beast" and winning him over to The Family. Virtually every older teenage girl and young adult woman grew up with "Heaven's Girl" as their role model. After 1987, this literature was pulled from circulation. It is no longer read and is not available in the homes.

No adult indicated direct knowledge of minor girls involved in Flirty Fishing. To be sure, parents would naturally be most reluctant to acknowledge any such activity. This study includes a good number of young adults who would have been teenagers in the mid-1980s. These young people were extraordinarily open about Family sexual practices and their own sexual history. The young women knew about Flirty Fishing, and many looked forward to doing it. However, none of them reported ever having become directly involved. Nor did they know of anyone who was involved in FFing as a young teenager. We can only conclude that as a matter of policy and standard practice, young girls were not employed in the Flirty Fishing ministry. Did it happen? This study produced no direct testimony about young teenage girls Flirty Fishing. Though it may have happened, it was certainly not the norm.

The entire issue of sexual activity by and with children is a menacing cloud that hangs over The Family. From the late 1980s, when accusations of child sexual abuse resulted in numerous harsh attacks, Family representatives were uniform in their declaration of innocence.

Although the laws in many countries do allow adults to have relationships with teens of legal age, communities in our fellowship strictly disallow it.

*****

*We are diametrically opposed to any form of sexual abuse or sexu-
al exploitation of children whatsoever, and all our membership are
resolute in their agreement to abide by and support this position under penalty of excommunication from our fellowship. Any and all
previous writings, philosophic and theological speculations, or individual opinions of members taken contrary to this position or that in
any way could be construed as lending credence, support or justification for any form of sexual touching of children, have been officially
categorically renounced and forbidden, and all printed materials
deemed objectionable have been ordered by our founder, Father
David, to be removed from use and destroyed. ("Position and Policy
Statement: Attitudes, Conduct, Current Beliefs and Teachings
Regarding Sex," Apr. 1992).*

This policy is firmly in place. I have closely observed a great many children in over thirty Family homes. I have interviewed scores of children
and young teens, a few in small groups, but most in private sessions.
Several more qualified academics and a number of social service agencies have made in-depth observations of a few Family homes. They
concur with my assessment. The Family, as a religious community,
does not abuse children. I am completely confident that any current,
isolated instance is dealt with by excommunication. I am confident
that child sexual abuse is less frequent in The Family than in society at
large.

However, this has not always been the case. The Family has struggled to come to terms with its history of the sexual exploitation of children. That struggle centered in a child custody battle in England,
known inside The Family as the "BI Case." The testimony of the central figure, though lengthy, illustrates the evolution of Family self-
understanding.

*My parents were divorced when I was fourteen. It was quite un-
pleasant. My mother was very difficult to live with. When I joined
The Family, I found love in my heart from the Lord for her.*

*I prayed to receive Jesus in India. I never touched drugs again after
that night. This was 1988 and I was twenty-two years old. I returned
to England in 1989. Initially, mother was OK about The Family. I*

tried to be more understanding of what she had been through. She started to feel love from me that she had never known before. Then she started to want to see more and more of me. I was acting in a loving way toward her and she tried to pull me in, take more and more of my time. She didn't work or do anything with her life—she was quite lonely. I had to pull back some, and she started to get worried.

I was pregnant when she made her first contact with the anticult movement. She invited me to lunch under false pretenses. An ex-member told me about her abuse in The Family. I listened, said that if it happened I was very sorry, but that was not my experience. I had never seen or heard of anything like what she was talking about. It became very unpleasant. They tried to prevent me from leaving. I was twenty-five years old at the time.

That was it for me. My mother acted very unreasonably. She was in touch with the anticult movement. She hired a private investigator who followed me for months. She started to say she was concerned for my child. I told her I was perfectly capable of protecting my own child.

A few days before my son was born, we began to feel the Lord giving us checks in the Spirit. The shepherds advised me to leave England. She began court proceedings and the police raided two of our homes in England. The judge had given care and control of my son to my mother. He was eight days old. The judged based his decision on the affidavits of three ex-members regarding things that happened outside of England ten years ago to other people. It had nothing to do with my son, but on that basis, he sent out the order to take my child.

I think my mother thought I would not be willing to give up my son, so I would be forced to go and live with her. Then, she hoped to convince me to leave. It backfired. I was not in the jurisdiction of the court. But, I had nothing to hide. And if not me, it would be someone else. I thought I was ready to fight, to dispel all these lies.

I had never experienced or known of any abuse of children in The Family. I told the judge I would return, if I could retain care and control of my son until the case was settled. He agreed. I was able to live in a Family home the whole time. It became a massive thing, kept es-

*calating. At first there were three affidavits, then two more. We
would answer one set of allegations, then another set would show up.
My mother had the money, and the anticult movement had the drive.*

*The Lord knows, and He allowed. I really believe the Lord used
this case to make us face up to the facts. Things did go terribly
wrong. People were hurt. All was not wonderful.*

*At first, I was happy to be persecuted for righteousness sake, to
stand up for Jesus, for The Family, for Dad being a Prophet, for the
spirit of The Family, what I knew to be true of us. If the judge had
evaluated the case on the present, then there was no case. There was
no evidence whatsoever that the home where I was living, or any
Family home now, is an unfit place for my son. But the judge said because The Family was unfit in the past in other places, he would have
to judge if The Family will be an unfit place in the future. It was very
frustrating.*

*There was no evidence of anything recent or current. After the
1986 memo on child abuse, it was an excommunicable offense. So all
the evidence presented at the trial was prior to 1986. Even the witnesses for my mother said nothing was going on like that today.*

*But, I learned a lot. The Law of Love is a very prominent part of
Family life. I believe in it. But my experience had always been with
adults. But in the past, some Family members applied it to minors. I
think that is plainly wrong. It is a shame on The Family, and I am
very sad that it happened. It is awful to think that Family members
abused others in the name of Love. But, I did come to clearly see that
some people hurt others. They had sexual experiences with minors.*

*I progressed through the issue of Father David's responsibility in
all this rather naïvely. Initially, I would not accept that Father David
was in any way responsible. Now, I know that he must bear some responsibility. I found it very hard to accept that people in The Family
would act abusively to children, or hurt any one. My experience has
been so good, so loving. But then they read some of those MO Letters.
I found some of it just wrong. I knew the Davidito Book existed, but I
had never seen it. When they read those sections out in court, it was
a real shock to me. The sections dealing with sexual experiences with
Davidito, him watching adults have sex, and Sarah masturbating*

him. I do not believe they were acting for their own gratification. But it was clearly wrong.

They used the "Little Girl Dream." Dad was in bed with Maria and an eleven-year-old girl. He was deciding who to have sex with, and finally had sex with the girl. But the whole Letter was Dad explaining what he thought the dream meant, that the girl was symbolic of the young church who needed his love. The court said people receiving this Letter would interpret it as OK to have sex with eleven or twelve-year-old girls. Maybe some people did interpret it that way at the time. I didn't. It was a spiritual application of a dream. It never would occur to me to take it literally.

To be honest, some of Dad's Letters are shocking. But we have the mentality that there is nothing wrong with using sex as an example for spiritual applications. But that Letter knocked me off guard. The court saw it as evidence that Father David was teaching people to have sex with kids. When I saw the judge piece all this together, it occurred to me that perhaps Dad did think it was OK to have sex with any age, any relative. He did say that in "The Devil Hates Sex."

I could not take any of that literally. I think it is only common sense that you do not do that sort of thing. When you read all of Dad's Letters, you see that he is extreme, bombastic—he uses wild statements to teach spiritual truths. The Letters also teach you should never harm another person. But, he should have stated very clearly not to have sex with children or relatives. That would have stopped those things that hurt people, things that were wrong.

Through the trial, the Lord was working on my life. I had to get rid of the bitterness, and I was gaining victories here. The Lord gave me a prophecy at the beginning, that I would not lose my son. I held on to that. Then, the judgment came. They were going to take my son and give him to my Mother. But the judge put a stay on the judgment for a few weeks, seeking World Services to address some concerns. If they would, he would extend the stay. In the end, he reversed his decision. I never lost my baby.

But when the judgment first came down, I read it. It was a very difficult, yet a very enlightening experience. He had pieced together some of the Letters to show that the MO Letters greatly affected peo-

ple in The Family to act abusively towards children. At that point,
it clicked with me. The judge was right! *The MO Letters* had broken
down taboos and opened the door wide for people to act abusively
toward children. These people who had given evidence of abuse, they
had authentic stories to tell.

With Father David's granddaughter, I thought: "What if I had been
in her shoes? Was that the way we were supposed to be as Christians?
Would I have thought that was loving? No, I would not!"[12] These people with these stories, this needed to be told for an accurate picture of
The Family to be made. I needed to accept that fact. I began to put
myself in their shoes.

Dad wrote the Letters. He broke down the taboos, opened the
doors without putting any safeguards. I do not think he believed anyone would really get hurt, but they did. And now, I admire The
Family for seeing that we were wrong. This needed to be changed,
and we did. So, yes, Dad was responsible. He wrote the Letters, and if
not, then it would not have happened. But all those who acted unlov-
ingly and abusively, they are also responsible. Some of the things that
were done are abhorrent.

I have learned a lot from all this. But, in The Family, we serve
God. We do not abuse children. We are not some cultish sex group.
We are normal people who love our children and are trying to serve
God. That is why God has fought for us, why God has had mercy on
us and forgiven us for our many mistakes and the wrongs we have
done in the past.

I know God's Spirit is with The Family, and that God did choose
Dad to lead us. But, I also know that within The Family as a whole,
we are flawed individuals. I think that is the major mistake Father
David made. He used to quote often, "to the pure, all things are
pure." That may be true. But I am not pure, and you aren't pure
either.

Dad was wrong. We were wrong. But that is in the past, and in
God's mercy we have been forgiven. A sincere apology was given to

12. In the court case, Father David's granddaughter gave testimony that she had
been sexually and physically abused by Father David, then subjected to terrifying or-
deals of exorcisms.

*those who were hurt. That was necessary. I truly believe we can go
on from here to serve the Lord together.*

The Family has come full face to the reality that literature such as
"Heaven's Girl," "The Little Girl Dream," "The Devil Hates Sex," and
"The Story of Davidito" did sanction adult sexual contact with minors.
The disciples have responded to all of this in various ways. For some,
particularly those holding a very high view of Father David, it has been
a difficult time.

*The court case in the United Kingdom has been very heavy. In
some ways, it is amazing that we survived as long as we have without some of this being known. See, we really are different. It is the
End Time. And the Bible says that persecution will come upon us.
Our doctrines are very radical. I understand how outsiders see us as
crazy. That is scary to me. I think we will get even more persecution,
now. My biggest fear is losing my kids. I can take prison, but it would
be very hard to lose my kids.*

*I don't know quite what to think about Peter's Letter "An Answer
to Him." I never saw that kind of abuse, never. I guess I heard some
things. But I never had teens talk of any specific incidents with me.*
* * * * *

*[How do you mean that you heard things, but never heard any
specifics?]*
* * * * *

*I guess if you press me on it, well, then I guess some teens told me
weird things happened. I cannot remember any specifics. I guess I
never asked any specific questions. I never heard of any really bad
things.*

*When we got that Letter, and it said that Father David was to
blame for some of these things. Well, I thought that was plain wrong.
Dad always said from the beginning that the Law of Love was our responsibility. The way I see it, if some others took it the wrong way,
that is not Dad's fault. To be honest, I was shocked when they apologized for Dad to that Judge. I was shocked. But I guess we had to.*
* * * * *

[Have you read the Heaven's Girl series?]

* * * * *

Yes. Most, of it. I don't see the problem. (Rebea)

Other disciples seem willing to face up to the past, but are quite certain that the sexual abuse of children was never widespread.

I was taken off guard when we apologized to the court about the sex with kids. I honestly didn't know. I always thought that it was not true. I guess I was wrong. But, up to the point of that Letter, The Family [leadership] always said the same, that it was not true. Now, we say it did happen. And that it was a very bad mistake.

I am concerned. If this gets public, and it will, even though it was done in the past, it might really hurt us. Our enemies will try and make use of it to hurt us.

I realize there were things in the MO Letters. But I never once supposed we were actually to do these things with kids.

* * * * *

[What about the Davidito Letters?]

* * * * *

Yes, I read the Davidito Letters. I accepted it as from Father David's household. But it did not shape my behavior. I sure thought it was different. But, if they wanted to do that in Dad's house, I guess it was OK by me. But I sure did not bring it down into my home, or teach my own kids like that. (Joy)

Beth is a European disciple who was heavily involved in the BI Case from the beginning. The experience was a difficult revelation for her.

During the trial, we really had to delve into the MO Letters. We had to come to terms with how others see us, and defend the Law of Love. I went in very positive. But then a flood of doubts came over me. Sex with children is not our policy. As far as I was concerned, it was never supposed to have been done. When it was pointed out to me that Father David said there were no boundaries, I said there was no sense in which that was something to be copied or implemented by Family members. I did not recall any statement in the MO Letters that said it was permissible to have sex with children. When the pas-

sage was first read out in the court, I said it was a lie, that there was no such thing in the MO Letters. But it was there. I honestly never recalled reading that. I certainly never did it.

That was the first time real doubts hit me. It was very hard on me, to analyze this whole thing. Then, I began to hear the testimonies of backsliders who had gone through very difficult experiences. I heard about things that had gone very wrong in other places, years ago. It was very demanding spiritually. Hearing those stories was very hard for me. Sex with children did go on in some places. People got carried away, and a lot of people got hurt. We were trying to live a heavenly existence in isolation. Some took it to extremes. It was not right.

I love The Family. You don't know how hard this is. I wish I could be a little deceptive right now. I wish I could do the PR thing. But I cannot. I prayed and heard from the Lord about this. I knew you would be asking these questions. The Family has PRed this in the past, evaded as much as possible. But now I know from the Lord that I must speak the truth.

The Family did do these things. To be sure, some of the stories have been exaggerated. Now, this was in the past, those writings were many years ago. But it was The Family.

Sex with children is not under the Law of Love. The Law of Love requires full consent from all. Children are not able to make free and informed consent.

I look back on all this now with great sadness. There was sex between adults and children. The sexual ethos at that time was to break down the barriers. I am sure that many who did these things would never have done so, if not for the sexual ethos of the time. And Father David created that sexual ethos.

I am sure we have young people who look back and wish that they did not experience what they did. Not just the sexual contact. That was terrible. But there was also far too wide exposure to sharing and sexual freedom in general. I know this firsthand. There was a serious lack of discretion. Some children were exposed to far too much, and it was not good for them. Sharing is now done with much greater discretion. We are in the present now, but it is our past.

Given the current strong prohibitions and the level of distress that these activities have created for the community, very few adult disciples were willing to discuss their personal involvement in sexual encounters with children. A number indicated direct knowledge of such events, but were understandably reluctant to offer any specifics. Most affirmed that it was neither a widespread nor a long-lasting phenomenon. Sari has come to terms with her past, and though at first quite reluctant, she opened her life.

I was in a place in the early 1980s that was most open to sexual experimentation and to following the lead of Father David. For example, there was a time when female-to-female sexual relationships were understood as perfectly acceptable. Now, you never see or hear about it. At one point, Father David sent a Letter that affirmed this, and my husband suggested that I and another sister have sex, so he could watch. We obliged him. It only happened once. Neither she nor I was into it at all. We only did it for my husband. But, that is the way we were back then. It was the way I was.

I cannot speak for others, but it was clear to us from the Davidito Letters and other Letters, such as "The Devil Hates Sex." Father David was teaching that adult sexual activity with children was acceptable. He did not say directly that we should do it. But he certainly sent the message that it was permissible.

There were Letters in which Davidito watched adults having sex, and as a two year old he had simulated sex with his care worker. There were references to her playing with him and kissing his penis. When the Letter came out about her masturbating this two-year-old boy, my husband said I should do it with our young son. I felt a little uncomfortable as his mother, so I asked another sister to do it. She did it once, then said she did not feel comfortable doing it either. After that, we stopped.

I think the "Little Girl Dream" caused problems. Father David had a dream of being in bed with Maria and an eleven-year-old girl. He had sex with the girl, as a vision of new things to come for The Family. Now, this Letter did not teach directly that adults should have sex with eleven-year-old kids. But, Father David did use it as a positive metaphor. Some people took it to mean sex with kids was acceptable. I know that it did occur as acceptable conduct in some places. Remember, this was a time when age twelve was considered an adult.

* * * * *

[You say that you know that it occurred.]

* * * * *

That is correct. I know that it did.

* * * * *

[four to five minute pause]

* * * * *

[You have an older daughter no longer living with you. She would have been about age eleven to fourteen at this time?]

* * * * *

Yes. That is correct.

* * * * *

[very long, thoughtful pause during which she looked straight into my eyes]

* * * * *

At the time, I accepted this. As a mother, I accepted Father David's teaching.

* * * * *

[long pause, her eyes began to tear]

* * * * *

[And?]

* * * * *

Please! This is very painful!

* * * * *

[silent tears were flowing down her face, but she remained composed and looked straight at me, saying nothing]

* * * * *

[OK. Let me rephrase it. Would you have sent your eleven-year-old daughter to another location, knowing it would involve her having sexual intercourse with an adult there?]

* * * * *

[long pause]

*****

Yes. At that time, I would have sent her. In those years, I would have done that. However, if I understood then what I know now, I certainly would not have sent her. Now I see that the Law of Love can not be applied to minors. And it never should have been in the past. Father David was wrong. I was wrong. Children are too young. They are not in a position to fulfill the consent aspect of the Law of Love. It is wrong and it is harmful. I see that now.

Living with this has not been easy. And these questions do not make it any easier. But, you must understand that all this is in the past. The Family is now very, very opposed to any sexual contact with minors. It has been banned since 1986. It has occurred since, but in very rare situations and the offending adult has been dealt with severely. I am sure that adult sexual contact with children is now much rarer in The Family than in the System.

I am ashamed of myself. I am not proud of The Family in this, either. But, I do feel good about how we have overcome this.

Sari is justified in feeling positive about the Family response to this truly shameful dimension of their past. Sexual contact between adults and children has moved from an accepted practice to one of the most serious offenses against community standards. There are no hard statistics regarding the current situations, but the disciples are quite committed to maintaining a high level of conduct in this area.

Sexual contact between adults and minors is not done in The Family. I can say that with no reservations. In the past, it did happen in a number of places with the full knowledge of leadership. Not any more. No compromise here at all. Once it comes to light, then we enforce the strict rule. Any offender is excommunicated immediately. There is no appeal. You know us. You know how serious a punishment that is.

I personally know of one case. No long-going affair and no intent to harm. The girl was in her mid-teens, mature and willing. Both were good disciples. It didn't matter. The adult was kicked out. That is the policy. The adult leaves. The minor is given strong counsel and a warning if it is willful. If the teen is a victim of the adult, then she

is offered help. We take this very seriously. I know our children are
much safer than those on the outside. And anyone who takes an hon-
est look at us now will know the same. (Alexander)

This era of life in The Family is now closed. The rules and regulations regarding the sexual conduct of minors are explicit and carefully
monitored.[13] Of course, the story will not be complete until we examine how the sexual revolution was experienced and is currently
processed by Father David's Grandchildren. We will address this topic
in a later chapter on the Second Generation.

Our excursion into the history of the disciples provides ample basis
to question Peter Amsterdam's "2 percent" assessment of the role of
sexuality. There have clearly been times and places where sexual
ethics and sexual conduct were significant and shaping features of
Family life. However, even those extreme moments do not fully reveal
the depth and scope of human sexuality in the Family ethos.

In the earliest stages of the movement, Father David began to envi-
sion spiritual realities in explicitly sexual terms, and to employ sexual
imagery as metaphor for spiritual truths. In August of 1969 he received
the prophetic dream "Love-Making in the Spirit!" It was not published
or released to the disciples for almost two years.

As the bride of the morning hath awakened thee with her kisses,
and as her soft touches hath aroused thee, so shall thou woo My
Spirit and touch the hem of My Garment, My Skirt: and as thy seed
shall flow out of thee into her to bring forth fruit, even so virtue shall
flow out of Me into thee to bring forth the fruit of My Kingdom.

And even as her breasts do satisfy thee, so shall My bosom satisfy
thee with the milk of My Word to the strengthening of thy sinews in
the Spirit. ("Love-Making in the Spirit!" ML #N, July 1971)[14]

---

13. Family rules and regulations are subject to change. The current regulations are
very explicit. No sexual intercourse is allowed for teens under the age of sixteen.
Sixteen- and seventeen-year-old teens are allowed to have sexual intercourse only with
others in that age category. People ages eighteen to twenty are allowed to have sexual
intercourse only with persons no more than five years older than they are.

14. This Letter is accompanied by a drawing of a figure who looks distinctly like
Jesus engaged in a sensual embrace with a nearly nude, attractive young woman. It is
primarily these types of illustrative drawings that arouse the charges of pornography.

From this point on, sexual imagery emerged as a principal vehicle for spiritual understanding and direct guidance from God. The clearest and most pronounced use of sexual metaphor came in recounting Father David's many dreams and visions. "The Goddesses" is perhaps the best example of how he intertwined sex and spiritual insight. Apparently, Father David was subject to erotic dreams in which he engaged in sexual intercourse with exotic females.

Sometimes the Lord uses strange symbols and mysterious identifications to show His prophets what's going on. It's like the prophets in the Bible. . . . A symbolic ravishing of the Queen represented the Common Market rape of England by Europe. I've had some other visions like this which I've not understood until now, like all those other goddesses I've made love to in the Spirit. I've even been a little shocked by some of these strange experiences because I didn't understand them and was almost afraid to ask the Lord what they meant: In each case, the one I was making love to would suddenly turn into one of these strange and beautiful goddesses, and I would immediately explode in an orgasm of tremendous spiritual power while at the same time prophesying violently in some foreign language!

I finally sought the Lord for an answer: Do you know what every one of those women was doing? Each was submitting herself to our love!—Each seemed like some sort of symbolic conquest!—Each is the Spirit of her country, like the spirit of their religion. . . . I was literally overcoming, or overpowering them, conquering each of them with God's love, loving each into submission by the irresistible power of the Spirit of God and His overwhelming love! Hallelujah! ("The Goddesses!" ML #224, Apr. 1973)

He describes his erotic visions with the Black Goddess of Africa, the multiarmed Goddess of India, the Queen of England, the Cat Goddess of Egypt, the shy Latin American Indian Goddess, the Pearl Goddess of Central Asia, even the Miss American Sex Goddess. Each was then interpreted as symbolic of the Children of God carrying Jesus to those locations and the power of God's love to overcome indigenous religious resistance to the message.

The level of overt sexual imagery in Family literature remained consistent through the 1980s. It was most graphic and almost always accompanied by illustrative drawings. It is quite understandable how outsiders would view much of this literature as pornographic. Further details or examples would serve no useful purpose. Sexual imagery continues to play a role in the religious language of The Family. To be sure, the literature of the 1990s has been far more subdued and less explicit. The disciples remain quite comfortable with this distinctive religious vocabulary that still inhabits their literature. Yet, as best as I could determine, sexually explicit language did not work its way into the day-to-day religious discourse of the members. However, a new emphasis in spirituality seems to portend a change in this area.

The link between sexuality and spirituality is still quite pronounced. In fact, Peter and Maria have made a conscious effort to strengthen that linkage. Maria has titled this new movement the "Loving Jesus Revolution." The stated purpose of the revolution is to encourage the disciples to love Jesus more and to experience and express that love as a true "lover" of Jesus. Peter Amsterdam explained the new movement shortly before it was made known to the community at large.

There is something the Lord has given us in prophecy, and it is not going to endear us with the churches.

* * * * *

[You are not endeared now.]

* * * * *

Well, this is not going to endear us even more. The Lord wants The Family to spend more time with Him, to be more prayerful. Actually, what He said is to be more intimate *with Him. The Lord said that in prophecy.*

* * * * *

[My mind is just racing.]

* * * * *

[we both laugh]

* * * * *

Okay, Lord help us. You must keep this to yourself until we have informed the whole Family.

* * * * *

[Agreed.]

* * * * *

He told us in prophecy that He has called the church the bride of Christ. Dad, in the Letters, talked about this subject. Dad often used sexual things to show the kind of relationship the Lord wants us to have. To be close, to love Him. The Lord said that the church is the bride. He said it's kind of a mystery, we are all His bride, collectively we're His bride, sexually if you will, and singularly we are His bride. He wants us to spend more time with Him. He is very happy with our service, the souls we have won. And now He wants us closer.

* * * * *

[I am OK, so far.]

* * * * *

He talked to us about praising more, hearing from Him in prophecy more. Our question was how do we do it. "What do you want us to do? How do you want us to love you?" He used the illustration of the man and the woman: the things they would say, words of endearment they would say to one another. He would like us to say those words to Him. "I love you." "I want you." "I desire you." So, the Lord told us to say these things to Him.

Now, it is pretty easy for the women to say "You are my lover" to the Lord. But the men, well we are quite opposed to homosexuality. The Lord told us in prophecy that it is no big deal. He calls everyone His bride. It is not a visible thing, there is no male or female in Christ Jesus. It is like role playing. The men will play the role of the bride.

* * * * *

[I am waiting for the punch line.]

* * * * *

Right. OK, how to do this? He called it a gift of the Spirit, to know how to love Him this way. He said that when we're lovemaking with your wife or sharing with a sister, we could say these words of endearment together to the Lord, as part of our lovemaking. Together we could say words to the Lord, like "I love you—I want you—I love your kisses." The other person kissing you is the Lord's love being manifest. So, that's basically it.

* * * * *

[Let me see if I have this. One, you wish to develop a language of

love and appreciation for God that uninformed outsiders might construe as sexually explicit with sexual implications. And two, you will begin to understand the physical sex act itself as an act of worship to Jesus.]

* * * * *

Well, not necessarily every time. But yes, you've got it.

Maria and I have done this and it is very precious. You do feel dear to the Lord. It is just very sweet.

Peter went on to state that this special language of love to Jesus should not be employed in front of children and is not something to be done as part of normal community worship.

It is private between you and the Lord, between the two of you and Jesus. Or, I suppose if you had a small group of people and you were going to praise the Lord, and there were no children around, then you could say these things. But we are going to draw a hard line here. It is just not wise for children.

* * * * *

[When you mention a small group together doing this kind of worship, are you also talking about the physical sex act?]

* * * * *

You mean a small group of people having sex together?

* * * * *

[That, or during the small-group worship, one couple having sex as part of that worship.]

* * * * *

I hadn't thought of that. From the prophecy so far and what I know, that has not entered in and we are not going to be suggesting that people start doing that. I cannot say that people, in some cases, might not do that. But, I don't think we are going to say, "Hey, this is a good idea." I see it as more or less a verbal form of worship when it is a group.

The "Loving Jesus Revolution" reached the disciples in 1996. Numerous Letters from Maria and Peter have implemented the new program along the lines that Peter described in 1995. The disciples I spoke with about the new movement were quite enthusiastic. They generally felt it was a needed change and would be a significant forward step in the spiritual maturity of the community. Though this movement is still fresh, it appears to be focused within the intimate setting of the private bedroom, and has not developed a communal or small-group dimension. However, as in almost every new initiative, a few disciples have found this one too much, and left.

The distinctive sexual ethos continues to inform and shape the daily lives of disciples. However, the relationship between sex and the spiritual enterprise is not limited to this life alone. Sexual fulfillment and sexual fellowship are also clearly understood as significant components of Heaven's final reward. The afterlife for God's special End Time disciples will be lived out in a perfected body. As in this life, sexual ecstasy will be both the substance and the symbol of spiritual union and ultimate bliss. The perfect joy, innocence, and sexual pleasure of the Garden of Eden await the disciples.

The first Family poster, "Space City," was a graphic depiction of Father David's vision of Heaven. The lower-right quadrant portrays a garden scene with a number of young, beautiful couples. They are fully nude and appear to be in perfect harmony and peace. In the background, several couples are clearly visible, fully engaged in sexual intercourse. Later editions of this poster were used for public witness, and clothes were added to the figures. However, the original poster remains the authentic vision of Heaven.

In one sense, Peter Amsterdam's "2 percent solution" starkly undervalues the role of sexuality. At one level, the unique sexual ethos virtually defines the community. It shapes personal and communal identity, communal values, and group loyalty. Sharply in the past, and to a lesser degree in the present, it places a strain on fundamental human relationships. Sexuality continues to play a significant role in defining the nature of discipleship, and continues strongly to inform theology, mission, and worship.

But in another sense, Peter is right. Since the late 1980s, Flirty Fishing has disappeared and sexual sharing has declined sharply in practice and value. Adult sexual contact with minors has been outlawed and virtually suppressed. The sexual conduct of teens and young people has been clearly defined and is much more successfully regulated than in Western society at large. The current sexual ethos is so normative that it is rarely discussed, and plays little role in day-to-day activities. The disciples are primarily focused on accomplishing their mission, while surviving in an increasingly hostile world.

We are not about sex. We are about Jesus. Everything we do and everything we are is about telling the world of the love of Jesus. That is our mission.

If people could really know us, they would see that. (Noah)

We now turn to consider that mission.

5. Mission Impossible

We began this inquiry with one central question before us: Who are these people? We have attempted to discover that identity by searching out their life experience and their own self-understanding. Clifford Geertz, in his admirable attempt to define religion, observes that religion is interesting, not because it "describes" the human condition, but because it "shapes" it (Geertz 1973,119). The Family is a distinctive and peculiar community. But beyond all other descriptive categories, the Children of God are a profoundly religious people.

Life in The Family is centered in and revolves around religious experience and religious motivation. A typical day in any home begins with a community "fellowship time." These services typically last from thirty minutes to an hour. Not just on Sunday, every day. They have consciously abandoned any semblance of formality associated with conventional "churchianity." But there appears to be a widely established, though very informal, liturgy. Leadership of the meeting rotates among the adults and older teens. The singing normally begins on schedule, with latecomers casually drifting in. Every home has at least one accomplished guitarist, the instrument of choice. The singing is always lively and enthusiastic, with selections from popular Christian hymns mixed with some of the hundreds of Family songs. A season of open and spontaneous prayer follows the singing. Often, special issues facing the larger Family and specific needs of the local community are articulated as prayer concerns. Occasionally, someone will pray in "tongues." However, the young people are much less disposed to this form of worship. Prayer is followed by "Word Time," a public reading of the Bible and the MO Letters or more recent Family literature. The "Word" is mostly read and believed. Discussion is not uncommon, but only rarely does a leader offer an exposition of the text. Lengthy text readings are the norm, but there is no sermon. The meeting is closed with song and prayer. The disciples then head off to their tasks for the day. But in no sense does this meeting end their religious focus.

Normally, all those who are at home gather two or three times a day for a brief season of praise and prayer. "We do this to keep our attention on Jesus, where it is supposed to be. It is not hard to lose that, to just let things go by and not keep our eyes on the Lord like we should" (Peter). I certainly would not question Peter's concern for the spiritual welfare of his flock. But it is difficult to see how anyone could live in a Family home and not keep your "eyes on the Lord." The disciples pray. They pray a lot. They pray before meals, and they pray before basketball games. They pray before any contact with the outside world. They pray before every car trip, even to the corner grocery store. They pray for guidance in all personal or communal decisions. And they pray before watching videos. Prayer is a central aspect of communal worship, and a vital component of the mundane activities of life. It is also the center-piece of personal devotion. Virtually all disciples related devotional lives that included daily periods of prayer in the privacy of their own hearts.

The Children are a worshiping people and a praying people. They are also people of "The Word." In the early years, the Bible was the sole basis of authority and guidance. As Father David's status as End Time Prophet evolved, his writings were fused with the Bible to form the scriptural foundation of the community, "The Word." The Bible is still very central to the religious life of the disciples, and they read it constantly. In addition to formal interviews and more casual interchange with the disciples, I spent a fair amount of time just observing carefully and noting every detail I could. I did not find any new Bibles. They were all worn and well used. From the wear, underlining and marginal notes, it appears that disciples center their Bible reading on the Gospels, Genesis, and the apocalyptic books of Daniel and Revelation. In casual conversation and the occasional off-the-cuff game of "Bible Jeopardy," disciples of all ages demonstrated solid and broad-based biblical knowledge. However, the MO Letters seem to have supplanted the Bible to a significant extent. Word Time in the communal services is almost always from the Letters. Most disciples, especially the young people, tend to relate more naturally to the Letters and spend more time in the "Word for this day."

Though the level of discipline varies from person to person and from home to home, most disciples spend at least a half hour a day in "Word Time," private reading and study. The children and teens have Word memorization as part of their educational curriculum. In addition, Family members regularly "go to the Word" for guidance and direction. One simply cannot enter into conversation without hearing a consistent refrain: "The Bible says" or "Father David has taught us," or "The Word tells us that." The vast majority of disciples have little sense of scriptural nuance or ambiguity. The message of God is simple and straightforward. And they are supremely confident that the full range of their beliefs and practices rests solidly on The Word.

The disciples worship and pray. They read The Word. But most of all, they are Jesus People. They see themselves as the last loyal soldiers in the Jesus Revolution, and this is the central component in their sense of self. Although they hold certain views about Jesus and the Trinity that are clearly innovative and considerably out of harmony with more orthodox traditions, they know themselves as true followers of Jesus Christ.

Look, I know we must seem fairly strange to outsiders. We have done some pretty strange things. I accept that. But if you concentrate on the weird stuff, you are going to miss who we really are. We belong to Jesus. The one thing that Father David taught us, the most important, was to hear from God, to stay close to Jesus. Now, I have to admit that we have not succeeded so well at that at times. Most of us don't walk as close to the Lord as we should. But that is what Father David really wanted. This is the most priceless thing about The Family, our close walk with Jesus. To be honest, most of the other stuff I can take or leave. But I stay in because it keeps me close to Jesus.

In a way Father David did want us to follow him, sure, but to follow him to Jesus. Is there strange stuff in the MO Letters? Yeah! Lots! But the MO Letters that we read over and over, the ones that are really at the heart of who we are, or at least what we should be, they are the ones that instruct us to know God better and to follow Jesus. Just

like the Bible, you can pull out pieces of the MO Letters and show al-
most anything. But what they mean to me is that they lead and guide
us to Jesus. (Harris—long-term European disciple)

The disciples pray to Jesus, and they sing to Jesus. They talk a great
deal about Jesus. When you spend time in a Family home, you constantly hear the name of Jesus. The disciples are supremely convinced
that they alone fully understand Jesus. They know they are Jesus'
Special End Time People. They are sure they have grasped the true nature of the mission of Jesus. And they have committed the full measure
of their lives to fulfill that mission.

From the beginning, Father David continually reaffirmed the fundamental purpose and ultimate goal of the COG, to carry the simple
message of salvation through faith in Jesus to a lost world.

"Go ye into all the world and preach the Gospel to every creature"
is not an option! It is a commandment! The message is clear! There is
no denying it, or excusing ourselves! We must simply have the faith
to obey, even if it means going out not knowing whither we go!

Jesus made it quite clear that all Christians are ordained to preach
the gospel. . . . [T]herefore it is just not a nice thing to do when you
feel like it, or can find the time, but it is the God-given job and re-
sponsibility of all His true Children.

That is why we are banding together and spreading around the
world. ("Witnessing!" ML #344, May 1975)

This mission is the very heartbeat of Family self-understanding. To be
a Child of God is, above all else, to be a "full time missionary in service to Jesus." Once Father David realized his worldwide vision, he sent
his young followers forth on a life of spiritual adventure, physical hardship, and genuine risk. They went. They went with loyalty, dedication,
intensity, and a sense of personal abandon that is at times hard to imagine. There is no typical disciple, and there is no typical story. Abner's
life history is illustrative of that of a Family missionary.

I dropped out, got into drugs, and was just wandering. I left Can-
ada for Mexico, hoping to find some answers for my life there, among
the Indians. I ended up in Mexico City, got robbed, and lost my pass-

port. I was in real bad shape. I met a guy from The Family, and he led
me to Jesus. Things changed for me instantaneously, suddenly. My
whole heart and mind was born again. I wanted to join right away, to
be in the Children of God.

I stayed there in Mexico for about six months. It was hard. No
money at all. We slept on the floor. But I could care less. I loved the
traveling and witnessing. But the fact was, I wasn't ready yet. It was
real hard. So, I hitched back to Canada. I witnessed to my relatives,
who were all traditional Catholics. But I lost contact with The
Family for about a year. Then, I realized for sure that God wanted me
to give my life full-time to serve Him. I rejoined The Family in
Montreal.

Then the RNR came. It was a difficult time for me. Everything
seemed to come apart. We began to drift a little. I took several jobs to
support my wife and kids. Then my wife wanted out. I met my cur-
rent wife shortly after. She was an exotic dancer I met and led to
Jesus. Then came the Fellowship Revolution in 1980. Father David
called us all back together.

We went to Ecuador, as English teachers. Mostly we witnessed.
The teaching got us a visa. After a year, our visa ran out. The Lord
was ready to move us. We met another couple. They had children
who sang and performed. We decided to team up and strike out in
faith across South America. We had this crazy idea of getting a horse
and wagon and living like Christian gypsies. And I guess we did live
like gypsies. Anyway, we made our way down, hitching and on pub-
lic transportation, witnessing all the way. We did a lot of performing
and witnessing in Chile and Peru. Often we would just hop on a bus
and start giving out our lit. We would sing, take a collection, and wit-
ness to whoever was open. We were all fluent in Spanish by then. We
would work one bus, get off, and hop the next one. We met and wit-
nessed to thousands of people like that.

We traveled thousands of miles by bus, train, boat, everything. But
after six or seven months, it began to get difficult. So we decided to
pioneer a new area in Argentina. We stayed a year and witnessed any
way we could. Then the MO Letter came out saying "go East."[1] *So,*

1. "Go East: And Grow up with the Golden Triangle!" ML #1088, Jan. 1982.

we made our way back north the same way we got down to
Argentina. It was quite an adventure with a new baby. It took us
months, but we finally ended up in Panama.

We stayed in Panama for two years, had a good ministry there. We
then went to Costa Rica for six months. By then we had enough of
Latin America. We made our way to Miami to raise funds. It took us
six months, but we got the money together and we left for
Bangladesh. I think by now this was 1985.

We got a tourist visa, and we were able to spend two and a half
years in Bangladesh. We did a lot of straight witnessing there, mostly
at the university. It was tremendous. Most of the people were
Muslims, but they were very warm and receptive. We got out a thousand Christmas tapes one year, tapes with Jesus' picture right on the
cover. We were able to get by there fine, even though it is a very poor
country. Many people prayed to receive Jesus. They were mostly
Muslims, so we didn't expect them to throw off their robes, abandon
the mosque, and start going to a church. But they prayed to receive
the Lord, and that was good enough for us.

We also developed a ministry to the ships that came to
Bangladesh. We would go to the docks and board the ships, giving
them lit and getting out tapes and posters. Most were Indonesians,
Burmese, and Filipino. Many prayed to receive Jesus.

We loved Bangladesh. Now, it was not paradise. We had to contend with real difficulties: no electricity, bad water, disease. Our kids
got sick a lot. It was a tough place. We had one child there—that
made three. The Bengali people treated us well, but there were a few
Muslim fanatics. Several times we had to flee in the middle of the
night, leave everything behind and start over in a new place. So, it
was pretty tough at times. But God really used us there to lead many
souls to Jesus.

Finally, we had to leave. We went to India for about six months.
But then our visa ran out. So we went to Japan for about six months,
and that looked promising. But then we started to get bad publicity
in Japan. Anyone who did not have a specific ministry was encouraged to leave. We ended up in France. It was the last place in the

*world we wanted or ever expected to go. But that was where the need
was. And at least I spoke the language.*

*We stayed in France and Belgium for three years. I was in leader-
ship there. We had a lot of teen problems in Europe then. I did not get
much opportunity to do a lot of witnessing. But God knows. Because
then, eastern Europe opened up. I got the call to pioneer there. I went
to Romania first, then on to Bulgaria and Hungary. I spent almost
two years on the road, moving around constantly and witnessing all
the time. I left my family in France. That was a real sacrifice, but no
greater than many others have made. It was hard to be separated
from my wife and kids. But it was the greatest, most exciting time of
my life. We would pass out gospel literature and be mobbed by people, they were so hungry for the Truth. And I witnessed constantly.*

*I could speak English, French, and Spanish. I would just sit down
in a park and start playing and singing. Crowds would gather, and I
could always find someone to translate. Thousands came to know
Jesus. And we made disciples in Romania. I might still be there, except for the persecution in France. The French government raided the
home of my wife and kids, arrested them, and held them. It is a long
and terrible story. I went to Switzerland and did my best to get them
out. They held my kids for months. Finally all the charges were
dropped, and we made our way home to Canada.*

*We have been in Canada for almost two years. We have seven
kids. I don't know what the future holds. I have never known. I think
we will probably stay here for a while. We have a good ministry
among the Asian immigrants. But things change. Things could
change for The Family in Canada. If so, we are ready to go. Ready to
go anywhere Jesus needs us. Canada is not our home. Jesus is our
home.*

Mexico, Canada, Ecuador, Peru, Chile, Bolivia, Paraguay, Uruguay,
Argentina, Brazil, Columbia, Panama, Costa Rica, the United States,
Bangladesh, India, Japan, France, Belgium, Romania, Bulgaria, Hun-
gary, Switzerland, and back to Canada. This is not an unusual story.
Truly, they are just passing through.

Though the disciples often struggled when talking about certain aspects of their personal and corporate history, they would light up and be filled with enthusiasm and joy when recounting tales of witnessing.

What is the best aspect of my life? That is easy. It is telling people about Jesus. From the start, I was always a very, very intense witness for Jesus.

I went on the road a lot when I was single. Just hit the road and tell people about Jesus. My first road trip, I went into a restaurant. I saw this lady sitting at the bar, and she looked very down. So, I went up and just started talking with her. She began to cry. She had just lost her husband two days before. She was lonely and had no one. I just encouraged her to share her heart with me. Then I shared my life with her, how alone and desperate I was before I met Jesus. And she got saved, right there in that bar. She was so bright when she left that place, so happy. And I was so happy. I knew Jesus had saved her. I never saw her again, but I will in heaven. That is one story. I have many more. I cannot begin to tell you the joy it brings, to know you helped someone to heaven. (Anna)

In the early years, the witnessing mission was characterized by a stark sense of urgency and sacrifice. Time appears to have softened the edges and the pace of life has clearly slowed, at least for the first generation. It was not uncommon for an older disciple to express nostalgia for those early days.

My first two years I spent witnessing in the streets twelve hours a day, seven days a week. We shared everything we had. But we didn't have anything. [laughs] You cannot imagine how poor we were back then. And I loved it. I remember this so clearly. After my first two years I moved to a different country in Europe. When I got there, the home had beds. I had spent my first two years sleeping on the floor, and I fully believed I would sleep on the floor until The End. I remember thinking, "These guys are really compromising with the world." Because they had beds.

* * * * *

[He begins to laugh, then grows silent and looks down at the floor for almost a minute.]

* * * * *

We are not like that now. I guess we can't be. But, those were great days. The best. (André)

The disciples no longer sleep on the floor. However, the radical rejection of conventional norms and values is still a vital component of disciple life. This disconnection from "the world" has set them free to fulfill their calling. Family homes are always rented. They are normally well equipped with a sufficient number of beds and furnishings and adequate kitchen equipment. But all these things belong to the home, not to any one individual. One can rarely encounter a disciple who could not be out the door and gone in ten minutes, carrying almost everything he or she personally owned.

The Children are remarkably mobile. Virtually every member has lived on at least two continents. Many have served in over a dozen countries.[2] They go where the Spirit and Father David leads them. And they generally have displayed little regard for potential hardships or legal restrictions.

China was a real test of faith for me. Only four or five Family teams were able to get in. But I was committed. My wife and I were hired by a university to teach English. Slowly we worked in some milky gospel material to our lessons. But we went very slow. Our main job was helping with conversational English. So we talked with the students.

I didn't do much out-in-the-open witnessing during the first year, we were cautious. But eventually several students got close to us, and we began to share Jesus. We had to be careful in the class, because they had monitors. But after the first year, our witnessing bore real fruit. We even made a couple of secret disciples. Since I am Asian, I could just put on my hat and get on my bike and blend in. It was hard for them to keep track of me. I was able to hold Bible classes three times a week, in secret locations.

Witnessing was hard there, but in some ways it was the best. In the Philippines, people would pray with you to receive Jesus with no problem. But nothing really changed much with them. In China it

2. I have personally interviewed approximately 15 percent of the adult disciples. These people have served in over eightyfive countries.

took a real commitment. So it was very fruitful there, because those who did receive Jesus made a life-and-death commitment. China was a great experience for me. My wife and I are trying to figure a way to get back. (Barnabas)

Although straight one-on-one witnessing was always the ideal method, the COG was flexible and creative. A wide number of strategies and techniques were employed to facilitate the basic mission. "Poor Boy Clubs" were one of the more interesting ventures. Poor Boy Clubs started in London, then spread through Europe and Latin America.

Poor Boy Clubs were like a Christian disco, I guess. We would come and dance with the kids, get to know them, and witness to them. We would also put on plays and skits, usually about the End Time.

They worked great. But, it was very time consuming. Most of us had other duties or ministries. Most of us were very young back then, with little family responsibilities. I have to say that the Poor Boy Clubs really were effective. We reached a lot of youth that way. We got a lot of disciples through the clubs. But after a while, most of us just couldn't keep up the pace. (Deborah)

Although the mission has always been foremost, the disciples must survive in the world. They "live by faith." They generally do not work in any secular capacity, depending on God to supply their needs.[3] Although there are numerous accounts of God's miraculous provision, many disciples survived the early years at a subsistence level. Though Father David despised the System, he always taught that the resources of the System were to be appropriated for God's mission. As the movement matured, the Children became more adept at liberating those resources. Many have developed a cadre of family and friends who send financial support on a regular basis. Some have been able to establish support networks with Christian organizations and churches. How-

---

3. Disciples will accept secular employment in order to obtain a visa or get access to an otherwise restricted country. There is no absolute prohibition on secular employment. Recently, a few disciples in the United States and South America have turned to part-time employment to help support their homes.

ever, these are generally unstable and often require the disciples to hide their Family identity. We have already detailed how Flirty Fishing helped to meet immediate needs and establish long-term supportive friends. But the most significant and universal means of sustaining life is "provisioning."

The disciples simply ask for help. They present themselves to potential donors as a Christian missionary group that depends on the kindness and generosity of others. A typical home will have one or two persons assigned to provisioning responsibilities. They will make friends and contacts at local wholesale fruit and vegetable markets, receiving donations of food that is edible but too marginal for sale. They establish relationships with dairies, bakeries, wholesale grocery and meat distributors. Virtually all the food is provisioned. Clothing is provisioned. Used furniture is provisioned from hotels and restaurants. The disciples have become so skilled at provisioning that they often have a surplus of some commodities. They share with other Family homes in their region and donate their surplus to inner-city missions or homeless shelters.

Provisioning is an important task in Family life. Some disciples clearly have "the gift," but most young people receive training in the finer points of the process. And success in provisioning is always interpreted as the faithfulness of God. They depend on that faithfulness. And they often demonstrate remarkable confidence that God will provide.

We try to make one or two road trips a year. I usually take five or six of the teens and YAs, and we just head out to witness in places where there are no homes. It is often the highlight of the year. We had one just a couple of months ago, and it was great.

* * * * *

[How do you finance a trip like that?]

* * * * *

The same way we finance everything we do; God does it. We get out lit and tapes, that usually brings in some needed funds. But mostly, God just provides.

* * * * *

[You mean you provision the whole thing?]

* * * * *

You got it. The last time we went out, I took seven kids in the van, and we were gone for almost a month. We provisioned the whole trip—the gas, food in restaurants, places to stay.

* * * * *

[The gas?]

* * * * *

Sure. We just stop at a station and explain who we are. Often the kids will sing for the guy. We tell him we are missionaries that depend on the donations of people like him, and that we don't have any money. Of course, we always pray first. And God provides. I have left on road trips with less than ten dolllars among all of us.

* * * * *

[Do you ever have doubts about making it back home?]

* * * * *

Doubts? *Why would we doubt God? (Paul)*

The world and all its material resources may be under the control of Satan, but the disciples are convinced that all these things ultimately belong to God. As God's End Time Army, they have a full right to those resources as their needs arise. I was along on several provisioning trips. The disciples never displayed even a hint of embarrassment or reluctance in asking for help. They were always pleasant, respectful, and thankful toward their donors. But it is quite clear that disciples interpret provisioning as God's action, justly caring for their needs.

On occasion, provisioning extends beyond simple needs. While visiting a home on the East Coast, one of the teenage girls had her sixteenth birthday. The other teens wanted to do something special. After a few calls, they were able to provision a full pizza supper, complete with soft drinks and dessert. I was invited along to "chaperon." After supper, we took in a movie. They provisioned me for the tickets.

Although provisioning remains an effective tool in providing for many of the necessities of life, homes still require some hard cash to survive. There are rent to be paid, car insurance and repairs, transportation needs. And the homes are required to "tithe" 10 percent of their revenue to the central headquarters. In most situations, gifts from friends and relatives meet only a small portion of the need. The early years were very lean. But in 1974, Father David introduced "litnessing" as a primary means of bearing witness to the world. Specially designed literature was to be distributed to the general public, for "a small donation." This fusing of the witnessing mission with fund raising has been the bedrock of financial stability ever since.

Interestingly, the disciples were quite slow to respond to this new initiative. Father David soon solved that problem.

I was working as a secretary at the International Office in London when litnessing first started. This was 1974, I think. Hosea and Jethro were the direct overseers. But they got their direction straight from Dad.

People did not seem to take to the litnessing thing right away. Maybe people just didn't feel right about asking for donations in exchange for the gospel. Apparently Dad went out on the streets and observed the local disciples. He wasn't happy at all, about how they were doing it or how much they were doing. That is when the Letter "Shiners or Shamers" came out.

Anyway, we came into the office one Monday, and Dad had given orders to shut the entire International Office down for a week. He sent everyone of us out on the streets with our lit. We were given a quota. We had to get so much money for each piece. The amount was very small. But, anyone who didn't get their quota should start praying about where they would like to go, 'cause they would be fired from the International Office.

I got mine, but some didn't. Then we went back to work, but we still had a quota. Had to work all week in the office, then get out the lit on the weekends. We were all young and mostly single then. It wasn't so bad. A few couples had small kids—that was tough. Quite a few people didn't make their quota, and they got sent off to other fields.

Quotas on lit lasted for a long time. Some of the other top leaders took the idea and made quotas into a tyrannical thing. Some area leaders were demanding 25 or 35 percent of home revenues, in addi-

*tion to the 10 percent we sent to World Services. A lot of people suf-
fered under that kind of abuse, while the leaders lived high. But most
of that was solved in the RNR. (Jasmine)*

The complete blending of mission effort and financial support has remained a hallmark of disciple life. Since 1974, the Children have rarely
faced financial hardship or deprivation, except at the hands of their
own leaders. In some instances, particularly during the early and mid
1980s, homes with successful "FFers" were able to establish a more-
than-comfortable lifestyle. Many communities, particularly outside of
North America, are still able to maintain very nice dwellings. But today, the vast majority of disciples live simple lives, with little or no dis-
posable income and few personal possessions.

In the current climate, local and regional leaders appear to have few
special prerogatives. Father David's household has been closed to outsiders for years. However, Peter showed me a number of "family pho-
tographs" of Father David, Maria, and the household. I am not sure
what I expected, but was frankly taken by the simplicity of the scenes.
In one photo, Father David was seated on an unusual piece of furniture.
Peter explained: "Oh that. A while back one of our couches broke
down. So we took the back seat out of our van and brought it in the
house. It worked fine. We didn't need it in the van, so we just kept it in
the house."

There is no doubt. Family leadership financially abused the disciples
in times past. They are very open about all this, even naming guilty
persons who are still active in the movement. But disciples now believe the organization is run properly and fairly. The homes still tithe
10 percent of their revenues to World Services. But they are confident
the money is used to sustain World Services personnel at an adequate
and appropriate level, to support their vast publication and recording
activities, and to support "pioneer" missionaries into new fields.

The basic concept of litnessing was quickly expanded into other
facets of Family ministry. Music was always a central component of
the witness. One of the more common early strategies was to invade a
public space, begin singing and dancing, and wait for the crowd to
come. Many homes formed small groups of musicians who went to the
streets, "busking" for donations and getting out the message in song.

The children were incorporated into this ministry at very young ages. Virtually every Family teenager has grown up singing in public and witnessing on a regular basis. They sang on street corners and in restaurants, in hospitals, and in schools all over the world. They sang for Jesus, and a "small donation."

In the early 1970s, Jeremy Spencer was the lead guitarist for the popular rock group Fleetwood Mac. He was converted and joined the COG. He remains a loyal disciple to this day, spending most of his life in South America. He has had a strong influence on the musical witness of the Children.

In the early 1980s, Father David instituted the *Music with Meaning* program. Several recording stations were established to produce music programs for broadcast. *Music with Meaning* lasted only a few years, but The Family set up professional-quality recording studios in South America and Japan. They remain active and highly successful. The Family now produces several music tapes a year and has gone into CD production. These tapes generally carry an explicit witness. They often center on End Time themes and carry a clear message of salvation through faith in Jesus. One of the more recent tapes is entitled "The Lion, the Dragon & the Beast." The selections include a number of Family songs with an apocalyptic message: "In the Time of the End," "The Antichrist Shall Come," and "The Abomination of Desolation."

In addition to the production of musical tapes and CDs, they established a video recording studio in Japan. Several series of children's videos have been successfully distributed all over the world. These videos are "wholesome entertainment for kids that teach the values of kindness, patience, honesty, and belief in God." The Christian witness is quite subdued, and the disciples have had great success with these videos in predominately Muslim and Buddhist countries. Distribution of these children's videos has often been the entry mechanism for further witness in hostile and generally inaccessible territory.

I went to Pakistan and got into printing again, also tape and video duplication. It was great in Pakistan. We really clicked with the upper crust. There seemed to be a famine for the kinds of things like our videos.

We spent five years in Pakistan, mostly ran a duplication ministry, all on our own. I was on a tourist visa. We never had a lot of trouble, just a few knocks at the door. We were very wise, low key. You have to go very soft sell with the gospel to Muslims. We did have a few government people come to our Bible classes.

Once while in Karachi, a sister and I tried different ways to get out the tools. We decided to visit the seaport. We boarded one ship and got out twenty-five tapes. And a number of the seamen prayed with us to receive Jesus. The next ship, same thing. This opened up a great ministry for us with the seamen. It was a springboard to the Gulf States.

We provisioned free tickets, and a sister and I headed to Dubai. We checked it out, and went witnessing. It was the biggest open door to get out tapes and videos we had ever seen. We would sometimes get out 100 tapes a day. We would go office to office. There were lots of well-paid office workers, mostly from India. They spoke English, and they all wanted tapes.

At first we smuggled in the tapes and videos from Pakistan. But then I began duplicating them right there in the UAE. Then we went to Abu Dhabi. Our stuff was like contraband, and they wanted it. We met a lot of sheepy people. We had Bible studies in the evenings, and a lot prayed to receive Jesus. But, we did not make any disciples. I finally got overseas burnout. I had achieved way beyond what I had hoped for there, and I needed a new challenge. And I became concerned about reconciliation with my parents. So, I headed back home. (Alex)

The disciples also use live performance as an avenue for witness. Talented young people regularly gather into strategically located homes and form themselves into "show troupes." They perform in all varieties of settings, bearing a muted witness and providing support for the community. The home in Washington, D.C. has performed for the President of the United States and at the Special Olympics. Homes in England and other European nations have troupes that perform for embassies.

Most of the homes have a singing group, or a group of children and young teens who aspire to that calling. In some places, these groups provide the primary income for the home. I spent a full day with such a group. This particular team consisted of three young women: a Mexican disciple, a disciple born to American parents who has spent most of her life in Mexico, and an Italian who seemed to have picked up Spanish overnight. Their home was located in an extremely modest section of Chicago that is home to over 600,000 Hispanics, mostly from Mexico. We spent the day going from one Mexican restaurant to another. Restaurant singing is an accepted activity in Mexico, and the young women seemed to fit right in. They would sing three or four songs in Spanish, usually only one with a specifically Christian theme. They would then go from table to table, "getting out" tapes for a ten dollar donation.[4] They made a six dollar profit on each tape. The Sunday I was with the team, they "got out" forty-five tapes. They did this every Saturday and Sunday, making enough revenue to meet most of the financial needs of the home. They also provisioned a delicious lunch.

However, these young people were not simply selling tapes. At each table they would share a little of who they were, giving out a poster containing an End Time and a gospel message. Late in the afternoon we visited an upscale restaurant. When the disciples approached a table of three young men, playful sparks began to fly. They handled the flirtations with ease and got out two tapes. Two of the men were still quite interested, so the disciples gave the posters and asked the young men to read them right there. They were at the table about fifteen minutes when everyone grasped hands and bowed their heads. Two of the men prayed to receive Jesus. They were given some additional literature and were encouraged to contact the home for Bible studies and to seek out a good church.[5] Afterward, the young women were pleased and excited.

It is great when someone prays to receive Jesus. That is really why we are out here.

* * * * *

[Is this unusual?]

* * * * *

4. These tapes are professionally recorded Family music by a Family team, not the young women who were singing in the restaurants.
5. I observed all this at a distance. The entire conversation was in Spanish, and the details were related to me afterwards.

Oh no! It happens almost every weekend. We expect it. People really want to know Jesus.

The disciples have developed many different strategies for combining their witnessing ministry with fund raising. Some homes are partially financed in the summer by weekend car washes, where donations are taken and literature is dispensed. Over the last few years, "clowning" has developed into a particularly fruitful ministry. Typically an adult disciple will dress as a clown, complete with multicolored wig and rubber nose. He or she is usually accompanied by several children. They set up a table or small booth at a shopping mall or a large department store. The clown makes colorful balloon animals. These are given to children, while someone asks the parents for a "small donation" to support the mission activities of the group.

I spent a full day with a clown team in a Toronto mall. The sign identified the group as "The Family Mission: an independent Christian missionary organization bringing Jesus to the world." They displayed a number of music tapes and children's videos, but only a few "got out." The balloons went like hot-cakes. And every donation merited a poster with a gospel message and phone number for further information. "We found that dressing as a clown really disarms people. It is amazing how we can get the posters out this way. Personal witness is not the best as a clown, but I usually get to pray with someone every time out. And my daughters get to be involved. They see the good we are doing for people" (David).

David and his children took in $175 that day. Support from family and friends, occasional distribution of tapes and posters, and two days a week of clowning provide the hard cash this home of six adults, two YAs, and ten children needs. And David is right, a clown is disarming. At midmorning a Sikh in full beard and turban came by the table with his wife and two small daughters. When he saw the "Christian missionary" sign, he offered a defiant look and hustled his family off to shop. But little children with balloon animals were everywhere. And in a short time the Sikh was back, each young daughter pulling on a coat sleeve. They got their balloons, the Sikh father came up with the "small donation," and the mother walked off reading the poster. David turned and commented: "Bet you don't see many of those in *your* church."

There are disciples who are more entrepreneurial in their approach to fund raising. A disciple in South Africa developed a successful operation. He established a friendship with a major car dealer and was able to provision a used car for Family business. In time, the dealer allowed him to choose two or three used cars a month at rock-bottom wholesale price. This disciple had the gift. He would shine up the cars and sell them at a profit.

I know motor cars, and I can sell. But I recognized right away that this could be a wonderful thing for The Family, but a dangerous thing for me. It could easily lead me off into materialism and a lack of dependence on God. So, I committed all the money I made selling automobiles to The Family. I would either send it to World Services, or use it to support other Family missionaries who were pioneering new areas. I would help with transportation costs and support money while they got established. I never used any of the motor car money for our own needs. Of course, we got on fine making other friends and getting out lit and tapes.

* * * * *

[How successful was this car thing?]

* * * * *

For three years, I made about thirty thousand of your U.S. dollars a year. (Ebed)

The disciples still do a great deal of "straight witnessing." They work the beaches and other resorts in the summer, congregate at major athletic events, and head out on road trips on a regular basis. But the synthesis of witness and fund raising is a fact of life. It sustains the community through the very act of fulfilling the mission.

As the disciples aged and matured, the nature of the mission evolved with the times. Change is endemic in the Jesus Revolution. Although a number of factors contributed to this overall process of maturation, nothing changed life in The Family as much as the coming of children. From the earliest years, Father David adamantly affirmed the beauty and God-given nature of sex. With equal force, he rejected any form of birth control as sin. So, the children came. They came in droves.

The COG had deliberately and self-consciously cut itself off from "worldly" values and influences. Many of the disciples were left with little direction or understanding about the care and nurture of children. It also appears that, at least in some instances, the infants and toddlers were construed as obstacles to the task of getting the message out before The End. Family leadership responded forthrightly to these problems. In 1978, Father David issued "God's Gift Is God's Work," one of the more significant and shaping of all the MO Letters. He reaffirmed, in his own bombastic fashion, that sex is God's special gift to his children. He then went on to make very explicit that the fruit of sexual activity is also God's special gift. Father David spelled out very clearly that the proper care and nurture of children would be a priority and a central component of the mission.

God's Gift *is God's* Work! *So don't ever tell me a child was an accident, or well, it's of some* fish *or something* fishy. *God's* gifts *are God's* works, *so get busy. If He's given you such a gift you better go to work at it and make that gift what He wants it to be, amen!*

He *gives you children, and you have to work* hard *at taking care of them and bringing them up the way they should be reared—Teaching them, training them, taking care of them until they can take care of themselves—and* someday *they'll be taking care of* you.

Remember what I once told you about children! I said they are the Kingdom of God. So while you're taking care of those children you're helping God's Kingdom come on Earth!*—As it is in* Heaven, *amen!—The Lord's Prayer! ("God's Gift Is God's Work—Part 3," ML #756, Aug. 1978)*

The basic thrust of "God's Gift Is God's Work" was repeated in a number of subsequent MO Letters and other Family writings. In response, the COG made a significant shift. Maria took the lead in investing substantial resources, time, and energy toward developing sound and consistent child-rearing policies and educational programs. The Family has developed its own programs and an extensive child-care manual. To be sure, Family child rearing has had its downside. We will explore that more fully when we consider the second generation in a later chapter. But the disciples generally took their responsibilities serious-ly. A few disciples have devoted virtually their entire productive lives to the development and continual refinement of child care and educa-tional programs.

"God's Gift Is God's Work" had a pronounced impact on the lives of many disciples. The care, nurture, and education of the children be-came the central focus of life and the avenue to fulfill their mission for God.

[As you think back over your life in The Family, what are your best experiences?]

* * * * *

Oh, that is easy. Every one of my eight children. Being able to have them, to have time with them, and to raise them in The Family with real Godly attitudes and outlook. I have been able to teach them that they are on this earth for a reason, to serve the Lord and to put others first. That is the best of my life. My older children have de-cided to serve the Lord full time in The Family. I am most fulfilled and blessed in that. My kids have been my life. I mean I am out and about witnessing and doing other things. But the responsibility of be-ing a mother is very stressed with us. That has been my main min-istry. Through the years our emphasis on child care has developed to a point where it is one of the priorities, and has been for many years. I really like that. (Sonnet)

The older children and teenagers are given training, experience in, and responsibility for the care of young children. Preschool and early grades are often taught by older teens or YAs. The girls seem to be drawn to these duties, but the teenage boys are clearly not exempt from child-care training and responsibilities. Gender-specific roles have their place. Almost all the secretaries are female and the handymen are male. But care of the children is a universal responsibility.

The emphasis on the children as "God's Work" has redirected con-siderable energy inward. The nature of the mission has also evolved with the changing fortunes and circumstances of The Family. In the early years, Father David's vision was to reach the "hippies, the out-casts of society." In an early vision, Father David heard God challenge him to become "King of the Beggars." People on the margins of society were clearly the focus of COG witness, right up through the early 1970s. But the hippies went the way of all things. And COG families were growing quickly, with ever increasing needs. The target audience shifted to the middle and upper classes, the "up and outs." The introduction of Flirty Fishing epitomized this shift. You do not find many "Beggars" checking into five-star hotels, or employing an escort service at $200 a night.

Father David also had a pronounced aversion to the "Social Gospel." With the ever present and impending End Time looming before him, he directed the Children away from any concerns beyond the explicitly spiritual welfare of potential converts. The many social welfare and social justice projects of conventional "churchianity" were portrayed as a fundamental weakness and a great distraction to the real mission of Jesus, the spiritual salvation of lost souls.

However, toward the end of his life, the Prophet had a change of heart. In the spring of 1992, Father David published "Consider the Poor!—Our New Ministry in the U.S. to the Poor!—To the people who don't care who we are!" Father David received a prophecy that was based on Isaiah 61:1–3.[6]

> *[referring to Isaiah 61:1–3] From that, what would you gather is the type of people the Lord is calling our folks to minister to now as they serve the Lord in North America? Does it sound like bigshots? . . . What economic class would you say those people are? The poor!*
>
> *I think we are going to have a very lowly ministry again . . . we are going to seek out the people that nobody wants—the lost, the lowly, the forsaken, the despised & the broken—"the castoffs, those which no man desireth, which others do not want & do not seek, the unwanted & the uncared for." That is what the Lord gave me—that we'll be doing just like we did when we first started! ("Consider the Poor!—Our New Ministry in the U.S. to the Poor!" ML #2755, Mar. 1992)*

6. This is the passage quoted by Jesus in Luke 4, inaugurating his mission.

"Consider the Poor" was received throughout the world as a very welcome change, particularly among the second generation. The Prophet cautioned the Children that "our main job is still to minister spiritually." However, the disciples were now freed to do all they could to meet all the needs of "the despised and rejected." Father David specifically suggested ministry to migrant workers, refugees, illegal aliens, minorities, unwed mothers, prostitutes, drug addicts, and those in correctional institutions, prisons, orphanages, and "old folks' homes." He cautioned the disciples very strongly not to lose sight of the spiritual mission, but clearly broadened the scope of that mission to include the care for people in need. He also noted that "these people won't care who you are."

"Consider the Poor" has created a minor revolution. The disciples are still focused on the End Time and the salvation of souls, but they are increasingly involved in active social ministries as an avenue for that witness. They have poured their energies into prisons and refugee camps all over the world. In a few instances, "Consider the Poor" has become the primary mission.

The Family has had a number of very long-term and faithful friends in the New York area for years. Our home has recently consolidated a lot of that support, and we focus it toward our Consider the Poor ministry. We have great resources; wholesale food companies, a health food distributor, a major clothing chain that donates damaged or obsolete items. It really takes up most of our time now. We consolidate and distribute to a lot of very needy people. We give to several inner-city rescue missions, detention centers, a couple of battered-women shelters, and a home for abused and abandoned children.

The rescue missions love us, and we get to witness there a lot. The women's shelters are a different story. They are secular, and they were very suspicious of us at first. So, we have been very low-key with them. But we are beginning to wear them down with our love. The woman who runs one of them is a Jew. At first, she didn't even want to talk to us. You know, "just leave the stuff and go." But we have loved her and kept bringing her things they really need. Finally, last Christmas, she allowed our kids to put on a program for the women in the shelter. We made sure it was real milky. And the kids were great. Even the supervisor had a tear in her eye. In time, they are going to know we are doing this for them because we love Jesus, and Jesus loves them. (Nathan)

To understand the degree to which the disciples have responded to "Consider the Poor," one only has to read the monthly internal publication "Worldwide Activity Report."

From Isaac, Ruth and Joanne in Burma[7]

* * * * *

Saturday morning we taught our weekly English class at a boarding school/orphanage for blind children. The conditions are desperately poor. Only two meals a day and the children sleep on the floor.

In the afternoon we went to a charity dinner we organized for the school for blind children. The dinner was attended by two of our friends, and they came to our home afterward. We explained more about the Lord to them.

Sunday a family came to inquire about the kindergarten school which we opened and operate. While these were visiting, another friend came to pick up 100 Family posters to send to a pastor in the mountains. About 6:00 P.M. a doctor who is a specialist at the government children's hospital came to our home. We had phoned him earlier to request his help with the sick baby of a poor widow whom we met in the course of our outreach activities. We showed the doctor our photo album, and he said: "You are so versatile, just like the missionaries that used to come to Burma. I'll do anything I can to help you." During the conversation, the director of the school for the blind dropped by to pick up the funds we raised through ticket sales for the charity dinner the night before—a busy but rewarding weekend of sharing God's love with others!

Although the Consider the Poor ministries has influenced the activities of many disciples, it is still understood as a means to an end. Witnessing remains the central theme. It was reinforced again by Maria

7. The nation of Myanmar (Burma) is legally closed to all Christian missionaries.

and Peter in the spring of 1995. Peter had just suffered a mild heart attack. During his recovery, he received this prophecy from Jesus:

[Maria speaking] After one time of crying out desperately to the Lord with intense tongues, I asked Peter if he thought maybe the Lord wanted to speak to us. . . . Well, I was right about the Lord wanting to speak.

(Prophecy:) [Jesus speaking through Peter] So does My *heart hurt!—For the lost! So does* My *heart pain!—For those who have pain and those who are lost and those who are brokenhearted! So does* My *heart hurt!—For the war-torn and the weary and those that thirst in the heat of the desert for My water, and those that freeze in the cold and seek for My warmth; and those that are lost and lonely, and seek for My love. My heart aches and My heart breaks for these. ("Go Ye Into All The World!" ML #2990, May 1995. By Maria)*

The Family is empowered and directed by a deep and pervasive religious conviction. The End Time is fast approaching. Though aware that others do spread the message of salvation, the disciples are convinced that they alone are uniquely qualified to reach the world for Jesus before the great cataclysm. They are Christian missionaries, but not just Christian missionaries. They are also Father David's Children. He alone has received God's final message for humanity. In "Go Ye Into All The World," the prophetic voice of Jesus spoke:

Go ye into all the world and preach the gospel to every creature, for this is the commission that I have given unto you, the children of David. Go and make disciples of all nations, for the children of all nations cry out for the Words of David. I open the door of all nations of the world unto you, that ye may plant the seeds of the Words of David, and that ye may feed them with the Words of David. . . . If I be lifted up, I will draw all men unto Me. Thus lift Me up in these lands, and lift Me up through the Words of David, that which has made you different.

Yes. The disciples are different. Their mission is to carry the message of the Love of Jesus to the world. Their mission is also to denounce the evils of this present World System and to warn of the coming of the Antichrist. Their mission is to proclaim the teaching, guidance, and example of God's Final Prophetic Voice. They are the Children of God. They are the "children of David." Both components of the mission have filled their lives with purpose and direction. And both have brought down ridicule, rejection, opposition, and oppression. We have already demonstrated how many disciples were mistreated and abused by their own leaders. They have also suffered at the hands of "the world." From the beginning, there was a steep price to be paid for being one of Father David's Children. We now turn to consider the cost of discipleship.

6. The Cost of Discipleship

Farom the opening shot in the Jesus Revolution, Father David set his young disciples against the outside world. He continually reaffirmed his passionate opposition to the System. He repeatedly identified that outside world with Satan and charged his followers with the task of bringing the System down.

Jesus Christ was a Revolutionary! *He was not a Reformist. He attacked the system of His day. . . . Likewise, we today are not mere reformists trying to improve or patch up the old, decrepit, false Systems of man! We are a* Revolution!—*For* Jesus! *And a real, red-hot, genuine revolution is not merely for something, but* against *something also! . . . Because we really* love *Jesus Christ, we therefore hate the God-damned anti-Christ Systems of this world with everything in us! The Bible says, "Ye that love the Lord,* hate *evil!"*

Therefore, we in our worldwide Revolution for Jesus have declared war of the Spirit against *the System's Godless schools, Christless churches & heartless Mammon! Like Jesus, "Who was manifested that He might* destroy *the* works *of the Devil" (1 Jn. 3:8), we are rebels against these anti-Christ institutions of man & the Devil & are rebels for the* Truth, *rebels for the true naked Word of God. ("Revolution for Jesus!" ML #1963, Mar. 1984)*

Father David was always careful to warn and instruct his Children regarding the nature of their self-declared war on the System. This conflict was to be a distinctly spiritual crusade. Violence of any kind on the part of the Children was not part of God's plan and would not be countenanced in God's End Time Army.

The Lie is the spirit of Antichrist—a spiritual force of evil that is invisible, but which has created the visible evil system. God's word says, "The weapons of our warfare are not carnal (Physical), but mighty *through God to the tearing down of strongholds! But you can't do that with physical force, with physical violence! You can only do that by the Word of His Truth, the "Sword of the Spirit, which is the Word of God!" (Eph. 6:17) ("Revolution for Jesus!" ML #1963, Mar. 1984)*

He did not say that the enemies of God and his Prophet would go unpunished. Quite the contrary. But they would suffer for their evil deeds at the hands of God and his avenging angels, not at those of the Children.

Then suddenly I saw America, just like it was going to happen there the same, only even a more horrible slaughter!—Plagues and people lying everywhere, dead and dying!

[Jesus speaking] O, Behold, how they kill their prophets, and how they stone their Saviors, and how they despise My messengers! . . .

O, even so would they have done with my David had I not overshadowed him, and protected him, and kept him, and sheltered him round about by My angles, and given him the aura of My wings, and the protection of My power! . . .

For I shall scatter their dead throughout the land, and they shall neither be lamented or buried, but they shall be dung upon the ground! (I saw people being slaughtered by the millions, like a great plague, scattered everywhere, piles of bodies! Most of what I saw seemed to be in America.)

All our enemies shall be swept away! Preserve Thy Children, Lord, and keep Thy little ones, Jesus, and guard Thy flock, O God, until we see that day that Thou shalt come! Thank thee O God! Thank You Jesus! Amen. ("A Prophecy Against Our Enemies!" ML #188, Oct. 1972)

Though Father David completely rejected any use of physical violence, he left no room for compromise with Satan. God's face is set against the System because the System hates God, and serves the Devil. To be a friend of the World was to be an enemy of God. The Prophet called his young charges to total opposition toward the educational, religious, social, political, and economic institutions of contemporary society. He also required them to abandon connections or relationships with anyone in the System who might tie them to those institutions, and thus deflect them from their true calling in Jesus.

> When Jesus walked by the seashore, He called to the fishermen . . . "Come now & follow me!" Did they stop to try to figure it out? — "Let's see now, what about the house? — What about the wife and the kids? — What about father & mother? Can I get all the bills paid?" NO! They dropped everything on the spot, forsook all, & followed Jesus! . . . It's a high privilege to be called by the Lord into His service, & when the time comes, it's urgent, & often He expects you to drop everything immediately! Time & time again, Jesus' acid test for His prospective disciples was if they were willing to forsake all, drop everything, leave it all behind & follow him! — And not even look back, not regret the past and not wish they could go back. And today it is the same.
>
> Jesus wouldn't even let them go back and say good-bye to their parents, much less bury their father! . . . Well, that was often one of their first and greatest tests, & this is why God still often brings division in families today. Jesus said, "Think not that I have come to send peace on earth: I come not to send peace, but a sword! He that loveth father or mother more than me is not worthy of Me!" (Mat. 10:34–38)
>
> So don't make the mistake of putting your hand to the plough, the Lord's plough, the calling & job that God has for you, & then looking back! He says, "forget the things which are behind, & press forward to the things which are before!" (Phil. 3:13) That's a commandment from the Lord — Forget the past! ("Revolutionary Discipleship!" ML #1965, Feb. 1984)

In the first decade of the movement, virtually all of the disciples heeded the Prophet's call to sever connections with the System. They turned their backs on employment, school, and family ties. They simply walked away. Many had already "dropped out" and had little attachment to those left behind. The majority of older adult disciples recounted ruptured or highly stressed family relationships prior to joining the movement. However, any attempt by family or friends to pull the disciples back from the COG was run through the revolutionary grid, and rejected out of hand as the work of Satan.

There are any number of adult disciples who look back to those "forsake all" experiences with very mixed feelings. On the one hand, they remain adamantly convinced of Satanic control of the System. On the other hand, many feel considerable guilt and remorse over the pain and sorrow they inflicted on their families. They would not make a different decision to "forsake all" and follow Jesus and Father David. But they also evaluate their actions as "immature," "unwise," or "unloving." Over the past decade, many disciples have reconciled with parents and with former spouses who deserted the movement.

However, in those early years, "reconciliation" was not in the COG vocabulary. Their rejection of family ties and their harshly disrespectful attitude toward established religious institutions generated distress, fear, and anger. And in response, FREECOG members and other parents began a crusade against Father David and the movement. Influential parents fomented a media campaign to discredit the Prophet and expose the harsher aspects of colony life. Numerous complaints were filed with local and federal law enforcement agencies, accusing the COG of drug usage, kidnapping, extortion, fraud, and theft. In 1972, the attorney general of the State of New York opened a full-scale investigation.

In general, the disciples followed Father David's lead in the face of these attacks. All opposition was interpreted as the persecution of the Faithful and the work of Satan against God's One True Church. It only reinforced their view of themselves as crusaders for the Truth. And in keeping with the Prophet's general policy, they got out of North America as quickly as possible. But they did not all escape.

Early in the history of the COG's battle with the System, FREECOG and others involved in the anticult movement developed a theory of "brainwashing" to explain how their otherwise normal children could be drawn into such a "cult."[1] Though brainwashing as a recruitment technique has little legal or scientific foundation, the theory was wide-

---

1. Brainwashing theory remains most controversial. For sympathetic treatment, see Delgado 1977 and Singer 1979. For a critique of brainwashing theory applied to alternative religious movements, see Richardson 1993. See also Shupe and Bromley 1980; Zablocki 1997 and Bromley 1998. I find the "brainwashing" theory of recruitment into religious movements flawed and inconsistent with the life experiences of the disciples I have come to know.

ly accepted by families who had lost their sons and daughters to Father David. It not only offered a logical explanation that relieved parents of any responsibility, but also justified extreme measures to "rescue" their children. Soon a small cadre of professional kidnappers and "deprogrammers" began to offer their services to distraught parents. No action could have alienated the Children further from their families or the System. They began to take security measures to protect themselves. It was not paranoia.

We made our way up to the U.S. A young Swedish brother was with us. We were out every day litnessing. We got jumped on the street by these big guys. Two huge guys jumped me, wrestled me to the ground, and held me down. My first instinct was that we were being robbed. But one of them held my face to the ground and kept repeating, "Don't move. His father is in the car." I couldn't see anything. But I heard this long fight, real violent struggle. Finally, they were able to force this Swedish brother into the van. He was about nineteen or twenty, and they just kidnapped him right off the street. I figured it out right away.

They let me go. I was really shook up. We had all his belongings and his passport. When I got home, I called the police. I told them that my Swedish friend, who had a very successful swimming career in Sweden, had just been kidnapped. They were very responsive, and the FBI got involved right away. But, as soon as they found out who we were, and that it was a domestic issue with a "cult," they dropped it. They did nothing.

I guess he got deprogrammed successfully. He went back to Sweden, and we never heard from him again. The kidnappers came to our house asking for his passport and things. We would not give it. We were really afraid, 'cause we knew we could not count on any protection from the police. But he signed a paper dropping all charges, so eventually we gave them his passport and belongings. And that was that. (Jason)

Father David was particularly incensed by the deprogramming efforts of FREECOG and the apparent cooperation of law enforcement agencies and the courts.

*That these fanatical and fascistic religionists also consider them-
selves above the law and the courts and the freedoms of the people
and willing to commit any crime in the name of national, religious or
so-called family security has been proven by the activities of the
black bastard renegade reprobate who leads the FREECOGers in
their blatant criminal activities of criminal assault, violence, kidnapping, abduction, illegal imprisonment and mental, physical and
spiritual torture against the members of any groups with whom they
happen to disagree!*

*Using methods akin to the communists and fascists themselves
and reminding us of the Roman, Turkish and Inquisitorial tortures
used in the past to force both Jews and Christians to deny their
faiths, the free-wheeling FREECOGers have been running rampant in
a rabid reign of terror across America amongst these poor little innocent, weak and defenseless non-conformist religious groups, snatch-
ing away their members by lies, deceit, violent bodily force, and the
hooks and crooks common to the lowest thugs in order to submit
these poor children to tortures and mental anguish not even conceived by the Romans or the Inquisition! Some of them have been literally threatened with death if they did not deny their faith!*

*It is a miracle of the grace and patience of God that some of their
tortured victims have not already erupted in violent retaliation and
self-defense against the ravenous attacks of these evil beasts!—As
God Himself no doubt will some day very soon when their vicious
cup of iniquity is full! ("State of the World," ML #270, Sept. 1973)*

Moses David certainly knew how to turn a phase. And he rarely
stepped back from exaggeration. But in this case, he does not seem to
have been that far off the mark.

*I met the Children of God and got the challenge to forsake all for
Jesus in 1971. I landed in Toronto, living very simply and witnessing
every day. My parents were never happy that I had become a "Jesus
person" to begin with, not the true Church, you know. I kept in touch
with them. But it just got progressively worse. Then they got in touch
with FREECOG. They got literature that played on their fears. Who
knows what was going on in their heads! I guess they were driven to*

*conclude that there was only one way to get me back. This was 1974.
I was age twenty-four by this time. Married with two kids.*

*I had been in contact with them. But to be honest, the way most
of us handled the "forsake all" was not too good. We were young and
immature. I am sure the way I handled things scared them and upset
them. I wish we had been a little softer and kinder back then, more
loving. But, we were very young in the Lord. But, mostly it was the
literature and the anticult people that made my parents act the way
they did.*

*I was out on a market pickup with my two little kids when they
picked me off. Six big guys jumped me and forced me into this big
car. I was fighting and yelling: "Help, I am being kidnapped." But
they were strong and tough, and mean. Took me to this safe house
and held me for over a week.*

One of the guys was this big ex-marine type. You know, strong like
bull and smart like streetcar. *[said in jest] About every fifteen minutes or so he would say something like, "Hey Ted, just give me ten
minutes alone with him, I can beat this COG shit right out of him."
He had this rubber-coated metal pipe he kept hitting in his hand, trying to frighten me I guess.* It worked. *[laughs—he related this whole
story with a remarkable sense of humor]*

*There was Ted Patrick, the marine, a guy named Randy who was
an ex-Hare Krishna, and another guy. They went at me hard from the
very beginning. "You are worse than slime. Your children are going to
grow up to hate you." They would say the most degrading things to
try and make me feel as if I were a terrible person. "Admit you were
never happy in the Children of God." "They wouldn't even let you go
to the bathroom by yourself." (That one was kind of funny, since
these guys really wouldn't let me go to the bathroom by myself.)
[laughs loudly] "You were never happy. Admit it. You were* brainwashed." *They called Dad's mother "Bitch the Witch." Stuff like
that. They just tried to humiliate and degrade me.*

*They pushed me around, but did not physically assault me, other
than when they kidnapped me. When I tried to pray, they would yell
at me: "There he goes in that trance again. Snap out of it." They just
tried to wear me down.*

It was all very bad, but Ted Patrick was the worst. He attacked my faith. He kept yelling at me that I was never saved. That I never knew Jesus. That there was no possible way that I could be in the Children of God and even remotely know Jesus.

The next day, I grabbed a glass globe and hurled it through a window, then began yelling for help. From that moment on, they took me in the basement and tied me to a chair. They were relentless. They would come at me in four-hour shifts. Attacking me, degrading me. It was a real spiritual battle. And by the third or fourth day, I was getting exhausted. They would only let me sleep four hours a night. There were times I felt I was holding on by a thread. Then I would pray and God would give me a boost.

They kept me tied in this hard chair all day. Then they would try to break me a little at a time. Offer to let me lie down for ten minutes if I would make one small concession. Then they would try the "bad cop, good cop" routine. I guess Ted Patrick must have learned all this from how they did the American soldiers in Korea.

It was getting to be a week, and I was really getting wiped out. And they had nailed all the doors and windows shut, so I knew there was no escape. And they never let up, constantly at me with the "evil cult" stuff. After a week, I prayed and it dawned on me, the idea of being wise as serpents and harmless as doves. I realized there would be no reasoning with these people. And they just couldn't hear the truth. So, I deceived them. I faked it. Said I had seen the light. [laughs and raises his arms in mock delight] I began to cry. "Where is my mom and dad?" They untied me and I ran upstairs. I saw Ted Patrick and gave him a big hug. Thanked him over and again. "You saved me, Ted." "I see the light." I really went for it. It was the performance of my life. [laughs] And they bought it, mostly.

I guess I was pretty convincing, 'cause Ted offered me a job. He said if I was really changed, I would want to rescue others. He told me there could be a real career waiting for me. Good money. "We will get you on radio and TV and all kinds of things." "If you really have changed, you must have a real hatred for those evil people who oppressed you and led you astray all those years." I said, "Sounds good, but do I have to decide right now. I am so tired." I dodged that

one pretty good. Said I wanted to hear some Elton John music.
[laughs]

They still kept two big guys with me. Maybe since I wouldn't com-
mit to kidnapping others, they were not absolutely convinced yet. We
slept in the basement. But I awoke early in the morning and sneaked
up the stairs. I knew this would be my only chance. I got my coat
and my shoes, but didn't put them on. I just ran out the door and
down to the highway. In the snow. The second car picked me up, and
I was free.

I made it north, to Thunder Bay. My parents found out I was there
and came again to see me. I was reluctant, but they promised to do
nothing. The whole thing had shaken them as well. It cost them over
ten thousand dollars. **What a waste.** *They must have seen a* lawyer
too.[laughs] They gave me some money and had this statement they
wanted me to sign and get notarized. I just said that all I wanted was
for them to promise from their hearts that they would never do that
again. And they did.

I went to India in 1982 and was gone from Canada until 1994. I
am back in the same town now with my folks. I have forgiven them.
They still don't like Dad or The Family, but that is OK. I visit once a
week now, shovel the driveway or mow the yard. We are fine now.

* * * * *

[Did you take any legal action?]

* * * * *

I filed a police report, back when it happened. But then I dropped
it. So, I didn't take any legal action.

* * * * *

[Thinking back now, do you wish you had?]

* * * * *

Not really. The police never help us. And besides, my parents, real-
ly they were victims too. And besides, it would have taken so much
time away from my witnessing for Jesus. On the other hand, this an-
ticult thing is such a racket. Playing on people's fears with misinfor-
mation. I was angry at the time. But, God knows. "Vengeance is
mine sayeth the Lord." (Jacob)

Jacob's story is widely known in The Family. He is certainly not alone. There are many others who were targeted for deprogramming, but avoided "the hit." These kinds of hostile and aggressive activities not only intensified the COG's already deep sense of opposition to the System, but also placed further strain on already stressed family relationships. Given their deep communal attachments, we should not be surprised that many disciples developed an enhanced sense of wariness and suspicion toward family members on the outside, even if they had no specific reason. However, though the disciples carry hostility against the anticult industry, they now appear to be remarkably forgiving of family or friends who may have orchestrated attacks against them in the past. Their hostility toward the anticult industry appears to be well earned.

My son left for Japan on business. He was gone for some time, then we got a letter from him. He said that he had "found Jesus," (whatever that meant) and had quit his job. He was living in a community of other people who "loved Jesus," and would not be coming back. He had never *been religious before. We really did not know* what *to think. He* seemed *happy in his letters. I kept them all, you can see them if you want. It just didn't make any sense to us. We didn't know what to think or what to do.*

Then my daughter somehow got in touch with some of the anticult people. They came to see us. They brought some of the literature of the group. It was very shocking. *They told us that almost no one joined the Children of God of their own free will, and they doubted very much if our son had either. They told us that most likely he had been either kidnapped or drugged, then brainwashed into believing in the group. We showed them his letters. They said the group forced him to write letters like that to fool his parents. Our son was twenty-five then, not a child. But, we love our son, and we were totally distraught. We believed these people. We were desperate.*

They told us they were professionals and that they could get him back for us. So we hired them to do it. We signed some papers. I do not know how much we paid them. It has been almost ten years now, but my husband still will not tell me. He won't even talk about it.

But, I saw some of the receipts for their expenses. They flew first class to Japan, stayed in a five-star hotel, had room service. We are not wealthy people. We don't travel like that.

Thank goodness, they failed. Somehow, he had found out about it. He wrote us and was really upset at first. Then he invited us to come and visit him in Japan. My daughter was still in contact with these anticult people. They called us and warned us not to go to "his turf." They said he probably would be drugged, and would not be allowed to be alone with us. We still didn't know what to think. But we went.

It was a wonderful visit. He stayed several nights with us at our hotel. He took us on a tour of Japan. He wasn't drugged. He was kinder and more affectionate with us than he had ever been before. Once they were all convinced we were safe, we visited the home where he lived. They all seemed very nice.

It wasn't all pleasant. He tried to explain himself, but we still could not understand what this was all about. (I guess I still don't.) Anyway, when we left Japan, we thought we might never see him again. But he continued to write faithfully, and last year he moved back to our city. I was overjoyed. He has a wonderful Japanese wife and has given me five precious grandchildren. We visit him now once a week, and he stops by when he has a chance. I cannot believe what we almost did to him.

Now, don't get me wrong. I still don't understand what his life is all about. I do not agree with much of what he believes. And that leader of his group is a very strange person. I still cannot say that I approve. But, he is happy. And he still loves me. What more can a mother really ask? (Mrs. K)

Some disciples continue to face the possibility of violent kidnapping and forced deprogramming. In 1993, Noah attended a national meeting of the Cult Awareness Network. He was not allowed to register and proved to be an unwelcome guest. However, while there he met a couple whose daughter was a member of The Family. They reported to Noah that they had been approached by persons offering to kidnap and deprogram their daughter. The price: thirty thousand dollars.

The Family still calls disciples to "forsake all" for Jesus. The extraction of young people out of the System still creates anger and serious opposition. The fear of kidnapping and deprogramming still haunts the Children. But, it can get much worse than that. The disciples report that they consistently experienced harassment, opposition, and repression from law enforcement agencies. In the United States and Canada, the prevailing ethos of religious freedom and civil liberties generally led to passive opposition from the justice system. However, the disciples ventured out into much more dangerous waters. In many parts of the world, they often faced harsh consequences for their call on young people to "forsake all."

We were in Mexico in 1978. FFing had just started then, and I had only FFed one guy. But the Lord blessed it. He had money, and his uncle was a lawyer who really helped us when the persecution hit.

When they hit us, it was well planned. They hit all the homes at five o'clock in the morning. Broke through the doors with guns drawn. It was terrifying, for us and the children. I had a sick baby, and I couldn't take her with me. They gave us one phone call. I was able to reach my friend, who arranged for care of all the kids.

They took us to prison and took our mug shots, which they released to the media. We were thrown into this deep women's prison, like a dungeon. No trial. They did not even tell us the charges for a month. Finally they charged us with prostitution and corruption of public morals. Can you imagine, that kind of raid and arrest and imprisonment for prostitution, in Mexico! If they wanted to arrest prostitutes, all they had to do was walk two blocks from the police station. [laughs]

Our lawyer found out what was really behind it. This young Jewish girl got saved, joined, and left Mexico. Her parents were terribly angry that she forsook all for Jesus. They stirred up the authorities. They wanted us to be in prison for ten years.

After two months in that terrible prison, our lawyer was finally able to convince the judge what was really going on. It was heart wrenching. Finally, they dropped all the charges. They held this secret immigration hearing in the middle of the night, ordered us deported, and put us on a bus right then. Again, we had one phone call.

We were able to reach the friend who had our baby girl. We were just so scared. Not what they would do to us, but for her, and that we would not get to take her with us. Just as the bus pulled away, the friend showed up with our baby. He pulled his car right in front of the bus, and handed us our baby through the window. Looking back on it now, it sounds exciting, like in the movies. But then, it was heart wrenching. We lost everything, money, all our clothes and possessions, our lit, all our pictures, everything. But we had our little girl.

Prison in Mexico was a terrible experience. But we did our jobs with joy, a real witness to the guards. A few prayed to receive Jesus. We sang and witnessed to the other prisoners. God gave us the grace for that. Many prayed to receive Jesus.

And prison strengthened us. It really makes you depend less on yourself and more on the Lord. I learned for sure that God is with me, and that His grace is sufficient. And when the End Time comes and the Antichrist is upon us, it will be a lot worse than what we went through in Mexico. And I know that God's grace will be sufficient for me then, too. It was terrible. But it was good to really walk with God, to depend totally on God. I would not change it now, even if I could. (Angela)

Only a small number of disciples have been the target of deprogramming operations. A good number more, like Angela, suffered harsh consequences for the "forsake all" call to new disciples. Most have some tale of persecution. Generally these incidents of intimidation, harassment, physical assaults, and arrests came in response to the disciples' witnessing strategies. Father David sent his young charges into all the dark and dangerous corners of the world to proclaim their message. He sent. They went. Even into the den of the dragon.

My major persecution came in China. I got hired to teach English in China. We went to Wu Han Technical Institute for three years. Or at least it was supposed to be for three years.

They had no idea who I was. I grew to love the Chinese people. And I witnessed how I could. In my free time I would go out to the city or to villages.

I went slow at the school, very cautious. I let the director know I

was a Christian. No big surprise. Half of the foreign teachers in China
are underground missionaries. But you couldn't trust anyone; anyone
could be a spy.

Toward the end of the second year we had two catacomb [secret]
disciples and over four hundred had prayed to receive Jesus. But we
got busted. The police came to our house at 11:00 P.M. It was me, my
wife, our two kids, and a teen visiting from Japan. Lots of cops and
officials came bursting in, with floodlights and TV cameras. They
were really rough. Searched our house and took everything out: all
our lit, pictures of friends and family, all our tapes and videos. Our
two boys were young, but we had prayed with them often and talked
about this possibility. They were scared, for sure. But they handled it.

At 1:00 A.M. they took me and my wife into custody. We agreed to
answer their "few questions." We told them we were Christians, we
were in The Family, and that we did witness. That was all we would
say. But it didn't stop there. They wanted names of all we had witnessed to. We decided to say nothing. Our response to all their questions was "no answer." They interrogated us for twelve hours a day,
then let us go home at night. We told our kids we could go to prison.
We decided to go to prison rather than give up the names of our
Chinese converts and other Family in China.

The interrogation got very rough. They did not torture me, but it
got very rough. Smashing furniture, smashing his fist on the desk in
front of me. Screaming at me constantly: "The American Embassy
does not want you." (He was right on that one.) "Father David does
not want you. No one wants you. You will go to prison for forty years.
You are at our mercy." It went on for five more days. And I would always respond: "No answer."

I was 75 percent sure my wife and I were going to prison. But finally, they just kicked us out. The two Chinese disciples we had, they
disappeared the day before we got arrested. Just gone. But they knew
Jesus, and I am sure the Lord cared for them.

I am making plans to go back to China now.

*****

[Isn't that a bit dangerous?]

*****

Sure. But I speak Chinese, and they need to hear the gospel. So what if there is some danger? I have been persecuted in the U.S., in Poland, France, and Denmark. There is danger everywhere if you are a Christian, more so if you are Family. And it will get far worse as the End approaches. We don't have a lot of time left. (Samuel)

[Samuel and his family returned to China in 1998.]

Though Samuel's adventure seems quite dramatic and very few disciples made their way into the People's Republic, his story is in no sense unusual. The disciples understand that they are at war with Satan, and that the Devil will do all he can to prevent them from bearing witness. Persecution is their lot. They expect it. They accept it. Most all have heard the "knock at the door" at one time or another. Each member is required to maintain a "flee bag." Flee bags contain the passport and other important documents, a few prized personal items, and enough cash to sustain them for a month on the run. They are prepared to suffer. Some have suffered dearly.

I have faced a lot of persecution. My two most difficult experiences were in India and Egypt. In India, it was my wife. We did a lot of street witnessing and litnessing in India. It all seemed to go well. Then we got rocked. It wasn't the Romans [the police] this time. My wife was getting out lit, and I guess she was near this Hindu temple, or something. Anyway, this Hindu fanatic threw a bomb at her, like a pipe bomb. It exploded right at her feet. When I got to her, I thought she had been killed. She was unconscious, and there was blood everywhere.

She was injured very badly. They did an emergency operation, then we made our way back to Europe and she had several more surgical operations. God has been good, and she has made a full recovery. She has no hate for the Indian people. We know who is behind all the persecution.

I love my wife dearly, and that was probably the worst moment of my life. Much worse really, than when I was imprisoned in Egypt. We were in Cairo, as missionaries, from 1984 to 1985. I loved Egypt. My wife did FFing and follow-up on catacombers. I did a fair amount of witnessing.

We had to be underground in Egypt. Then this MO Letter came out, getting on all of us for not getting out the Word. It said everyone needed to get out at least ten posters a day. The area shepherd in charge of Egypt said, "OK, this is what Dad said, so you will do it." Huge mistake! *(You know, our biggest problem has always been bad leadership. I had leaders who were arrogant, or cruel, or selfish. This guy wasn't like that, he was just* dumb.) *But, we followed orders. We always followed orders. We started getting our posters out, right in the open on the streets of Cairo.*

It didn't take long. One night we were in a club, passing out posters, when eight Romans came and got me. They interrogated me like a criminal, really rough. I had a legal tourist visa, but that didn't help. They threw me in prison, without any charges. The interrogation was hard and relentless. No sleep. Little food. The pressure was immense. I got very weak, very quickly. It was just like in the Book of Acts. I did feel the power of the Holy Spirit. In fact, I witnessed to the interrogators. That is how I responded. Looking back, that probably wasn't the wisest strategy. *[laughs]*

They held me and three other brothers in this old maximum security prison for two weeks. It was really bad. Hard to describe, really. Most of it I have tried to put out of my mind. If you don't mind, I would just as soon not go into those details. We went on a hunger strike until they moved us to a more civilized jail. But we still had to sleep on the floor. When they moved us, they put us with a bunch of American Presbyterians who were also underground Christians. At first those guys were mad. They thought they were in prison because they had been mistaken for us. They were not happy about it. At first they didn't like us much. One guy said: "How bad can this get? Rats, cockroaches, and now the Children of God!" [laughs] But after a while, they saw our sample and our faith in Jesus. They changed. They discovered we were *Christians like them. I think it was some of their parents who helped get us all out.*

We were held in prison for over a month. They treated us very badly.

*****

[In what way?]

*****

I really don't want to go into the details. I began to face the possibility that I might not get out. There were never any official charges that I know of. There was nothing about the FFing. I don't think they knew anything about that. It was just about the witnessing, getting out the Word. Then, one night they moved us to another jail in Cairo. We didn't know what was about to happen. Early in the morning, they put us on a plane to Greece. And that was it.

After this, Maria came out with a Letter saying Muslim countries were dangerous. (I guess that was news to some people.) [laughs] We had to get them the gospel, but we had to be very cautious. I thought: "Now you tell me!" (Amos—a French disciple)

The disciples generally bear a forgiving spirit toward the countries and peoples who persecuted them for their witness. There is nobility in suffering for the cause. They generally do not view such people as intentional agents of Satan. They carry a much less generous spirit toward anticult groups and the news media that have attacked them over their sexual practices. These attacks are understood to be intentional attempts to harm or destroy them, because of who they are. And they are absolutely convinced that a conspiracy exists to smear them with deliberate distortions and lies.

They know that it is lies. I guess that is what really makes me angry.

I was in Denmark in the early 1980s. We got attacked as a "sex cult." In Denmark. Anything was accepted in Denmark back then. Why us? The police raided our home. Of course there were no drugs or guns or anything. So, they had nothing. But, the newspaper people came along on the raid. (It is amazing how many times our homes are hit by the police, and the media is along for the show.) They took pictures of the raid and ran this terrible article about us. Of course they didn't mention that no arrests were made and no laws were broken. They got a lot of information from a European anticult group. They didn't bother to interview any of us. It was a vicious article. This article was picked up by a lot of other newspapers, and the TV got into it. We were getting killed.

We decided to invite one of the TV stations to visit our home, investigate us, and do interviews. They promised to be fair. Right! It was a hatchet job. I remember one example, because I was sitting right there. The reporter asks this sixteen-year-old girl when she first had sex. She said: " At age 12 I had a real good talk about sex with the other girls." Then she went on to talk about kissing at a later age, and so on. She told the guy she had not had full sex yet. When the show aired, you saw him ask the question, then her answer, "At age 12." He edited the tape to make her answer that. He deliberately used it to lie about us. We get that kind of thing all the time. (James)

Through out the 1970s and 1980s, the disciples were battered and harassed by the anticult movement and the media. Almost everyone has some tale of the injustice of anticult or media "persecution." Only on rare occasions did they attempt any kind of counterattack. Mostly, they just kept their flee bags handy. When things got too hot, or when their "enemies" were able to instigate official action against them, they fled to less hostile fields.

Given the frequency and intensity of their corporate persecution experience, the disciples have a remarkable lack of bitterness. It is not quite a "turn the other cheek" mentality. There is surely no love lost with the anticult folks. But their profound sense of special calling and their all encompassing communal support seem to have buoyed their spirits over some very troubled waters. At times their lot has been harsh, even tragic. But they seem to understand it all. Their enemies may be "liars and cheats, irrational people." But the persecution itself is not irrational. It has only confirmed what Father David has taught them about God and the System. And most of all, though Satan has the upper hand now, their day will come.

However, toward the end of the 1980s, the rules of the game dramatically changed. The anticult movement had always been aided and empowered by hostile ex-members of the COG. Some of the most bitter denunciations of the movement came from former members.[2] But the

2. The most damning is a "tell-all" work by Father David's oldest daughter: Deborah Davis, *The Children of God: The Inside Story* (Davis 1984). The most recent is Miriam Williams, *Heaven's Harlots: My Fifteen Years as a Sacred Prostitute in the Children of God Cult* (Williams 1998). Ms. Williams floated in and out of The Family from 1971 to 1986. This is a well-written and reasonably accurate first-person account, though from a decidedly post-Family, feminist perspective.

confluence of two factors raised the stakes considerably. The sexual abuse of children had exploded into the public arena as a critical social problem. In the summer of 1984, prominent members of the American anticult movement manipulated law enforcement and social services agencies in Vermont, fostering a brutal raid on the Northeast Kingdom Community Church.[3] The children and adults were released by the courts the next day. No abuse was found and no charges were filed. But the anticult movement had discovered a new and devastating weapon. As the legitimate concern over the sexual exploitation of children spread through the Western world, alternative religious movements became susceptible to attack. None were more susceptible than The Family.

In roughly the same time frame, scores of older teenagers and young adults began leaving The Family. Some bore the scars of emotional and physical abuse, as well as evidence to very serious sexual exploitation.[4] When the anticult movement rolled out the heavy artillery of the sexual abuse of children, the COG proved to be an exceedingly target rich environment.

There is a bitter irony in what follows. By 1986, The Family had renounced adult sexual contact with minors, eliminated any possible theological justification for such practices, and established strong regulations against this formerly accepted behavior. The Children had repented, and they were confident that God had forgiven them for these "mistakes." By 1989 the sexual abuse of children had, for all practical purposes, ceased. Some have questioned Family motivation in this change. Assessing the full range of motivation on the part of a complex community like The Family is futile. No doubt, the leadership was becoming aware of their high level of vulnerability. And older children were now maturing to the point of speaking out, inducing serious reconsideration of past activities. Whatever the reasons, the change was in place by the end of the decade.

When the first raids motivated by accusations of child sexual abuse began in 1989, the practice had all but disappeared from almost all communities years before. A number of young people and older adult

3. For details of this tragic episode in American religious history, see George Robertson, "Island Pond Raid Begins New Pattern," in Lewis and Melton 1994.

4. We have dealt with this issue previously but will fully explore it in the next chapter.

former members came forward with horrendous accusations. Homes all over the world were raided commando-style. Adults were brutally seized and incarcerated without trial. Hundreds of innocent children were literally ripped from their mothers' arms. And no instance of child abuse was uncovered. The anticult forces screamed "fraud and cover-up," and occasionally tried to manipulate or manufacture evidence for crimes they knew had been committed. Family leadership cried "lies and more lies," proclaiming their innocence and denouncing the persecution as evidence of their faithfulness to God and Satan's evil control of the System. And all over the world, disciples bore the yoke. Especially the mothers.

I know there were things that did happen in the past. I was never personally around the sex with kids. I would not have tolerated any such thing in my home. It did happen in some places. But that in no way justifies what they did to me and my children.

I was living in Belgium, and my husband was in Eastern Europe. The French authorities had been spying on the homes for some time, they had our phones tapped. So, I was coming in with my six kids for a visit, and another sister was leaving in a few days for the States with all her kids. They knew that I could not possibly have been guilty of abusing my children in France, because I didn't even live in France. They intentionally timed the raid so they would capture as many children as possible.

They hit the home early in the morning, came through the door ready to shoot. There had been no actual investigation. They could have come and checked out the accusations. But no! They took us to the police station and questioned us. They took my children and put them in holding cells. They said we could have them back the next day, then changed it to a couple of days. It stretched into two months. All four of my older children were taken from me. I kept the baby and the toddler.

I was charged with child sexual abuse and contributing to the delinquency of a minor. I was charged, without one shred of evidence. And they knew I had only been in France for four days. They investigated us for two months, dragged it out as long as possible. When they knew from the beginning there was nothing. There never was even a trial, because there never was any evidence. They held my children for two months in institutions, all the time telling me I was a child molester and I would never see my babies again.

They put the women under house arrest; we had the babies and toddlers. The men went to jail. They kept my children for two months. But then they wouldn't let us leave. They made our kids do a "socialization project," and the social services people continued to investigate and monitor our activities. They examined the kids and found nothing. There was nothing.

Finally, I was brought before this judge. He asked me all kinds of questions. He was really interested in the FFing. I tried to tell him that had not been done in years, but to no avail. Finally he said, "Your presence is no longer necessary in France to further this investigation." That was it. No apology. No, *"you're not guilty."* Just, *"you are no longer* necessary *here." They gave me back my passport, and I left to rejoin my husband in Switzerland.*[5]

* * * * *

[How were you affected by it all?]

* * * * *

It was very painful, very hard at the time. But, ultimately God worked it for good. Before, I was always fearful. Fearful of persecution, of having my kids taken away. I know it was the Devil behind all this. The anticult people in France did this to us, we know that. But I made it through. God was *faithful.*

It made me stronger, and more committed than ever. Sometimes I actually prayed, "Lord, should I stay in The Family and risk this happening again?" And I would always get this verse from Jesus, "to whom shall you go?" God carried me through. I know that when the End comes, I will have the Lord and The Family. I will be able to stand. (Ruth)

Accusations of child sexual abuse spawned similar raids on Family communities all over the world. They were hit in England, Italy, Spain, other parts of France, Australia, and Latin America. Hundreds of chil-

5. This case was finally resolved in January of 1999. According to a Family press release, Judge Phiippe Assonion of the Tribunal de Grande Instance of Aix-en-Provence closed the file, stating there was no grounds to pursue the case.

dren were subjected to all levels of examination. Scores of adults were
arrested, interrogated, and incarcerated. The fear of harsh persecution
and losing their children swept through The Family. And just when it
appeared that things could not get any worse, American and Canadian
ex-members affiliated with the anticult movement made their way
down to Argentina, carrying their stolen video tapes and documents.

*The American Embassy was really against us. The anticult people
had gotten to them. The anticult movement, the Catholic Church,
and the government were together, working against us. Seeing the
pattern in France and Australia, we started to really get concerned.
We made the decision to evacuate most of the families. So, a lot of
people began doing passport work at the American Embassy. From
what we heard, the Embassy alerted the prosecuting judge that the
raids had to happen soon, or there wasn't going to be anybody left to
raid.*

*I heard pounding at 2:00 A.M. We opened the door, and they came
through with guns drawn: "Put your hands up or we will shoot!"
They actually pointed guns at the children. They were very mean.
They wouldn't tell us what the charges were. One of them actually
told me that they had gotten some training from an anticult group in
Argentina. They were told not to look in our eyes, 'cause we would
hypnotize them. If we were sweet to them, it was part of our "brainwashing" technique. We started praying and singing, 'cause we knew
what was coming. They brought social workers. We knew vehicles
would soon come to take the children. The press was there too, of
course. It was all coordinated. At about 8:00 in the morning we
turned on the TV and started seeing the dance videos that had been
stolen from the Philippines. (We learned that later. We had never seen
those things.) It was very well coordinated, just a few hours after the
raid, and the videos were already on TV.*

*They tore through the house, searching everything and confiscat-
ing a lot of important material. (In the end, the police stole all they
wanted and left the homes unprotected. When we finally got out of
prison, everything was gone. I lost everything I had but the clothes I
took to prison.)*

Then it was time to go. They wouldn't tell us where we were going, not anything. What we were charged with, nothing. At first, we couldn't call our lawyers. They took the children off in another car. I wouldn't see my son again for a long time.

We were being held "incommunicado." We were kind to the officers, and witnessed to them. They began to like us and would slip us notes about what was happening to our brothers and sisters. We were held there for ten days. Never left the cell.

We were held for ten days without charges. Then the judge called us to court and wanted us to declare. Our lawyers advised us the whole proceeding was illegal, and we should say nothing. They held us at court all day, until our lawyers left. We thought we were going to be released. At about 6:00 P.M., they brought us in again and came down with theses horrendous charges. They said our children had been examined, and they found that the children had been raped, sodomized, all these horrific *charges. (It was a lie. The people who examined our kids found no evidence of any abuse. That is in the court records. It is* one reason *why this judge is in so much trouble in Argentina today.) We were absolutely* furious. *We refused to sign the charges. They then told us we were such dangerous people, we would be "preventively detained." We were going to be held in prison before any trial.*

This was a very heavy *moment for me. The prosecuting judge was outside giving a press conference, telling all these horror stories of sodomized children, abuse, "evidence" found. And then the prison guards came to get us. They were very rough.* They thought we were child molesters. *They brought us out to the prison van, one by one, through this horde of press asking these* horrible *questions. It was* awful.

(The Argentine people are not like this. There were many people there who cared about us, and cared about this abuse of liberty in their country.)

They took us to prison, and it was very bleak. *They read off the charges to me.* Unbelievable. *One of our detractors, an ex-member, accused me of sexually initiating all the minor boys that came through our home. I was just shocked. He had never lived in our house. I had never, even as a minor myself in the world, ever had contact with a minor. It was just total, blatant lies. I thought, "Well Lord, these kind of lies cannot stand, not by God's Word."*

They brought us to the women's side of the prison. It was brutal. There were like thirty guards with machine guns. You could see the hate in their eyes. (The effects of the media.) When the doctor came in to examine us, the guard said, "Watch out. These are very dangerous people." The doctor was very nasty. "Take off all your clothes." We obeyed, and he just left us standing there, totally naked in front of all these male guards, while he went off and chatted for a while. It was very degrading.

The next day we were sent to the main women's prison and put in an isolation cell with five other prisoners. The word was out that we were "child abusers," and it was not safe to put us with the general prison population. When the other prisoners would see us, they would scream at us and threaten to kill us. And that is where we stayed for the rest of the time, for three and a half months.

The children were in institutions, and we were not allowed to see them for a month, which was also illegal. We had our visitation rights taken away, and they wouldn't even let us have Bibles.

Then, after about a month, the appeals judge came to see us. That was the turning point. He was accompanied by one of the prison supervisors. I told him we couldn't see our kids, had no visitation rights, nothing. He didn't believe it. He turned to the prison supervisor and said, "Could this possibly be?" The guy says, "Yes, sir. We received an order from the prosecuting judge." He went to see our kids. (You know what our kids are like.) He could see our kids loved us and had not been abused. Before that, the prosecuting judge refused to allow our defense to present any evidence or any expert testimony. The appeals court judge found that out and reversed it. When that happened, the prosecuting judge's "expert" witnesses knew they might be in trouble, so they backed off completely what they had said before, saying what they meant was their examinations were "inconclusive." Eventually, the appeals court ruled in our favor. All charges were dropped.

It was a terrible ordeal. For the children, it was even worse. But

the Argentine people did not do this to us. It was the anticult people.
They flew our detractors down to Argentina, paid their expenses,
used stolen and false evidence. They got to the American Embassy.
One of the ex-members who went down to testify, I know her. I
helped raise her.[6] *When she finally realized what terrible things we*
suffered, what she had done to our kids, she repented. Of course, we
love her and have forgiven her. But they [the anticult forces] are still
out there. They hate us and will do anything to destroy us. (Claire)

* * * * *

[I interviewed Claire one week after her release from prison and
about one year later. At the first interview, she was still experiencing
the shock of the events. Her physical well-being had obviously been
affected. She was quite emotional and showed signs of real anger. By
the next interview, she had processed the events through her faith
grid and had arrived at a very forgiving place. Most of the above ma-
terial was taken from the second interview.]

To date, there has been no credible evidence of current child abuse,
and no Family member has been convicted. But now that the children
are the target, the disciples have heeded Father David's orders to "stand
and fight." The Family has attempted to counter these attacks in the
courts, and in the court of public opinion. They have opened their communities to legitimate scholarly inquiry. They have invited social services agencies into their homes to investigate them, in hopes of avoiding
a police raid. The Family does not allow firearms and is committed to
nonviolence. Yet, the specter of the Waco raid on the Branch Davidians
is ever before them. And Family leadership has gone on the counterat-

6. This woman is Abigail Berry. She has not reconciled to The Family but is no
longer active in efforts against the community. Bithia Sherman is another person who
had been active in anti-Family efforts. She has not rejoined, but has come to a reconciliation. She wrote a moving letter of apology to the children taken in the Argentine
raids: "To the Children I Hurt: You Led Me Back to the Arms of Jesus!"
    "You see, I was there too—watching. It was I who wounded you. I believed the
battle I waged against you was a righteous one. I had hoped to rescue you from a life of
presumed harm and abuse. For those of you who were captured in battle, I watched in
horror as you were ripped away from your loved ones and placed in dangerous faith-
destroying environments. It was not long before I saw that I had become the abuser that
I wanted to rescue you from. Then you did something that was truly astonishing. You
forgave me! Not only did you forgive me, but you also loved me! And you have kept on
loving me!"

tack against the anticult industry. In October of 1993, they published
the first issue of *PEN-Persecution End Time News*. It is published by
"The Family—An International Christian Missionary Church," and is
intended for wide public distribution. The headline article leaves no
doubt who the enemy is.

WHO WAS BEHIND THE TERROR!

*Why did the authorities act against our peaceful Christian com-
munities in such a brutal manner? [referring directly to the French
raids] Why were our members forced to undergo the anguish and almost indescribable heartbreak of having their small children taken
away to they knew not where? Why did the authorities feel justified
to perpetrate such raids against our homes and abductions of our
children?*

*They had been grossly misinformed by a so-called anticult group
known as ADFI (the Association for the Defense of the Family and
the Individual). ADFI was directly responsible for inciting the authorities to act against our communities.*

*ADFI is part of an international network of similar groups bent on
persecuting a wide range of churches and religious groups. Its coun-
terparts in other countries include CAN (Cult Awareness Network) in
the U.S., FAIR (Family Action Information Rescue) and Cult
Information Centre in the U.K., and Projuventud in Spain. Together,
these so-called anticult organizations form what sociologists have
termed the Anticult Movement (ACM), which is publicly committed
to the total dissolution and destruction of a large number of religious
movements, including ourselves. (PEN, No. 1, Oct. 1993)[7]*

It is difficult to know how successful Family countermeasures will
be. What is certain is that current attempts to attack The Family
through the children have traumatized the entire community. The disciples are more certain than ever of satanic control of the world and of
the imminent arrival of the End Time. It is also certain that they have
suffered.

7. The subtitle of the first volume reflects the Family commitment to nonviolent response and the theological interpretation of their current woes: "The Pen is Mightier
than the Sword." "All that will live Godly in Christ Jesus shall suffer persecutions" (2
Tm 3: 12).

The videos of the women dancing topless, the ones stolen from our archives in the P. I. and then taken down to Argentina. Some were released to the news media and shown on TV all over the world. Did you see it on American TV?

*****

[Yes, I did.]

*****

I was on one of them. The young girl dancing is my daughter.

*****

[I see.]

*****

Yes. You did see. And so did a lot of other people. Those videos were done a long time ago. We turned our back on that, quit it and erased all the tapes. At least we were supposed to erase them all. But that *is not the point.*

*****

[No?]

*****

You know our teaching on "One Wife." That we are all one family.

*****

[Yes.]

*****

Those videos were private, family *things, my extended family, I mean. They were done* as a family, *and meant* only *for my family. They were our private, personal things. What would you think if someone broke into your house, took some of your most private family things, family secrets even, and gave them out to whoever. Then, had the news media broadcast them all over the world.*

*****

[pause, waiting for an answer]

*****

Right!

*****

And not once *did any of those media people, or the authorities, or the anticult people, or anybody, question the appropriateness, the* rightness *of doing such a thing to me and my daughter. See, James, when you are in a "cult," they think they have a right to do anything to you they want,* anything. *And somehow, you are not really a person. Somehow you won't* feel *it like other* people *do.*

*****

[I'm sorry. I honestly never thought of that.]

*****

Why should you? I am not a human being. I am a "cultist."

*****

I love my children, just like any other mother. *You know we don't have many things, right? Well, I do have something very* special *to me. I have this big scrapbook that I have kept of all my children, all twelve. I would love to show it to you. It is the most precious thing I have in this world.*

*****

[Her eyes grew moist, but she continued to speak with intense resolve.]

*****

I have had to go through my book and destroy *any picture that might in* any *way be used against me. Many of the baby pictures were without clothes, like a lot of baby pictures in the world. I destroyed them all, and other things too.* I *had to.* 'Cause if we get raided, then I knew they could be used to make false claims about me, to take away my kids. I have almost no pictures of my babies.*

*****

[long, emotional pause]

*****

God knows. And I am ready, even for that, if the Lord requires it. When The End comes and the Antichrist takes control, it will be terrible for us, and for many other Christians as well. What could be more terrible? I don't know. But, God knows.

It is a good question. What could be more terrible?

The disciples have endured great pain and suffering over the attacks on the children. Any parent would suffer. But, these are not just any children. They are also Father David's grandchildren. And the future of The Family now rides with them. They are now the life of the movement. And what a life it has been so far.

7. Children of the Revolution

I t is difficult to define success for an alternative religious movement that resides well outside the mainstream culture. The Family's radical opposition to the "System," the powerful ideology of the End Time, and the extraordinary sexual ethos virtually preclude any possibility for broad-based acceptance as a "legitimate" religious enterprise. In general, the disciples suffer no illusions here. They are sometimes confused and often distressed that other Christians consider them completely outside the fold. Father David having constantly denounced "goddamned hypocritical churchianity," their desire for toleration and even acceptance may seem disingenuous. And though The Family has moderated recently in their hostility to the wider church, disciples still demonstrate no desire to "fellowship" with anyone who does not accept the prophetic role of Father David or his message as God's Word for the Last Days. Their general self-understanding remains that of an elite corps of highly disciplined and fully committed spiritual warriors who will lead the larger body of Christians through the terror of the Last Days and on into the Millennium.

In the early years, numerical expansion through the recruitment of new disciples was a well-articulated goal and a significant component of individual and corporate success. However, a shift occurred before the close of the first decade. The number of souls saved and the maintenance of internal discipline remained the top priorities and most important measurements of achievement. New disciples did continue to join from the outside, but the pace of recruitment slowed measurably. The emphasis moved to the second generation. Raising the children properly, training them, incorporating them into the life and ministry of the community, and retaining them as "full-time missionaries" became primary goals, and thus singular marks of God's blessing. These grand expectations had a powerful influence on Father David's grandchildren.

Toward the mid 1980s, the children started to come of age. As might be expected in an intense religious community, many young people left the movement.[1] A fair number were expelled, but many more left of their own choosing. Some departed with their entire families, whereas others made individual decisions to join the System, leaving parents and siblings behind. Those who remained faithful have taken up Father David's mantle with enthusiasm, dedication, and personal sacrifice reminiscent of the early years of the COG. They are on the cutting edge of almost all new missionary ventures. As significantly, they have been entrusted and empowered with leadership roles and responsibilities that place them at the center of life in The Family. They now seem poised and prepared to carry the movement forward until The End. But the journey that brought them to this point is an extraordinary one.

My task from the beginning has been to construct an image of The Family through an exploration of their own life experiences and self-understanding. In one sense, I could tell the story anew, through the eyes of the children. But for the sake of space and focus, I will concentrate on dimensions of life that most relate to the second generation, and on those aspects of their lives that the youth themselves deem most significant.

The Family expended enormous effort to ensure that the second generation would conform to its peculiar religious orientation and ideological commitments. Those young people unwilling or unable to do so had little choice but to leave. The four most distinctive components of Family ideology are the ongoing interaction with the Spirit World, the place of Father David in God's grand economy, End Time expectations, and the sexual ethos. In general, the youth who remain faithful have been fully socialized into the norms of the community.

There appears little or no doubt about the fast approaching of The End or The Family's role in God's plan for the climax of human history.

1. I have not been able to obtain hard statistical data on the numbers or the percentage of the second generation who have left the movement. The Family takes great pride in the children and claims that, unlike other NRMs, most have remained. My own observations and conversations with the young people lead me to believe that a large number of the oldest children have departed. The older children would be in the twenty-three to twenty-seven-years age range as of 1997, and I encountered very few disciples of that age. I spoke with a good number of adult disciples who have lost older children to the System. There have been losses of young people born after 1975, but the retention rate here seems to be much higher, with a good number having left and then returned.

*I really don't know how the Lord is going to work out everything
in the End Time. Most of the cities will be controlled by the
Antichrist, so we will be in the wilderness. But the Lord will provide.*

* * * * *

[What do you see for yourself?]

* * * * *

*I think a big part of our witness in the End Time will be dying for
our faith, like in Roman times. If I have to die in the End Time, I
want to die smiling for Jesus. I hope I will be able to witness for Jesus
to the end. Being killed for my faith is not what I want. But, I think
many will be witnesses that way.*

* * * * *

[What will be your role in the Millennium?]

* * * * *

*I think the Millennium will be fun. Grandpa said it will be us who
will do the training of other Christians. The way we live now pre-
pares us to lead the tons of Christians who will reject the Beast.
Grandpa says all will be destroyed and God will build a new earth.
We are the ones to get it ready for people to live in. Grandpa said all
our hardship and training now will be used at that time. It is really
exciting. (Cindy, age twenty-one)*

End Time expectations are fairly uniform among younger members.
But as with the adults, there is a significant range in both their experience with and understanding of the Spirit World and Father David.
With regard to the Spirit World, a few border on the skeptical, with
considerable reservations about the spiritual causation of any and all of
life's difficulties. Jack is seventeen years old. He was born of American
parents, but raised in the Orient.

[What are the most vivid memories of your childhood?]

* * * * *

*I guess one of the things I remember most about my early child-
hood was getting sick. We got chicken pox, measles, mumps, whoop-
ing cough. I think we got almost everything.[2] I remember we did a*

2. According to Noah, Father David's sister had a bad experience with an inoculation
for polio. As a result, he was opposed to the whole concept. To this day, Family children
are not inoculated against childhood diseases, and infection is common.

skit once, how all these diseases were given to us by the Devil. You know, because we were his main enemy. [laughs]

*****

[You find that amusing?]

*****

You don't? *[We both laugh.]*

*****

[What do you think about that now? Were those diseases caused by the Devil?]

*****

How should I know? Maybe it was the Devil, maybe the Lord. My guess is they just came. Everybody gets sick. Most of the others think those things happened for some big deal, spiritual reason. Not me.

*****

[That surprises me a little.]

*****

Listen, man. A lot of the stuff we were taught about the Spirit World back then was just plain weird.

*****

[Can you give me an example?]

*****

Sure. Like, we always got around on the bus, right. We always took public transportation, 'cause we didn't have any money for cars. So, as kids we were taught that cars were the curse of the Devil. [laughs] Now, how dumb is that?

And it wasn't just that. Every time something went wrong, or we got into trouble, it was the Devil in us. Now, I know the Devil is real. But come on, we were just being kids.

Though many of the youth expressed resentment about the attribution of their childhood misbehavior to the Devil's work, Jack seemed far more skeptical than most. Or, at least he was more open about his skepticism. Like their parents, the majority of the young people appear to have a profound sense of living in the immediate context of the Spirit World. The tragic auto accident in Austin, Texas, seems to have triggered a more serious attitude about these matters in many of the teens.

Austin really sobered me. I knew many of the kids in that accident. One of the girls killed was a good friend. Sometimes I feel her presence.

* * * * *

[How does that happen?]

* * * * *

I am not sure. I have always been very sensitive to the Spirit World and to spiritual presence. Recently I was having a hard time, and I just felt my friend's presence there with me, to comfort me. It was neat.

Since Grandpa went to heaven, The Family has had a lot more communication with the Spirit World. But I have always been like that. When I was younger, I had a lot of connection to the wrong side.

As a kid, I didn't have a good standard. I think that left the door open for different spirits to enter my life. As a very young teenager I had two very bad experiences. It was the same each time. A strange light would appear, and out of it would come this very strange man, like a spirit. I was pushed down on my bed by this weird spirit. I was totally awake, but not able to scream for help. He didn't assault me or hurt me. He would just push me down, let go, then push me down again. It was awful.

* * * * *

[Are you talking about a dream?]

* * * * *

No, it really happened. I definitely believe in spirits. I know they are real. Recently, I have begun to feel good spiritual presence, like the thing with my dead friend. Before, I had a lot of fear in my life. And, I was not close to God. I really think the bad spirits came into my life to get me closer to Him. (Abby, age sixteen)

Spirit World communication is endemic to life in The Family, and the overwhelming majority of the youth have adopted this general pattern of interface. The prophetic role of Father David is the bedrock of communal identity and the central ideological commitment. The COG spared no effort in attempting to inculcate into the second generation a deep reverence for and loyalty to the Prophet. Most have sung songs about being one of "Father David's Children" from the time they could talk. Virtually every teen and young adult read constantly from the "Life With Grandpa," a series of childrens pamphlets published for internal use. They were fed a steady diet of MO Letters and other Family literature, along with videos and skits that extolled The Prophet as the very model of a true Christian. A good number were subjected to intensive, "boot camp" style training and indoctrination events. But all this sustained effort did not produce a uniform understanding of The Prophet.

All of the over one hundred teens and young adults interviewed for this study were asked about their impressions and understanding of Father David. Only a very few spoke about his prophetic role and office. Though all of the young people refer to him as "Grandpa," there is a wide range of views about Father David. Given the intensity, consistency, and often deadly seriousness of the indoctrination efforts, some seem quite casual.

[Do you have a lot of memories about Father David?]

* * * * *

Of course. Who doesn't? We sure heard about him enough. The MO Letters were read all the time, and there was lots of lit from him and about him. I read the "Life With Grandpa" series all the time. And the adults talked a lot about him. There is no kid raised in The Family that did not hear about Father David a lot. I mean, all *the time.*

* * * * *

[What did you make of it all?]

* * * * *

I thought he was a big lion.[3] *(laughs)*

* * * * *

To tell you the truth, as a kid, I didn't pay a lot of attention to it all. I just wasn't that interested. As a JETT, I got a little more into the Letters. They were interesting, at least some of them were. I liked the stuff about world events and the End Time, different stories he told. I began to like him more at about twelve or thirteen.

* * * * *

3. For security reasons, Father David's face was always overlaid by a lion's head in all literature.

[Who was Father David? What did you think he was about?]

*****

I am not sure. I mean, to me, he was like my grandpa.

*****

[What did that mean to you, as a child?]

*****

Not a lot. It was not like he was actually there.

*****

[What about now? What is his role now?]

*****

What do you mean? He's dead.

*****

[What about his role from the Spirit World?]

*****

Oh that, sure. He is in heaven. He watches over us and helps out Maria. And I guess he still speaks through his Letters. Is that what you mean?

To tell you the truth, Father David did not have such a big impact on my life. I never saw him or met him. He was just there, sort of. It did not really affect me emotionally when he died, not like a lot of others. (Jordan, age sixteen)

"Grandpa" is the term used by the youth to refer to Father David, but it carries a variety of meanings. Unlike Jordan, most Family youth have warm and positive memories of "Grandpa." Jordan is an exception that proves the rule. Luke, age eighteen, was born to American parents who each attained high leadership roles. Luke spent most of his life in Europe and Asia. His outlook more generally conforms to the majority view.

I have a lot of early memories of Father David. I think I learned to read with the "Life With Grandpa" stuff. I mean, he was always there.

I have always really loved and respected Grandpa. When I was younger, he was like this person that really cared about all of us, watched over us, kind of. As I got older, his role in my life has been more like a father, or like a teacher. A lot of what I know is from reading what he says. He will correct when needed, but it's very lov-

ing. I guess I really want to be like him. The more I can be like Father David, the better.

A few of the youth expressed not only sincere respect and admiration for The Prophet, but also a deep emotional attachment and a very high view of his role in the Spirit World. As with the adults, this sense of intense personal relationship was most evident among female disciples.

I grew up really loving Grandpa. And now that he has gone to the Spirit World, I sometimes feel his presence. He gives me a certain security. I know I am not alone. I wake up in the middle of the night and get verses from the Lord. I think Grandpa being in the Spirit World has something to do with that.

*****

[Does he give you a sense of comfort or support?]

*****

Yes. I know I am not perfect, that I have sinned. But, Grandpa is there to comfort me and to encourage me. I know that he loves me, and I can feel his love. He is very forgiving. Now that he is gone, I can look at his picture.[4] And when I do, I know that I am in love with him. He is my hero. He is everything *you could ask for in a man. He is so sweet, compassionate, understanding . . . [she drifts off into thought for a moment] I* really *miss him.*

But, he is not like really gone. *I talk to him now. He is like a mediator between Jesus and me. I feel that since he was so human, he understands me. So, I talk to Grandpa and ask for his help. I actually feel that I know him* better *now that he has gone to the Spirit World.*

*****

[Can Father David hear and see and speak with many different people all over the world at the same time?]

*****

You know, I have actually thought about that a lot. I am not sure if it is him, or his presence. Then, I am not sure what the difference

---

4. As earlier stated, before Father David's death his face was always overlaid by a drawing of a lion's head. Before October of 1994, virtually none of the young people knew what he looked like.

is. It is pretty confusing, isn't it? Certainly Jesus can be a thousand places at once. I mean, we know that. I think Father David can comfort many people at once, but I am not sure he can actually be many places at once. I really don't know how it all works. Do you? (Janice, age seventeen)

The young people who have remained loyal have adopted the broad religious and ideological commitments that mark out the community. And as with the adults, there is a substantial range in the meaning and depth of those commitments. If anything, the range is broader among the second generation. In the current climate, there does not appear to be any sustained effort to normalize these various interpretations of Family doctrine. Freedom of thought and expression is an extremely important value to the youth. Most of the teens and YAs were asked to reflect on what made their life distinctive. That proved to be a delicate issue. They know full well that their lives are far from the norm of "System kids." But, they repeatedly encouraged, and occasionally admonished, me not to view all "Family kids" alike. "I think that is the most misunderstood thing by outsiders. Sometimes it really bothers me. We all were not *stamped out* by some *machine*. We are all very different people. We are not all the same. Maybe, at one point, the adults tried to make us all the same. But it *didn't work*" (Anna, age nineteen).

Anna is right. But, Family youth are bound together. They are bound not only by a shared belief system, but also by a shared life experience that is truly distinctive. Growing up in The Family can be described only as a remarkable and often perilous adventure. Most seem to understand and to have come to terms with the peril. And most take great satisfaction in the adventure.

There is no typical second-generation disciple. The best way to understand their lives is to hear their stories. There are joyful stories and sorrowful ones. Mercy is a seventeen-year-old young woman. She is attractive, talented, articulate, poised beyond her years, energetic, deeply spiritual, and filled with the joy of life. If The Family wanted a "poster child," she would be the one.

I grew up in India, was there from age four to age ten. We moved around India, but we were in Bombay a lot. I really liked it. I did a lot of singing and shows as a little kid. I loved it. Most of the people really loved us, especially the kids. I feel like I grew up singing for Jesus in front of tons of people. Neat, huh!

Anyway, after India, we moved to Japan for two years. I don't mean to sound prideful, but I was a pretty good dancer and singer, at least for age eleven. So, I helped make some of the different kids' videos that The Family did in Japan. I did acting and dancing and singing. It was like being a movie star, sort of. But, my parents were great. They helped me keep from getting a prideful spirit. It is not like I was some kind of perfect kid or anything.

I have four brothers and sisters. Actually, my birth mom left us back in India and went to be a secretary at a World Services unit. I have a step-mom, and the three youngest ones are from her. My dad got together with her not long after my birth mom left. I was about nine. One day they sat us down and said: "You know mommy and daddy love each other and really love all of you. But, we don't want to be together anymore, and mommy is really needed somewhere for her secretarial work. That place can't have kids, so you are staying with daddy." It was done with a lot of love and understanding. I don't remember it being very, very hard on me. I've kept up good contact with her. But, I haven't seen her in years. But, that's OK.

My new mom was young, about ten years older than me. We had known her before. She was actually like my best friend, and we had lots of fun together. I guess the Lord made it easy for me to get another mom. I know that not every Family kid has had such an easy time when parents split up. But, my new mom has been great.

Anyway, from Japan we went to Mexico for about a year and a half. I was in a big combo home with a lot of JETTs. Mexico was a great place to witness. I really liked the Mexican people. I didn't have any problem there. But Letters came out about going back to North America. So we went to Canada when I was fourteen. I was mostly with a teen group in Toronto. We did shows at detention centers and at young people's centers. It was super neat. I had really great friends there. Then, we went to Chicago.

I liked it in Chicago. It was big with lots of kids in the home and lots to do. We did restaurant singing. (I speak Hindi and Spanish.) I also worked with kids, teaching and caring for the little ones, which

*I love. I got a lot of good training there. I was very happy. But then I
got a chance to go to the D.C. home and join the show troupe. The
shepherds invited me. They said, "Think and pray about it for a little
while." I was like, "Hey, I can give you an answer right now. I'll go!"
I have been here since then, in the show troupe. We do shows, sing,
and witness at a lot of different places. And we are making a tape of
our music. There are not a lot of little kids here, so I help on kitchen
and laundry, and I do a lot of personal witnessing. This is a great
home. I get along with the people here really well. I love it here.*

* * * * *

[Thinking back, what has been the hardest thing about your life?]

* * * * *

*That's easy. Leaving people. You go to a home, make good friends,
then you have to leave, or they have to leave. I think the longest I
have been in one house was two years, and that was when I was real
young. But, there are always new friends to make in your new place.
So it isn't all that bad.*

* * * * *

[What is the best thing?]

* * * * *

*There are so many. You are constantly with people your age. You
always have a lot of friends. Real friends. And, at least for me, there
have always been a lot of love and understanding with the adults. (I
know that is not true for everybody.) But the best thing is that I have
a reason to live. We have a vision, or a goal, to reach people with the
Lord's love. I can't see just living for nothing, going to school or to
work every day, just living for myself. I live for Jesus. What could be
better than that? I could say a lot more, but that's it in a nutshell.*

Mercy has many positive memories of her childhood and teenage
years, and feels genuinely blessed to have been raised in The Family.
Life has rarely been easy for these young people, and never dull. Many
of the teens have developed positive interpretations of certain life experiences that others could easily see as hardship.

*We were in a big home in India, with a lot of national disciples. I
think I was eight, and the Heaven's Girl Series was coming out then.*

My name was Maria at that time. Anyway, Heaven's Girl was also named Maria. All the girls wanted to change their names to Maria. We all fantasized about being Heaven's Girl.

One night the police came. My mom hid and was destroying all the Selah lit and reports. They arrested the American adult disciples and told the rest of us to wait at the home, and they would be back to take us to jail. When the police left, mom came out of hiding and grabbed us kids and a young national disciple. We split. It was a miracle we got out. By that time, I was sure I was Heaven's Girl. [laughs]

We hid out for days, just like in the movies. Eventually, we made it to the train station. It was a super exciting adventure. We hid behind a door, then dashed out to get on the train, just as it pulled away. I am not sure why that persecution came. FFing, I would guess. It was pretty hard on the adults. But for us kids, it was just so much fun, really exciting. I was sure it was the End Time, and I was Heaven's Girl. (Glory, age nineteen)

Whereas Glory has romantic memories of some of the more stressful times in her life, that is not true for everyone. Two consistent themes emerged from the stories of these young people, instability of place and insecurity in family relationships. Most, like Glory, have been able to see parts of their past as a great adventure. A few have a much less positive memory of all the dislocation. Page is nineteen, born into The Family of American parents.

I lived in the U.S. till I was about six. My folks lived in a mobile trailer. Usually they hooked up with some home, but lived outside in the trailer. Then we went to Mexico. We moved around a lot. We would come back to the U.S. every six months for a visa trip and to see our supporters.

Then we drove down to Guatemala with this van and trailer and lived on the road. My dad was sick all the time. And we always got robbed. And the guerrillas or the regular army were always around. We would get stopped and searched a lot. I found it very scary. I never felt very safe as a little kid. I didn't really understand it all. But it seemed like we were always in some kind of trouble. I think I grew up thinking something bad was always going to happen to me.

Then, we went back to Mexico, and my older sister left for a while to join Bob and Sue. I guess my parents were struggling. But, we all got back together, and we finally went back to the States. It was terrible. The homes in the U.S. back then were not good. There was a real double standard. The shepherds were very harsh. And there were questions about money. It was like before the RNR, I guess. There was a lot of foul language and drinking. I hated it. I was desperate to get out. Bob and Sue agreed to take me and my older sister and keep us. So, we went back to Mexico to live with them. I was age eleven, and so happy to be getting back to Mexico, even though it meant leaving my parents and younger brothers and sisters.

I didn't see my parents again till I was sixteen. I was basically adopted by Bob and Sue, though not legally of course. I guess I missed my parents. But as the years passed, they faded. Basically, my folks got kicked out. Back then, it was policy not to have any personal contact with TSers. It was also policy that kids under fourteen had to go with TSed parents. But I really didn't want to leave The Family. Thankfully, my parents agreed that Bob and Sue would be my new parents, which they are. It was hard, not being able to see them for years. But I could write. Finally, at age sixteen, I went to the U.S. to visit them. I hardly knew them or the younger kids. But, Bob and Sue have been great to me, and it has all turned out all right, I guess.

Dislocation from parents remained a very common feature of Family life. Until the reforms of the charter in the mid-1990s, virtually every second-generation disciple spent considerable time apart from parents before the age of sixteen. The breakup of many marriages and numerous short-term relationships, the strong communal ideology of "One Wife," and the consistent emphasis on ministry responsibilities often left many young people adrift. However, even for those who were raised in a relatively stable family unit, adolescent development was often problematic. In the late 1980s, The Family began to experience serious problems with some of the youth. There appears to have been considerable regional differences, with the Orient having the least difficulty. Europe was the real trouble spot.

I was in Denmark from 1989 to early '94, age eleven to fifteen. My folks were area shepherds, gone all the time. I got some adult guidance from a couple that was sort of like foster parents, but mostly I

was just with other teens. I sort of drifted there. Then we went to
Switzerland, then to Italy, and my troubles really started.

I was already becoming very independent, and there was very little teen control in Switzerland. We would go off on our own to discos,
do drinking, listen to System music. There was fighting and a lot of
disrespect for the adults. And almost no witnessing.

In Italy it was even worse. There was pretty wild sex, and a lot of
birth control. General disrespect, rejection of the MO Letters, just not
much discipline at all. I was really into my own independence. I decided Father David was just another guy. I mean, how can you know
he is some kind of Prophet? I doubted the MO Letters. I wouldn't
work, wouldn't listen to or respect the adults. I got into drinking,
even into drugs. I would sleep during devotions. I stopped reading the
Word. I had constant trouble with the adults. They just gave up on
me. Then, the "Back on Track" Letters came out. The message was
simple: get the victory or get out. This was from Maria, but she
meant nothing to me. I wanted them to kick me out.

When my parents left for the U.S. I was not allowed to go, until I
changed. No way. Finally, I got my excommunication notice: "You
are out!" [points his finger in mock anger, then smiles] I wanted to
leave. But that night, I finally began to really think it through. I am
an Aquarian, very analytical. I started to realize that I would be giving up a lot, to get things I really did not want. So, I got desperate
with the Lord. Then I got mad at the Devil, 'cause I had given in to
him. I promised Jesus I was going to change. The next day, I threw
out all my System music and computer games. They were going to
ship me back to the States, to my uncle who is in the System. I just
decided to change. I got up, cooked breakfast and did the dishes. I
was friendly and polite. It shocked everyone in the home.

It wasn't easy. I rejoined my parents in December of 1995. It took
a whole year to clean up my act. I began to read the Word every day,
to pray, listen to Family music. At times I didn't think I would make
it. I had a lot of trials. I really didn't deserve to still be in The Family.
But my parents were always there for me, encouraging and not judgmental. I knew they loved me. And, eventually I got the victory. I
think I have made it through the hard times. I will stay. (Trace)

It is difficult to assess how widespread were the "trials" reflected in
Trace's life. The initial interviews for this study were with young people living in homes more geared to public relations. They had some experience in encountering inquiring outsiders. These young disciples
were generally very upbeat, and they reflected little of the struggles and
trauma of young people trying to come of age in The Family. As my experience deepened and my access to the teens broadened, some of the
more troublesome dimensions of Family life began to surface. It was often enthralling to discover how these young people had traversed some
very rocky terrain on their way to maturity and stability within The
Family. Other stories were simply heartbreaking. Casa is nineteen. She
was born in North Africa, but is of European descent.

*I really had a happy childhood. At age six, I was performing in
schools and all kinds of places. I have loved singing and dancing all
my life. I always loved my dad. He is a great musician.*

*We were in Nepal from my age six to nine. I did a lot of performing
and street witnessing. My dad had a contract to sing on the weekends
at a hotel. And my mom FFed. From there we went back to India for
a short time, then on to Pakistan for almost three years. I loved
Pakistan. We did a lot of road trips, singing and dancing. We went to
embassies, restaurants, prisons. But, our visas ran out, and my dad
got invited to work in a Family music studio in France. I guess that is
when things started to go not so good.*

*I was only twelve, but I got sent to a teen home. 'Cause the leader-
ship didn't allow kids at the home where my folks went. I was there
a year and a half. It was OK, I guess.*

* * * * *

[Really?]

* * * * *

*Actually, it wasn't. It was hard being away from my dad. There
was a mild Victor Program, some silence restrictions for bad behavior. But not me. I tried very hard to stay out of trouble. I stayed focused on my spiritual life. I memorized the Book of James. I studied a
lot from most of the New Testament and the Letters.*

*Then I was asked to go with the area shepherds to take care of
their kids. I was with that family for almost two years. I did weekend*

singing, shows in pubs, and concerts. Mostly I did child care.

Then, I got sent to Belgium, I thought I was to help with the trans-lation and typing of our lit into French. But, they put me on kids duty again. I had a hard time opening up and telling them I wanted some-thing else. That would be murmuring. And that could get you in a lot of trouble. I was very disappointed. And I was lonely. Then, it got even worse. A shepherd came and told me my folks were splitting up. It was a real shock. I blamed my mom, 'cause it was her decision. My mom started working with another uncle, and they just got together. I still don't really understand it.

I finally got back to France to be with my dad. But he was having real problems with leadership, too independent, too open with his opinions and criticisms. I only got to stay with him for a very short time. Then, the French persecutions hit. The area shepherds got missed. They asked me to escape with them, so I could take care of their kids. They had no interest in taking care of their own children.

The whole time the French case was going on, I had six kids full-time, twenty-four hours a day, seven days a week. It was real hard. I hardly had any time at all for myself. I didn't say anything then, but I see now that I really got taken advantage of. But, this was the time when some of the really harsh discipline was coming down on the teens and YAs. And the worst thing a kid could do was to question leadership. Also, the adults were really into prayer sessions back then, you know, like exorcisms. If the kids had any problems, the adults would pray over them and lay hands on them. You know, to get the evil spirits out. I sure didn't want any part of that. So, even though I was miserable, I kept my mouth shut.

I was basically on full-time child care from age thirteen to sixteen. I tried to keep up with my scholastics, but it was hard to find time. I did get to do some occasional singing and performing, but not much. I really got fed up with taking care of other people's kids. I had to sac-rifice a lot. There were a lot of tears. I felt very alone. I had no sense that the adults were sensitive to what I was going through. Basically, I had been apart from my parents since age twelve. And I found it embarrassing to talk with other adults about my problems. I really missed my dad.

Of course, they were very pleased. They always talked about how "responsible" I was. Then things got even worse. My mom came with her new mate. I was really bitter against her for abandoning my dad. I did not accept her new mate. He talked all the time about my dad, really criticizing him. I was nice and respectful, so he thought I was accepting of him. All the time, I kept thinking, "You stole my mom." It was awful. Finally, I couldn't take it anymore.

*****

[She began to cry. The rest of the interview was accompanied by tears and frequent pauses to regain her emotional control.]

*****

[I'm very sorry. You did get to leave that place?]

*****

They finally let me go to rejoin my dad in Belgium. This time with my dad was great. We did shows and performing and prison ministry. It was the best time of my life, but it was far too short. Then a shepherd asked me to go to Switzerland with him to do child care. I didn't want to go, but I didn't really feel like I had a choice. I went, then shortly ended up in the United Kingdom, doing child care. I have been here ever since, except for a short road trip into Hungary.

I guess I am pretty discouraged right now. The Austin thing really shook me up. I guess I feel that I am just not really appreciated.

But, I am happy in this home now. I am doing child care, and the adults really appreciate me. I think I will probably stay here for a while.

*****

[You say you are happy now. I don't mean to be offensive, but you don't seem happy.]

*****

[after a long emotional pause, she completely broke down in tears]

*****

So many times I feel like giving up. I don't really have a vision for what to do or what to be. And yet, there is so much I want to do.

I feel like I am just holding on, making it through life another week.

We talked about Grandpa. I don't pray to him, but sometimes I think in my mind, "Why did you have to go?"

At first I had a sense that Grandpa was still around. Now, I don't *think about it like that. I really miss him. I just don't know what to do or what to think.*[5]

The joyful, purposeful Mercy and the confused, tearful Casa stand at two poles. The majority of young people are much closer to the Mercy pole. The youth generally express a positive assessment of their lives, and seem to have come to terms with the stress, dislocation, and eccentricity of their shared journey. Like the adults before them, they have accepted the hardships endemic to life in The Family. For the most part, they have subsumed their "slings and arrows" under the banner of Father David's grand vision to reach a lost world with the message of the love of Jesus. And they are prepared to continue to pay the cost of discipleship.

However, two specific "cost factors" stand out as particularly shaping and occasionally traumatic aspects of their path toward adult discipleship: sexuality and discipline. As we have already noted, both of these factors have generated serious attacks on numerous communities over the past several years. Also, many adult disciples and the current leadership have some very serious regrets about certain aspects of the sexual experiences and the discipline of the children. Not surprisingly, disciples of all ages were generally reluctant to speak openly and frankly about activities that have caused such personal and communal distress, and which are now repudiated by the movement. It took almost two years of my learning the culture and slowly building friendships and a trust relationship before memories and experiences of such a personal and often painful nature began to emerge.

In contrast, talking with the young people about sexuality was an astoundingly relaxed enterprise. It is quite evident that they have been raised in an environment in which sexuality is viewed as a wholesome, positive, and natural aspect of life, a true gift from God. This observation came home most clearly in the fall of 1995, while I was visiting a home in the upper Midwest. I was introduced to two fifteen-year-old girls who had just come up from Latin America. The three of us spent

5. I have maintained contact with Casa and a number of other young people. In early 1997, Casa went to visit her father in Belgium. She decided to leave and remain with her father.

almost four hours together, talking about their lives as children and teenagers. Eventually the discussion turned to issues of sexuality, and we ended up talking at length about their views, their experiences as children growing up in an open and permissive environment, and eventually of their own personal experiences. And when the topic shifted in this direction, absolutely nothing changed in their demeanor, the tone of their conversation, or their body language. Here were two teenage girls, talking to a fifty-year-old total stranger about the most intimate details of their parents', their peers', and their own sexual attitudes and experiences. And not once was there even a hint of a blush, or a giggle, a raised eyebrow, or even a pause. We might as well have been talking about the weather.

Whereas the young people proved open and relaxed in speaking about the sexual mores of the community as a whole, the legacy of the sexual exploitation and abuse of children was another matter. We have already established that throughout the late 1970s and early 1980s, sexual activity between adults and children was an accepted practice in a number of communities. The majority of the teens interviewed in this study did not recount a personal history of sexual abuse or sexual encounters with adults, but almost all were aware of these activities and knew personally of others who had been involved.

Sure, I know about all the sex things that went on between adults and kids, back some time ago. What kid in The Family doesn't? That doesn't go on now. I never personally got into it, but I know some who did. I think it happened a lot, at least in some places.
* * * * *
[Is this an open topic of discussion among the teens and YAs?]
* * * * *
Yes and no. The guys talk about it a lot more than the girls. You know guys, right? "Yeah, I had sex with this older woman when I was only eleven." Stuff like that. Some of them seem almost proud of it, even though The Family now says that it was a mistake and should not have happened. With the girls, it is different. We don't talk about it much, even among ourselves. You can understand that, right? (Rita, age nineteen)

Rita's observation is on target. The young men are more apt to be open about their experiences. However, they are also much less inclined to attribute a great deal of significance to these events from their childhood.

I first had sex when I was twelve. The girl was a lot older, not sure really how old. She was Japanese. That is a little hard to remember exactly. She wasn't a kid, that's for sure. [laughs] When I turned twelve, that was the age of becoming an adult. Then, after a few months, it was changed and I was a teen. That was in 1986. Sex between adults and kids was common back then, at least where I was. It wasn't like a secret or anything. I was very shy, so I was not involved that much. But I know others who did it a lot. It was common really, kind of like the "in thing." But, it is not that big a deal now, not like it comes up all the time.

Then, after 1986, everything really changed. In Japan, even though people were still very loving and affectionate, we kids were encouraged to wait to have sex until we were mature enough to handle it. And the sex between the kids and adults stopped completely, as far as I could tell. Actually, after '86, I did not have sex until I was eighteen, and betrothed to my wife. Like I said, I've always been shy. (Amaal, age twenty-two)

In general, the young women have considerably more emotional investment in this issue. A number spoke with passion and conviction about the harmful effects of adult sexual contact with children. Such openness was sometimes the case, even for young women who were not directly involved. Amara is eighteen. She is European and has lived her whole life in Europe and Asia.

Before the BI Case, I think there was a lot of pressure to keep it quiet, even among ourselves. I mean, this is not the kind of thing anyone would want to talk about, right? I heard things from all over the world. I did not have it happen to me—my parents were very protective. But, I have heard some very, very bad stories from other teens about sex abuse. Now, I am going to tell you this stuff, as long as it is clear that this is about stuff that happened in the past. It is not going on now.

When I was six or seven, we had this older girl who lived with us.

I was seven and she was twelve, so she was "older," right? She took care of us a lot and slept with us younger kids at night. One night, I woke up, and she wasn't in the room. I ran around the house, and found her having sex with one of the uncles. Even though she was older than me, I still knew that something about it was not right. It scared me. I always looked at that uncle a little different after that. It really upset me, at the time.

I am not sure if that kind of thing was actually approved or not, but it sure did happen. And how many secrets can you really have in a Family home? For the kids, whether it was officially approved was really not the main deal. See, we were all raised to really respect and honor the adults. So, when an adult did something with a kid, we usually assumed it was OK. Kids or teens would never report on an adult, 'cause then you were out of it with all the adults afterward. You know, I am not really sure how true that was. But it is the way we thought back then.

Things are different now.

Most of the youth have come to terms with this dimension of their history. Athough virtually all take pride in the new direction, some still harbor considerable pain and resentment over their childhood experiences. Virginia was born in North Africa to European and American parents. She spent much of her early life in Asia.

I think I know a lot about the sex abuse of kids in The Family, far more than I wish I did. There was a lot of that kind of thing going on in India when I was there. I was sexually abused. When I was about age seven or eight, an uncle would come to our room when I was sleeping. He would wake me and fondle me. It happened a lot. And not just to me.

I had no dad then. I honestly think that when a kid did not have a father living in the home, then that kid was at greater risk. At first, I didn't tell my mom. I guess I just thought these were really weird uncles. I did tell my mom a little about it, later. But she took it really hard. She cried a lot. She felt it was her fault. It hurt her so much that I didn't want to tell her any more. And, there was no one else to talk to about it.

I guess I am not overly traumatized by all this. It just happened. I

*am pretty open-minded about sex; I saw it all the time growing up.
There were lots of very graphic pictures of naked sex in the lit back
then, and a fair amount of nudity in the homes. And I saw adults
having sex all the time when I was growing up. Maybe I am just not
as affected by it as much as you might expect. I can handle what
happened to me OK. But knowing what happened to some others really bothers me.*

*I know that there were young girls who had sex with adults back
in those days. I think there were uncles who wanted to have sex with
me, but by the time I turned twelve it was not happening anymore. I
know one girl personally. She was thirteen, and began having sex
with an adult uncle. He was married, and the girl actually joined up
with them as a threesome, when she was only fourteen. That was so
out in the open that everybody had to have known. I think she is really bothered by it, even today.*

*To be honest, the teens and YAs who went through all that don't
talk about it much anymore, even among ourselves. And a lot of the
older ones are gone, anyway. But I tell you what really bugged me.
When the persecutions came in France, Australia, and Argentina, and
our enemies brought out the sexual abuse of the kids. Well, The
Family kept saying "No, nothing like that ever happened." A lot of
teens talked among ourselves over that, saying: "Yeah sure, right!"
We all knew that it happened, a lot. I was super upset that The
Family was lying about it. The leaders had to have known. And they
denied it.*

*One of the reasons I can talk about this now is that The Family
has really changed.[6] All the sexual stuff with kids has definitely
stopped. There may still be some weird person left, but it is much
more difficult to hide that kind of stuff when you live together like
we do. So, I think there is far less now in The Family than in the
System.*

Certainly not all children raised in The Family were subjected to
sexual abuse. Though the practice was spread throughout the world-

6. This young woman was previously interviewed by a social scientist investigating
The Family in California. She did not relate any knowledge of sexual misconduct in
that earlier interview.

wide community, individual homes and individual parents were able to minimize, if not eliminate, the exposure of many children. But even for watchful parents, the cost paid for the experiment in child sexuality could run very high.

I knew about the views of some regarding sex with the kids, but neither my husband nor I were ever into that kind of thing. I think we always made that very clear to others, so I guess we thought we wouldn't have a problem. We were wrong. We have one daughter. When she turned sixteen she left us for the System. Right away she became a stripper in a really low-class club in London. We loved her, but she just couldn't forgive us for what she went through.

She claims that she was sexually abused often while we were in India. Not by us, but by others that lived in the homes. I am sure she was taken in by the anticult movement. They promised her money and a vacation to Kenya if she would testify against The Family in the BI Case. And she did. But, now I am sure that some of what she claims is true. She never told me about it, not even when she left. The first I heard it was when she testified in court. In her mind, we allowed it to happen. But I honestly never knew. But, maybe I should have been more watchful, more careful. (Martha)

Although many, if not most, children escaped direct sexual involvement with adults, none were exempt from the sexual ethos of the community. Throughout the late 1970s and early 1980s they were constantly exposed to sexually explicit literature. Nudity was common in many homes and affirmed by Family leadership.

During the RNR we had a trailer and were mobile. My parents found this nudist camp in Florida, owned by Christians. The owners let us stay free, 'cause we were missionaries. I was like five or six, but I remember it very clearly.

My mom got in Playboy. *The wrote her up as the "nude Christian." Reporters came down. We were still in The Family, reporting and getting the Letters. We just lived in this nudist colony.*
*****
[What do you think of that, now?]
*****

It didn't bother me back then. I was just a kid. But, if I was asked to do that now? Forget it! No way. (Miles, age eighteen)

In addition to the nudity and sexually explicit literature, the children were consistently allowed to witness sexual activity between the adults. All the teens were aware that their mothers were Flirty Fishing, and that their parents were involved in sexual liaisons with other "aunts and uncles." A substantial percentage of the young people observed these sexual encounters on a regular basis. Their interpretation of those events varies considerably.

As a kid growing up I was very aware of the FFing and sharing. I do remember my mom was gone a lot at night. But I guess I don't remember all that much about the FFing. I would help her pick out her dress, fix her hair. I took it as quite normal. They all did it. For a while my mom had a close fish who supported us really well. He would come over to the house a lot. He was very sweet to me.

I guess I have a little more mixed feelings about all the sharing. For a while there was a sharing schedule. My folks had to share with whoever was on the list. The kids could see the lists.

That kind of really wild stuff only lasted for a few years. But man, it sure was wild and free while it did last. We were in Latin America, and all the different homes in our area would gather together for Sunday fellowship. I was like five and six at the time. The adults would have this dance, then all pair off and have sex. Us kids would just wander around, taking it all in. A lot of times the place was crowded, so all the adults couldn't find private space. They would just have sex right out on the grass, as we kids were playing around them. We just thought it was funny. (Cindy, age twenty-one)

Others found far less humor in an environment that was permeated by sexual promiscuity.

My flesh father was a fish, from Tunisia. I sometimes try to imagine myself with a stable father. Really, this has been the worst part of my life, not really having a dad. I used to be bitter when I was younger, 'cause I never had a stable father. Bitter at the situation, not at any individual. For a long time I had negative attitudes toward marriage and relationships.

I think I was always bothered by the sharing. I remember the sharing schedules, back when I was a kid. And I was a light sleeper. I often slept in my mom's room, and many times I would wake up while she was having sex with one of the uncles. It really hurt me. I did not want my mom hurt any more than she already was. I remember crying in my bed while my mom shared with different uncles. It really affected me. I have never talked to her about it. I don't want to hurt her. I am sure I will get over it. (Miriam, age eighteen)

* * * * *

I never liked the sharing or the FFing. We knew. We knew who our parents were having sex with. Sometimes it was even posted in the home. They would have this little dinner; then the music would come on. The adults would split up and go to different rooms. We were supposed to be sleeping, but we weren't.

I thought it was very strange then, and I still do. Sometimes I would be in the room when my mom would have sex with another guy. I hated that. The dancing would start. Then they would come into the room and just start doing it. I acted asleep. I really hated it. My mom and I never talked about this, but how could she not know? (Iris, age nineteen)

Family young people were raised in an extraordinarily open and permissive environment. Sex was constantly affirmed as a natural and God-given human need that should be fulfilled like any other normal human need. Today, they often live in communities of mostly teenagers and young adults, with very little adult supervision. And they are not only permitted to engage in sexual intercourse at age sixteen, they are officially encouraged to do so. One can only imagine that when the hormones begin to flow, there would be nothing to stop them. But that is not the case.[7]

7. In a 1998 study of adolescent sexual activity in The Family, Nancy Vogt found no significant difference in the incidence of sexual intercourse among Family teenage girls and among the general population. In fact, the percentage of girls reporting to have had intercourse were higher in the general population at every age level, but the differences were not significant. Vogt also correlated the level of sexual activity with self-esteem, closeness to parents, importance of religion and religious activity. All of these factors tended to be lower with increased sexual activity, in the general population. Vogt found that sexual activity had no impact on these factors among Family teenage girls. Vogt gathered her data through a written survey of 100 Family girls aged thirteen to eighteen (1998, 24–28).

The Children of the Revolution have developed their own sexual ethos, quite apart from the first generation. They differ from their parents in two significant ways. The first is the use of birth control. From the beginning of the movement, Father David was adamantly opposed to any form of birth control. If we judge by Family literature, the testimony of adult disciples, and the large number of children born into the community, virtually all of the first generation followed his teaching. In 1996, Maria issued "Go for the Gold." This Letter generally affirms God's strong displeasure with birth control and states that those who seek God's best (gold or silver) will not use it. However, those satisfied with God's third best (bronze) could use birth control and still be accepted within the community. To this point, almost all the first generation are "going for the Gold." Many in the second generation have been wearing bronze for some time.

A fair number of the youth confirmed being sexually active from their early teen years, even though it violated Family rules. More strikingly, a significant number reported using birth control measures on a regular basis, even though it broke a specific and very significant Family theological commitment.

Beyond the issue of birth control, the youth generally have what they term a more "conservative" view of sexuality. They respect the first generation, and often speak about the "sacrificial" nature of Flirty Fishing. But many seem equally eager to establish their own sexual ethos. Angel is a nineteen-year-old Australian who has spent her life in The Family, mostly in Asia and Canada.[8]

The sharing thing has calmed down a lot with the adults. I don't have a lot of clear memories of that. When I talk with other kids, I think my folks must have been more careful than most. I did have some memories and talked recently with my mom. She told me she had been in a threesome. I was shocked. I don't know of any teens who would even consider such a thing.

Don't get me wrong. Teens like sex. But I don't think we look at it

8. She is the daughter of June, the Australian disciple who narrowly averted suicide by joining The Family in New Zealand.

the same as the adults. It used to be they would take anyone and have sex with them. They are not so much like that anymore. And the teens I know have no interest in that kind of thing.

Most teens I know are not all that anxious to get involved sexually. From fifteen on down, it is not allowed. Recently, Maria sent some letters encouraging the teens sixteen and over to do more sharing, be more sexually involved in the fellowship of the homes. But, I think most teens are still pretty cautious. We have no interest at all in bringing back the old days of our parents.

I personally have had sex with only one guy. We were together a few times, but have stopped now. I am pretty sure I am going to wait now, until I am ready to marry. I want to get married to someone who will stay with me for my whole life. I want the right guy, and I don't want to do anything to mess that up. And I don't see myself being all that anxious to share him, either.

I am sure that most of the teens are more conservative about sex than the adults. I have heard a lot of talk. I have heard girls say, "I don't want to be a baby factory." We want to have a life as teens and YAs, do things for the Lord and be free to go anywhere before we get married and get tied down with kids. But most of all, girls do not want to be a single mother. And not just the girls. A lot of the guys feel the same way. I think we have all seen way too much of that.

This more restrained attitude is not limited to young women who fear pregnancy. There are a considerable number of young men who share the general outlook of Angel.

I grew up with the Law of Love. I have only recently realized how unusual it is. I believe The Family teaching that everything done in love is of God. But for me personally, well I am not sure I want to do that. Sharing is still a part of The Family, and I accept that. But it is not what I want to do.

I am twenty now, but I have never been sexually active. I could. There are girls in my home who would have sex with me tonight, if I asked them. But I have made a choice, to wait until marriage. And I am not the only one. If I get some girl pregnant, then I would be ex-

pected to marry her. If not, you are really looked down on. And you should be. It is terrible, not having two caring parents. So, I am not going to have sex until I find the girl I will marry.

I don't think I am all that unusual. I bet most of us are more conservative about sex than teens in the System. Sure, The Family has a lot of sexual freedom. But we are also very idealistic, at least a lot of us. We have a calling from God and want to make our lives count.

We are different than the older generation. Most of them came into The Family as hippies and whatever. I think maybe the teens and YAs who have decided to stay in are more serious minded than our folks were back in those days, at least about sex. Most of all, we are very concerned that our kids have a mother and a father, solid, there for them as they grow up. That didn't happen for a lot of us. Sure, there are exceptions. But I bet you won't find many teens who are into the kind of bed hopping that our folks were into when they were young. This is a different time. And we [second generation] are different. (Carson)

There is a wide range in the sexual ethic of Family youth. One twenty-year-old woman reported being sexually active since the age of fourteen, with approximately fifteen different partners. Yet, she professed to know girls who are "sluttish" compared to her. However, the second generation is markedly more conservative than their parents, and overwhelmingly more so than in the days of Flirty Fishing and sharing schedules.

Two dynamics seem to be at work here. Almost all the older teens and YAs grew up in large families with younger siblings. Most were given child-care responsibilities very early. Many love children and genuinely enjoy their child-care responsibilities. However, each has come of age with serious firsthand experience of the time, effort, and energy required to care for a child. A good number are far from eager to leap into parenthood.

More significantly, these young people are the product of a genuine revolution that pushed the boundaries of sexual freedom to the outer edge. They understand, at the deepest personal level, the cost of that freedom.

*Yes, I am eighteen and a Family kid all my life. And no, I have not
had sex. I do have a boy friend. I mean, we do more than hold hands.
But, I have made a decision to wait until I find the guy I will marry
and be with the rest of my life. See, I know what it is like not to
know who your real dad is. And I know what it is like not to know
who is going to be making decisions for you, or having sex with your
mom next month. It is not that my mom didn't love us, 'cause she
does. And there have been good times, and some of my dads have
been good to me. But my kids aren't going to grow up like that.
(Geena, age eighteen)*

The unique and constantly evolving sexual ethos profoundly shaped
the second generation. But, when they talk about their lives, the roller-
coaster ride of Family discipline often stands out as the most significant component of personal history. It is impossible to chart the flow
of the practices regarding child discipline. There were considerable differences in various regions of the world. Additionally, contrasting
waves of very strict and quite relaxed approaches rolled through The
Family during the 1980s and early 1990s. In general, adult disciples
sought to balance an emphasis on love and understanding with the discipline necessary to maintain strict community standards. Whereas
Father David clearly supported the use of physical punishment, he also
warned the disciples against cruelty and undue harshness. However, it
is very clear that there were times and places where the discipline of
the youth was harsh and extreme.

In general, the youth look back on their childhood experiences positively—though not all of them.

*My mom was mostly single the whole time we were growing up. I
really think we got more strict, more harsh discipline from the other
adults. The kids who had dads to stand up for them had it better. We
got more spankings, worse spankings, and more discipline in general.*

*I tried to stand up for my little sisters. A few times my little sisters
were beaten badly by other uncles. An uncle would get really upset
or angry and just beat on a kid. I saw that way too much. I guess that
is the one thing I am still bitter about. Especially when it happened*

to my little sisters. I know some of those uncles are still in The Family. I still hate them for what they did. (Cassandra)

Cassandra appears to be an exception. Most of the youth affirmed that they received spankings as young children, but few saw them as excessive or cruel. In general, the second generation appears to be at peace with The Family's approach to early childhood discipline. However, when problems with openly rebellious teenagers began in the mid-1980s, Family leadership responded with programs and approaches that still lay heavily on many young people.

I've been in trouble a lot. When I was thirteen, in Japan, I got mixed up with some older teens. (They all ended up leaving.) These guys were giving the shepherd a lot of trouble, and I thought it would be cool to go along with them. I started using foul language, no Word Time, being disrespectful. I was pretty much like that for my early teen years. Nothing like real serious.

* * * * *

[What happened?]

* * * * *

We got public exposure. They brought us all before the whole home and really gave it to us. It was pretty humiliating.

* * * * *

[No physical punishment?]

* * * * *

Oh no. When I was younger I got spankings and stuff, nothing out of this world. Normal, with the hand or occasionally a belt. But when you get older, it is more like the public exposure, or taking away privileges.

I got in trouble in Peru when I was fifteen. I got put on a Victor Program, where they get all the bad guys together. We had extra work, extra Word Time. They worked us pretty hard, for a while. They put us all in one room and gave us a lot of extra supervision. I guess it wasn't that bad. (Luke)

Victor Programs were common throughout the late 1980s and early 1990s. The offending youth would be grouped together and given close adult supervision. Often, their regular academic work was suspended and the "Victors" were given extra studies in the Bible and MO Letters. Recreational activities were usually suspended, and they were assigned extra labor to fill their time. Many of youth reflect Luke's general attitude. They feel that the Victor Programs were too strict, but effective in building character and dealing with their misbehavior.

However, some of the young people remain quite troubled over the harshness and uneven nature of attempts to shape them into reliable and loyal disciples. Charity is a European who spent her early years in Asia. Her story gives some sense of the ebb and flow that many experienced as they moved toward adult status.

I was in Thailand, age twelve, and I got into a big training center for teens. Things were always pretty strict in Thailand. I think that is where my first real trouble started. See, I have these thick eyebrows, so people think I am scowling. I was in a Word session, and the leader yelled at me, "Get up here!" He said I was doubting the Word, because of my expression. I didn't know what he was talking about. He tried to make me wear this big button that said "I am so happy." I was disrespectful toward him, and I got a spanking. (This shepherd was known to be short tempered.) I got put on a Victor Program. No get out [recreation], lots of calisthenics, scrub the house all day, and lots of Word Time. And I had to wear this badge that said "I am happy." Because of my "countenance." I really never understood that one.

I went to Italy, a big Combo home with lots of kids from all over Europe. Some of these kids were really out of it. There was vandalism, disrespect for leadership and even Father David, lots of sex. Things got very strict there, strict and harsh on all the teens because of the actions of a few. It didn't affect me all that much. I tried to stay out of trouble. But, it caused a lot of resentment, particularly among the older teens. A lot of them left. Back then, that was like a death. So they did their best to keep as many as possible. But they made real mistakes. It didn't work.

From Italy I got sent to Switzerland. I got good schooling there. I did mostly child care. But, I had problems with an adult that I worked with. And the benefit of the doubt was always given to the adult. I complained, and that was "murmuring." So, I got another

Victor Program. I had to spend one hour each day with the shepherd, which was OK. He was pretty nice and understanding, at least for those days.

I was fifteen when the real problems with the teens in Europe hit. (I was part of the problem.) I was sent to the Budapest Training Center. So, they made all these very strict rules, like in Rome. We were not allowed to wear jeans. We had to paste our hair back, so we wouldn't look "worldly." It was really bad, and there was a lot of resentment and rebellion. Then, we had this big meeting of teens from all over Europe. Leadership from World Services was there and they were surprised about all these rules. They cleared it up, and we went back to only a very few rules.

But, by this time I was ready to leave. I was really down on Father David, even on Jesus. I didn't want to read the Word. Then the SUR [Shepherding Europe Revolution] happened. Leaders came and got all the teens of Europe together with all the shepherds. Things got cleared up and seemed to work, so I decided to stay and see. By this time, all the real problem teens had left. We had eight leave in one week in Budapest. I think the majority of us are now pretty settled in. We have come through it. And the leadership has learned a lot about teens.

Victor Programs were employed in most locations, with varying degrees of intensity. Toward the end of the 1980s, Family leadership was facing a crisis. Substantial numbers of older teens were in open rebellion against Family ideology and lifestyle standards. It began to look as if most would desert the movement. The problem was not simply a matter of keeping the organization going.

I know some not-so-good things went on a few years ago, trying to straighten out some of the teens and keep them in The Family. Look, you have to understand. We love our kids. And they didn't know about the System, but we did. It is cruel, and materialistic, and evil. And soon it will all be caught up in a great devastation. Who in their right mind would want their kid to go out into that? So, we were desperate. And mistakes were made, bad ones. We have learned from that. We have a whole different approach now. But, some things just cannot be taken back. (Alan, age forty-six)

As various programs seemed to be having only minimal success, The Family reached a point of desperation. Teen Training Centers were established in Europe, Asia, South America, and Mexico. The directors of these centers were given the task of reshaping the youth into loyal and productive disciples. Few recall this episode with pride.

I was thirteen and living in Mexico at the Teen Training Center [TTC]. It was a very bad time for me. I had never been a problem. It seemed OK the first day. The next morning we had an emergency meeting. There was this nine-year-old girl on the "hot seat." Poor thing! I had never seen correction given like that before. They said she had serious problems: a rebellious spirit, daydreaming. They yelled at her. She began crying, but no matter. They said she needed silence restriction. I was like: "What is that?" *I was scared. I didn't understand what she did, but I sure didn't want to do it.*

One of the leaders said she had bad thoughts about the JETT shepherd. Well, who didn't? *This guy claimed to have the "gift of discernment," could see through teens, tell what we were thinking. We all gathered around her and had this desperate prayer, laid hands on her, to drive out her prideful spirit. She was on silence restriction and had talked once, so she had this diaper over her mouth. Then they put her out cleaning the cobblestones. I prayed she wouldn't get sunstroke. I felt really bad for her. But, I believed what I was told, that this was the way The Family was to be.*

One day the head guy, John, called all the JETT girls into the bathroom. He was extremely critical of the cleanness. He looked at me, and I said nothing. All of a sudden he started shouting: "You! You are goddamned self-righteous!" *I was stunned. He yelled again:* "You are murmuring right now. I can see it in your eyes. You are a goddamned murmurer!" *I didn't know if I should cry, or say I'm sorry, or what. No one had ever talked to me like that in my entire life.*

That night I cried for two hours. I prayed: "Jesus, I really want to do what is right. Please help me be good. I didn't know I was goddamned self-righteous. Please help me not to be." *I was really afraid.*

Next morning I hoped he would forget. But he went off on me again. It was a terrible experience. I never got further discipline. I didn't know my attitude was bad, but thought it must be. I tried to be yielded to the Lord every minute.

Once we were sitting around for our weekly public exposure. John came in with a paddle. He really exposed this one JETT. Then he paddled him. It wasn't vicious or anything. But I am sure it was humiliating. Then he hung the paddle in the girls' bungalow. I guess to scare us. We hid it, and he had to make another one. [laughs] I was there about eight months, and he was the only one I saw get paddled.

I hated my time there, but I guess the Lord used it. We learned how to take correction, and I am sure I got some benefit from it all. Some couldn't take it and left. Maybe the Lord used it so those who weren't fully committed would leave. Everything works for good in the Lord. But, it was very hard to see it then.

I was really afraid of John. I don't know if the Lord would ever let me hate someone. But, it was close.[laughs] He wrote me a letter. He said he had been wrong, the way he treated me. He apologized. I appreciate that.

When I left the TTC, I moved to a new home outside of Mexico City. It was a very happy home. There was absolutely none of the stuff that went on at the TTC. We made a summer road trip, and it was super fun. I haven't had any problems at all since I left the TTC. (Dawn, age twenty)

Dawn made it through those trying days with only minimal difficulties. Some had more trouble figuring out just what the Teen Training Center experience was about, or how to conform to the expectations of the adults. Others had more spirit than Dawn, and they paid for it.

I had a really happy childhood. Then, when I was twelve, my folks moved to Guadalajara. I ended up in the Teen Training Center. Man, that was a tough time. I went from shiner to like the worst person there is. And I'm still not sure why.

I got in trouble for murmuring. We were playing this game and the shepherd said he heard me say something against the game. I said: "What did I say?" He said, "You know." They took me off get out for punishment. For forty-five days I was on "get out restriction." Just for one comment. And I never found out what it was. I guess they figured me for a bad attitude. Things sure went downhill after that.

I got accused of murmuring against Work Call. Honest, man, I re-

ally have no *idea what I said. They put me on silence restriction. No special activities, no get out, no videos. I couldn't talk to anyone but the shepherd, and then only when he asked me a question. I got a lot of talks from John. He was one angry guy.*

* * * * *

[Sounds tough.]

* * * * *

I was on silence restriction for seven months.

* * * * *

[No!]

* * * * *

Yeah man, seven months! *And they worked me* hard, *too. I had to dig ditches. The worst was picking grass out between the cobblestones in this huge courtyard. When you saw someone out there, you knew they had done something* really *bad.* I *was out there a lot. [laughs] I had to do OHRs [Open Heart Report]. I was supposed to become more yielded. I never understood it.*

I had no school the whole year I was there, just work and Word Time. Lots *of work. It was the way I acted, my* attitude. *I got lots of XL [extra labor]. For murmuring, disobedience, being late. It was just nuts. To be honest, the silence was the worst part, a lot worse than the work. I have no good memories of that year at all.*

Then, I got saved. *My folks were allowed to visit me. After they left, my little sis got the mumps. I had to leave, 'cause I had been exposed. God got me out of there with the mumps, and I didn't even get them. That is grace.*

I never actually got paddled, but other kids did. I really hated *it there. But looking back now, it was not all that bad. It was tough, but I guess I learned a lot too. When I left, I went with my folks to this big farm-type home. It was great. Then, John wrote me a letter of apology. He even came to our home and asked my forgiveness. I could tell they all were really sorry for how they treated us.*

When I was fifteen, my folks got TSed out of The Family. I was out in the System a little over a year. But, I rejoined as soon as I could. I am really happy to be back in The Family. And I don't hold any grudges. The Family knows that was really wrong. And nobody gets treated like that anymore. (Jeremiah, age seventeen)

Second-generation disciples who remained have come to terms with the excesses of the Teen Training Centers for two primary reasons. First, they all affirm that the TTC experience was not normative. Virtually all religious communities like The Family face the challenge of retaining the loyalty of the generation born into the movement. Family youth have certainly been consistently subjected to constant and intense indoctrination into the ideology and norms of the group. But the harshness and occasional cruelty that characterized the Teen Training Centers has passed.

Second, Family leadership and the individuals who orchestrated the whole TTC affair seem genuinely repentant.

I was put in charge of the teen training in the Philippines. Things weren't going as well as we hoped they would. That was where the worst mistakes in the teen training were made. I was in charge.

*****

[What kind of mistakes?]

*****

Far too harsh disciplinary action—prolonged silence restriction, just way too harsh with the kids. Looking back on it is pretty painful. I was not close to the Lord, too independent in my attitude, and thinking I knew a lot more about how to deal with kids than I really did.

Back then, if a teen left, well, that was as a very, very sad situation. We viewed it as rebellion against the Lord. Unfortunately, I had very strong feelings about that. I was missing the unconditional love we should have given to the kids, no matter what. I was convinced the Lord wanted a certain standard from all our kids. We had a lot of high expectations of them too. It had been prophesied they would be the princes and princesses of His Kingdom. Many were a real disappointment. Then, if they didn't stay, they were headed to the System. We knew how bad that could be. And, we felt they were not prepared for that at all, they would really suffer out there. I was wrong about that, too. Most of the teens who have left have done well.

I was the problem. And when we left the Philippines and went to Mexico, I did the same thing there. I ran the TTC in Guadalajara. It really is hard for me to talk about. To think about how many kids I hurt. Finally, it all caught up to me. I got fired. It was a shock. I thought I was operating by Family policy. If I had been so wrong, how come no one had told me. But, I had become like a Pharisee. You know, keeping to the law while forgetting what was really impor- tant, like faith and love. I got put on manual labor. I call it my "rock pile" time. I was a failure.

Once I finally realized how off track I had been, how much I had hurt some kids, I apologized to as many as I could. And I got right with the Lord, too. (John)

From the beginning, the COG was a highly disciplined movement. Authoritarian leadership was the norm. When the first wave of chil- dren flowered into typical teenagers, The Family responded by at- tempting to force them into conformity. It did not work. The Victor Programs and Teen Training Centers alienated large numbers of older teens, and many fled the movement. Facing up to this failure helped turn the approach to child discipline, and overall leadership style, in a new direction. This shift culminated in the Love Charter of 1995. Homes are far more democratic, and individual rights are spelled out clearly. The Love Charter has had a substantial impact on the second wave of teens and YAs.

Life has really got better over the last couple of years. The Love Charter has made a big difference in my life. Before, we were always subject to like a king or something. The shepherd ruled the sheep, and I never had much say in anything. What the shepherd said was law.

But then the Charter came out. Things are much, much better now. Whatever you have the faith for, you can do. There is no one person in control of your life. You have the right to speak up, to dis- agree. And, if you don't like the place where you are, you can move. The Charter has really changed my life for the better.

* * * * *

[Is that what keeps you in?]

* * * * *

Well, yes and no. "Many are called, but few are chosen." I feel called to serve the Lord in The Family. I know I could not do nearly as much for Jesus in the System. But the Charter sure has made it much easier to stay. I enjoy my life now. I love the people here. And I get to do the ministry that I want to do. (Michael, age eighteen)

Leaving is now a much more accepted option for the young people. Many have given the issue considerable thought. But, it is clear that the bleeding has stopped. Relatively few of the first wave of children born in the early 1970s have remained. Retention is almost certain to be much higher with the second wave.

A lot of older teens and YAs that I know have left The Family. It has been hard. I am glad I am still here and am pretty sure I will stay. Some of the ones who left didn't have The Family vision. A lot of them were in it for themselves and didn't have an interest in helping others. Some were just not cut out for Family life. Others got real confused. The adults were really hard on those older kids, and a lot of them really resented it. I don't blame them. Kids in The Family now have it much better.

There has been a real change in attitude toward the teens. We have a lot more freedom now. We are taking over the outreach more and more, and there are all kinds of neat things we can do. And there is a lot more trust of the young people. I think The Family has matured a lot. The approach to the System is not so condemning now. There is a lot less of the "goddamned America" talk. Now, we are more into just trying to help people, and give them the love of Jesus. It really is better now. (Jordan)

The Love Charter has revolutionized life for the second wave of the younger generation. Though still self-consciously members of a structured and highly disciplined organization, they feel a sense of freedom, responsibility, and opportunity that was unknown to their older brothers and sisters. They carry a significant portion of the ministry load and leadership in the homes of Asia and the Americas. Recently, eastern Europe and Africa have been the primary focus of Family ministry and growth. The young people are the primary vanguard of outreach in these newest mission fields.

Michele is twenty. She was born in France to American parents. Her father was one of the original members of Les Enfants de Dieu. She was raised in Brazil.

In Brazil, I did mostly outreach. Actually mostly fundraising, not a lot of direct witnessing. It wasn't that exciting or satisfying. I really wanted more action, more direct witnessing. I got a vision for Russia.

I really began to pray. I am no big prophet, but I committed not to sleep until I heard from the Lord. This guy also had a desire to go to Russia. He got a prophecy that we would meet someone the next day to pay our way. I didn't take him seriously. But, the next day, we met a guy. (We were on a road trip in Bolivia.) We shared our vision for Russia, and he gave the money for both of us to go. I couldn't believe it. I was not used to God speaking and providing like that. I heard stories all the time from the adults about this kind of thing, but it was my first experience. We left for Russia right away.

We landed in St. Petersburg in a totally YA home. The oldest person there was twenty-five. We did skits on the streets. We made a very simple Russian video and gave it to the TV stations. We did lots of street witnessing, giving out three thousand posters a day and thousands of New Testaments and copies of the Gospel of John. We didn't ask for money. We got our support from World Services and homes in the West.

It is very rough there. But it is great, lots of witnessing. We go to the universities, give out posters and witness. We are getting lots of new disciples. It is just like the beginning in the U.S. back in the '60s. And, it is all us, all YAs.

Russia is a very fruitful place to witness. I have prayed with hundreds of people to receive Jesus as Savior. In St. Petersburg, a large kindergarten gave us a room to teach English every Friday. We do it with the Bible. The parents are starting to come and many are getting saved.

We have homes everywhere, about fifty in Russia. We also have homes in several of the Republics: Ukraine, Latvia, Khazikstan. I took a trip to Mongolia, did concerts at the university. We had eight or ten conversions.

All of Russia is very receptive to the Gospel. We go to prisons, mor-

*bid camps were no one else goes. We fill up the halls with five hun-
dred guys, do concerts, mingle and pray with many of the prisoners.
Most of the Russians are Orthodox. We don't try to change that. Our
task is to get them to pray and receive Jesus as Savior.*

*We do a lot of humanitarian aid in Russia. We approach Moscow
businesses and get help for orphanages: washing machines, beds,
food, clothes. I was able to clothe one whole orphanage through my
contact with an Indian company in Moscow. We now have a huge
warehouse in Sweden. We gather up donated clothing from all over
Europe and send it to Russia. We get toys from a French company. We
get TVs and VCRs from an Iraqi company. A lot of Westerners have
come to Russia to take. We have come to give, and they know that.
You just can't believe how exciting it is there.*

* * * * *

[Has life always been this good?]

* * * * *

*No. I was in a Victor Program for a long time. I was "negative."
They said I had a "critical attitude." [smiles and rolls her eyes] I can
look back on it now and laugh. Then, it wasn't so funny. I thought it
was* horrible. *I decided to leave a couple of times. But, I got over it.
Now, I am very committed. I doubt I will ever leave. I have a very
good life now, serving Jesus. I have much more freedom now under
the Love Charter. I don't have to leave The Family to do what I want,
the way I want to do it.*

*I am engaged now. As soon as I raise my funds, I will head to
Norway, where we will be married. Then, we are headed back to
Russia to serve the Lord.*

The life of Family young people has changed dramatically over the
past decade. The initial approach of hardwired indoctrination and
harsh discipline was a failure. It fractured relationships between many
teens and their parents, and it was singularly ineffective in retaining
the loyalty of the youth. As Peter Amsterdam often says, "We make
mistakes, but we learn from them." Today, the approach is to love the
teens into staying. And by providing trust, responsibility, variety, self-
expression, and opportunity for genuine adventure, The Family is prov-

ing to be an inviting place for the youth to live out their lives. In the past, Family leadership portrayed the System as an evil alternative. The evil of the System did not seem to deter many teens from giving it a try. In the present, the System looks far worse than "evil" to youthful eyes. It appears dull.

The Family is a constantly evolving religious society. Retention of the youth is now a major objective. Achieving that objective has been costly. And in many ways, success has reshaped the very nature of the community. And if The End does not come, the children of the Children of God will be The Family. Who can even imagine what that will be?

Epilogue

The Future of The Family

Historians are woeful prognosticators. In the case of New Religious Movements like The Family, prediction of the future becomes even more problematic. Although clearly a definable religious organization, The Family is also a complex of interrelated actions, beliefs, doubts, and dreams of a very wide range of individuals. Looking back over the past thirty years, who could have predicted the present situation from any given point of Family history? In 1987 Roy Wallis, a most competent sociologist who knew the movement well, confidently asserted that The Family would not be able to survive the death of Father David. Could anyone, insider or outsider, have foreseen the smooth transition of leadership or the extent to which Family members would continue to remain "connected" to The Prophet after his death?

However, there are some observations that can offer highly tentative insight into the possible trajectory of The Family. The two greatest challenges facing any New Religious Movement are the transition of leadership after the departure of the founding figure and the integration of the second generation. Father David still speaks to the disciples from the Spirit World. Queen Maria and King Peter have assumed the mantle of spiritual and political leadership, effectively placing their own stamp on the movement through the installation of the Love Charter. Through trial and error—some very serious error—the community has come to terms with the second generation and has found effective ways not only to maintain loyalty, but to integrate the young people fully into community life. In doing so, they have rekindled the initial drive and spirit of the Children of God. The two major hurdles seem to have been overcome.

The years 1996 and 1997 were the most statistically successful in Family history. It seems fairly certain that the movement will survive for some time. But survive as what? From the beginning, the Children composed an intense, highly disciplined, and "world denying" religious movement that has maintained a high level of tension with the surrounding cultural matrix. More particularly, they understand themselves to be the New Church of Jesus, who will lead and guide the rest of Jesus' followers through the trauma of the End Time. On the basis of The Family's understanding of the satanic nature of the System, End Time ideology, Spirit World communication, extraordinarily high commitment level, and the virtual sacrality of sexuality, it is likely that a significant level of tension will continue between the disciples and the world, as well as between the disciples and "church Christians." They hold this tension as a positive value. Conscious that living in contemporary North America has proven to be a temptation to compromise with the outside world, Family leadership is again urging American and Canadian disciples to leave their homeland for new challenges on the mission fields of Asia, eastern Europe, and Africa. Between 1997 and 1999, hundreds of disciples left North America.

However, recent developments demonstrate a capacity to soften the edges considerably. The Consider the Poor ministry has been the single most instrumental development in bringing the Children into a more constructive relationship with the outside world. Several homes have developed cooperative relationships with rescue missions, refugee programs, and various shelters for battered women or abandoned children. In 1996, disciples gathered in Washington, D.C., for a "Sackcloth Vigil." Harking back to the heady, confrontational early years of the COG, they donned their sackcloth robes. Disciples of all ages grabbed their staves and warning scrolls, and stood for hours before the White House in silent protest: warning America of its evil nature and imminent destruction. At that very moment, youthful disciples in Siberia were actually working under contract to the U.S. Agency for International Development to distribute humanitarian aid to needy persons. The "radical, revolutionary Children of God" are now engaged in a joint project with the Swiss Red Cross. From the earliest days on the road with "Uncle Dave," the COG refused any entanglement with government at any level. As late as 1995, Family representatives were adamant that any form of registration with the state would compromise their independence and freedom from the System. However, in January of 1997, Family leadership and several nonmember supporters established the Family Care Foundation as a 501(c)(3) human services and grant-making organization. The Family Care Foundation (FCF) channels funds and support to Family missionaries and humanitarian projects around the world. In March of 1997, the FCF received tax-exempt status from the Internal Revenue Service of the United States. The System is still the System. But, the disciples are beginning to find ways to work within it.

In March of 1994, The Family began the Ministry of Reconciliation: pouring considerable time and effort into bridging the gap between committed disciples and both marginal and former members. At the initiative of Bithia Sherman and other former members, Family leadership published an "Open Letter to Former Family Members" in the *No Longer Children* newsletter.[1] This letter offered to assist outside relatives in locating and establishing contact with Family disciples. The letter also offered an apology to former members for not maintaining appropriate contact. As the "BI Case" (the child custody case in England) unfolded, Family leadership became even more sensitive to the concerns of former members. In July 1996, Maria issued an open letter of apology to TSed (dismissed) and former members, asking forgiveness for mistreatment received at the hands of Family leadership. Peter Amsterdam made personal visits to group meetings of TSed and hostile former members, seeking forgiveness and reconciliation. The Family also established an 800 number to facilitate communication with outsiders; for the past three years, it has averaged 135 calls per month. Disciples all over the world have substantially increased the level of their communication and involvement with their biological families.

The attempts at restoring marginal members to a higher level of fellowship and commitment has worked well. Whereas in former times Father David castigated anyone who "turned his hand from the plough," The Family now speaks of "concentric circles of service." Peter has formally apologized to TSers who were mistreated or scorned by Family leadership.[2] TSed disciples are now referred to as "Fellow

---

1. No Longer Children was a loose organization of generally hostile former members that had actively campaigned against The Family.

2. "The Ministry of Reconciliation," *New Good News* No. 653, Oct. 1995.

Members." Though unable or unwilling to live at the full level of disciple commitment, they are now almost fully integrated into community life.

More than any other factor, the exodus of young people has caused Family leadership to rethink their relationship to the outside world. The Family has accepted the inevitability that a good number of the youth will leave the movement. Maria made this clear in 1994.

> We may have a hard time relating to the fact that in most churches and denominations, very few missionaries' children remain forever with their parents on the mission field. At some point or another, most of them go back to their home country, and they often choose to pursue different careers entirely.
>
> We've done our best to try to hang on to them, even to the point of trying to persuade some of them to stay with us long after it was obvious that their heart was not in The Family and that everyone would be better off if they were elsewhere. . . . [I]f they still decide they want to go, then we should say, "Okay, praise the Lord! You go out there and do the best you can, and we'll pray for you and we'll help you as much as we can. . . . We hope you'll be successful." . . . [N]ow is the time when they most need to know that we love them. ("When Teens Leave The Family!" ML #2942, Sept. 1994)

In 1997, with encouragement from World Services, one couple returned to the United States from South America to establish a "halfway house" to assist their own teens and others to transition out of The Family and into the System.

The Family has slightly blurred the formerly very sharp line between discipleship and living in the world. The ever increasing contact and relationship with relatives and their own children in the System will further erode the wall of separation. This reduction in "tension level" is already evident with adults and youth alike. In the early years of the COG, The Prophet regularly castigated the "goddamned hypocritical churchianity" of the System. Today, Family leadership is concerned to establish better understanding between their movement and other Christian communities. At some point, a limited level of humility, unknown in previous days, will pop up. "I love The Family, 'cause we really serve the Lord. But, it is not like we are the only ones. Our parents used to think that. I guess most still do. But I don't. The Lord has other groups of people who are also out there, sharing the love of Jesus. We are different than them. But, God has lots of people" (Peace, age nineteen).

However, the dominant self-understanding is still as God's Special End Time Army. The Family remains quite critical of the compromise and worldliness of virtually all other organized religion. Their hostility to the System church and their rather distinctive theology and lifestyle being what they are, there is no chance of joining the National Association of Evangelicals or the World Council of Churches. And there is no desire to do so.

Perhaps the greatest challenge facing The Family comes from within. Radical eccentricities are theologically justified and the mission is energized by the firm and passionate expectation of the imminent End Time. Like the first-generation Christians and the Adventists of mid-nineteenth-century America, they will have to come to terms with the delay of That Day and the continuation of history.[3] Although End Time expectations are a most central component of Family ideology, structures are in place for radical theological adaptation. Adjustments will certainly be required. But, there is no reason to believe that the disciples will be unable to accommodate an extended future in this world.

The Family has demonstrated a remarkable capacity to survive repression, persecution, radical theological shifts, self-inflicted wounds, and terrible mismanagement. They have survived the death of The Prophet. A dazzling racial, national, and ethnic array of Children has retained a surpassing level of coherence and mutual commitment while spread across the globe. Having come to terms with the loss of many youth, The Family has begun a flourishing recruitment of new disciples from the outside in some areas. Energy level is high. The Love Charter has substantially increased the comfort level of many, most particularly the second generation.[4] The bureaucracy appears to be stable, and the communication infrastructure is extraordinarily effective.

---

3. Unless they are right. Then, discussion of their future would be superfluous.
4. See Bozman 1998 for a brief but perceptive exploration of the changes brought about by the Love Charter.

Since new disciples still must "forsake all" and commitment level remains exceedingly high, it is doubtful The Family will ever be a large movement. But that has never been their purpose. They hope to share their distinctive understanding of the love of Jesus as broadly as possible, then stand as God's brilliant beacon in the Dark Night of The End. That hope has carried the Children through a past filled with hardship, dislocation, repression, and persecution. There is no reason to suppose it will not carry them well into the future.

Appendixes

Glossary

References

Index

Appendix A
Statement of Faith

1. The Scriptures

We believe the Holy Bible to be the inspired Word of God, given to us by God our Creator to be a "lamp unto our feet and a light unto our path" (Psalm 119:105). We assert that the Scriptures are a sacred revelation, written by holy men of old who spake as they were moved by God's Holy Spirit; and that these writings are the divinely appointed standard and guide to our faith and practice. Holding fast this truth, that "all Scripture is given by inspiration of God, and is profitable for doctrine, for reproof, for correction, for instruction in righteousness" (2 Timothy 3:16), we strive to study, memorize and obey it, that we may grow in faith, wisdom and spiritual strength through our knowledge of and adherence to its tenets.

God's Word as revealed in the Holy Bible is the basis and cornerstone of all our beliefs and practices. It is the mainstay of our spiritual strength and nourishment; its principles are the foundation of the instruction we give our children, and its truth is the basis of the witness we give to others. We come to the Bible not merely as a source of knowledge, which indeed it is, but much more importantly, through a prayerful reading of its pages we are able to "partake of the Divine Nature: (2 Peter 1:40), to commune with Jesus, Who is Himself the living Word. "The Words that I speak unto you, they are Spirit, and they are life" (John 6:63). (See also Matthew 24:3–5; Romans 15:4; 2 Peter 1:19–21; John 8:31,32; 1 John 2:5; Romans 10:17; Psalm 119:99,100; Jeremiah 15:16; 2 Timothy 2:15; 3:15;4:2; John 1:1,14.)

2. God

We affirm our belief in the one true eternal God, the all-powerful, all-knowing, ever-present invisible Spirit of Love, Who is the Creator and Supreme Ruler of the Universe and all things therein. We believe in the unity of the Godhead, that there are three distinguishable but inseparable Persons: the Father, the Son, and the Holy Spirit. (See Isaiah 43:10,11; John 4:24; 1 Timothy 1:17, 1 John 4:8; 5:7.)

3. Creation

We believe the Biblical account of Creation as outlined in the Book of Genesis, that it is to be accepted literally, and not allegorically or figuratively; that God, not chaos, created the Heavens and the Earth. We also believe that on the sixth day of Creation, God formed Man in His Own image and after His

Own likeness, and breathed into him the breath of life; thus Man became a living soul by divine Creation, not by random evolution. We also believe that God's visible creation provides clear testimony of His invisible existence. As our Creator, God deserves thanksgiving, reverence and obedience from us, His creations. (See Genesis 1:1; Romans 1:20; Psalm 33:6–9; Jeremiah 32:17.)

4. The Fall of Man

We believe that Man was created innocent by his Maker, but through the temptation of Satan he voluntarily transgressed and fell from his sinless and happy state, in consequence of which all Mankind are now sinners, and are absolutely unable to attain to righteousness without the saving power of Jesus Christ. (See Genesis, Chapter 3; Romans 5:12–21.)

5. Jesus Christ, the Son of God

We believe in the Deity of our Lord Jesus Christ, the only begotten Son of God, Who was miraculous in His divine conception and birth of the Virgin Mary, was sinless throughout His life, and made a full and vicarious atonement for the sins of the world by His death—the substitutionary sacrifice and death of the Just for the unjust. We affirm that Jesus Christ is the Mediator between God and Man, Who gave Himself as the only ransom for sinners. We believe in His physical resurrection and His bodily ascension into Heaven, His perpetual intercession for His people, and His soon coming personal visible return to the world in power and great glory, to set up His Kingdom and to judge the living and the dead. (See 1 Timothy 3:16; Philippians 2:5–11; Hebrews 4:14,15; 2 Corinthians 5:21; 1 Peter 2:24,25; Romans 1:3,4; Matthew 28:18; Acts 1:9–11.)

6. The Way of Salvation

We believe that all men by nature are sinners, but that "God so loved the world that He gave His only begotten Son, that whosoever believeth in Him should not perish but have everlasting life" (John 3:16). We believe therefore, that all persons who personally accept God's pardon for sin through Jesus Christ will be forgiven of sin, reconciled to God, and will forever live in God's presence.

We believe that the Salvation of Mankind is wholly by grace [God's love and mercy], through the mediatorial ministry of Jesus Christ, the Son of God, Who, in infinite love for the lost, voluntarily accepted His Father's will and became the divinely provided sacrificial Lamb Who alone can take away our sins.

We steadfastly adhere to the following Scriptural truths regarding Salvation:

a) All Mankind are sinners, and in dire need of a Savior. "For all have sinned and come short of the glory of God" (Romans 3:23). "For the wages of sin is death, but the gift of God is eternal life through Jesus Christ, our Lord" (Romans 6:23). (See also Romans 3:10; 1 John 1:8.)

b) Salvation is only by grace, and no one, by virtue of any goodness or mere work of their own, can become a child of God. "For by grace are ye saved through faith, and that not of yourselves, it is the gift of God: not of works, lest any man should boast" (Ephesians 2:8,9). "Not by works of righteousness which we have done, but according to His mercy He saved us, by the washing of regeneration and the renewing of the Holy Ghost" (Titus 3:5).

c) Salvation can only be acquired through Jesus Christ. "I am the Way, the Truth and the Life; no man cometh unto the Father but by Me" (John 14:6). "For them is one God, and one Mediator between God and men, the Man Christ Jesus" (1 Timothy 2:5). (See also Acts 4:12; 1 John 5:12.)

d) We are saved by believing on and personally receiving Jesus Christ into our hearts and lives, thus becoming spiritually regenerated or "born again". "As many as received Him [Jesus], to them gave He power to become the sons of God; even to them that believe on His Name: Which were born, not of blood, nor of the will of the flesh, nor of the will of Man, but of God" (John 1: 12,13). "Except a man be born again, he cannot see the Kingdom of God . . . That which is born of the flesh is flesh; and that which is born of the Spirit is spirit. Marvel not that I said unto thee, Ye must be born again" (John 3:3,6,7). (See also John 11:25,26.)

e) Once saved, the believer shall be kept saved forever. We believe it is the privilege of all who are born again of the Spirit through faith in Christ, to be fully assured of their Salvation from the very day that they receive Him as their Savior. Just as the believer is saved by grace, so is he sustained by grace; "Who are kept by the power of God through faith unto Salvation" (1 Peter 1:5). "The gift of God is eternal life" (Romans 6:23), and that which is eternal cannot be terminated; thus the one who has been cleansed and redeemed by the Blood of the Lamb has been purchased and eternally adopted by God, and therefore cannot be lost. "All that the Father giveth Me shall come to Me, and him that cometh to Me I will in no wise cast out" (John 6:37). "I give unto them eternal life, and they shall never perish, neither shall any man pluck them out of My hand" (John 10:28). "He that believeth on the Son hath [now possesses] everlasting life" (John 3:36).

(Although we firmly believe that the soul which God has saved and granted His free gift of eternal life can never be lost, this is not a license for sin to the believer. Because God is a holy and righteous Father Who cannot overlook the sins of His children, if they persistently sin, He will chasten and correct them. "For whom the Lord loveth, He chasteneth, and scourgeth every son whom He receiveth . . . for what son is he whom the Father chasteneth not?" [Hebrews 12:6,7])

7. The Holy Spirit

We believe that the Holy Spirit came forth from the Father to "reprove the world of sin, and of righteousness, and of judgment" (John 16:8). We hold the Holy Spirit to be the executive power of God by which believers are born again, taught, instructed, inspired and empowered for their God-given mission; and that every believer should be filled therewith. "Be ye filled with the Spirit" (Ephesians 5:18). The Holy Spirit is also known as "the Comforter", Who—like a mother—loves, nurtures and comforts the born-again child of God. (See also John 3:5-8; 14:15-18,26; 15:26; 16:7-11; 7:38,39; Acts 1:8.)

8. The Baptism of the Holy Spirit

We believe that the baptism or complete filling of the Holy Spirit is a baptism of Love, "for God is Love" (1 John 4:8), and that it may be freely obtained by all believers who simply ask God for it, and that it is often given after the Scriptural "laying on of hands" of other believers. The primary purpose of the baptism of the Holy Spirit is to empower the believer to witness the Gospel of Jesus Christ to others. "Ye shall receive power after that the Holy Ghost is come upon you, and ye shall be witnesses unto Me" (Acts 1:8). Other ministrations of the Holy Spirit are to guide the believer into all truth, to comfort the believer, to bring all things that Jesus has said to the believer's remembrance, and to assist the believer in prayer. (See Luke 11:9–13; Acts 8:15–17; Acts 1:8; Luke 4:18; Galatians 5:22,23; John 14:16,26; Romans 8:26,27.)

9. Gifts of the Spirit

We believe that it is the privilege of the Spirit-baptized believer to enjoy the benefits of the various spiritual gifts outlined in 1 Corinthians chapter 12. We believe that God gives different gifts to different people, according to their specific ministry and His particular plan for them. "Now there are diversities of gifts, but the same Spirit. And there are differences of administrations, but the same Lord. But the manifestation of the Spirit is given to every man to profit withal. For to one is given by the Spirit the word of wisdom; to another the word of knowledge by the same Spirit; to another faith by the same Spirit; to another the gifts of healing by the same Spirit; to another the working of miracles; to another prophecy; to another discerning of spirits; to another divers kinds of tongues; to another the interpretation of tongues: But all these worketh that one and the selfsame Spirit, dividing to every man severally as He will" (1 Corinthians 12:4–11).

We hold all of these to be gifts which are freely bestowed by the Heavenly Father upon His children, to be used and freely exercised in the congregation by both male and female members, that the Body of believers may be strengthened, encouraged and edified thereby. "If ye then, being evil, know how to give good gifts unto your children, how much more shall your Father which is in Heaven give good things to them that ask Him?" (Matthew 7:11.) (See also Joel 2:28,29; Acts 2:17,18.)

10. Fruits of the Spirit

We believe that Christians who are filled with the Holy Ghost should manifest the fruits of the Spirit as detailed in Scripture: love, joy, peace, longsuffering, gentleness, goodness, faith, meekness and temperance. (See Galatians 5:22,23; Ephesians 5:9; James 3:17,18.)

11. Angels

We believe that God created an innumerable company of sinless spiritual beings known as angels (a word which literally means "messengers"). Angels are powerful immortal beings whom the Lord has assigned to watch over Man, es-

pecially to protect and to minister to God's people. "Are they not all ministering spirits, sent forth to minister for them who shall be heirs of Salvation?"
(Hebrews 1:14). Although angels are usually invisible, they can materialize and
appear in human form and even walk amongst men without our being aware of
it, which is why God's Word tells us, "Be not forgetful to entertain strangers—,
for thereby some have entertained angels unawares" (Hebrews 13:2). (See also
Psalm 34:7; 91:11,12; 2 Kings 6:15–18; Genesis 19:1–2; Judges 6:11–22; 13:2–21.)

12. Spirits of Departed Saints

We believe that in addition to angelic ministering spirits, God on occasion
also uses the spirits of departed saints to minister and deliver messages to His
people. Scriptural evidence of this is found in the account of the spirits of the
departed prophets, Moses and Elijah, appearing and conferring with Jesus on the
Mount of Transfiguration; the appearance of the departed prophet Samuel's spirit to King Saul; and Saint John's account in the Book of Revelation of his conversation with a Heavenly messenger sent by God to reveal to him mysteries of
the future: "And when I had heard and seen these things, I fell down to worship
before the feet of the angel which shewed me these things. Then saith he unto
me, 'See thou do it not: for I am thy fellow servant, and of thy brethren the
prophets, and of them which keep the sayings of this book: worship God'"
(Revelation 22:8,9). (See also Luke 9:28–33; 1 Samuel 28:13–20; Revelation
19:10; Hebrews 12:1,22–24.)

13. Satan and His Demons

We believe that one of the angels, "Lucifer, son of the morning" (Isaiah
14:12), who was the mightiest of the archangels, through pride, jealousy and
ambition, sinned and fell, and thereby became Satan [the Devil], the infernal foe
of all righteousness. A great company of angels followed him in his immoral
fall, and thus became demons, evil spirits which are presently active as his
agents and associates in the execution of his malignant and God-defying purposes. We believe that Satan is the original perpetrator of sin, and that he,
through subtlety, tempted and led our first parents, Adam and Eve, into trans-
gression and their fall from their sinless state; thereby subjecting them and
their posterity to his own power, which can only be broken and defeated by the
power of God. Satan's evil spirits are now in possession of many, and are largely
responsible for the rampant rage of crime and wickedness presently flooding the
world.

We hold Satan to be the open and avowed enemy of God and Man, who, as a
usurper, now rules as the unholy "god of this world" (2 Corinthians 4:4). He
will be absolutely defeated at the Second Coming of Christ in the Battle of
Armageddon, at which time he will be bound and cast into the Bottomless Pit
for a thousand years, after which he will be loosed "for a little season" to again
"deceive the nations" (Revelation 20:1–3,8). He will afterwards be "cast into
the Lake of Fire where he shall be tormented day and night forever and ever
[through ages of the ages]" (Revelation 20:1–3,10). (See also Isaiah 14:12–15; 1
Peter 5:8; Revelation 12:7–9.)

14. Spiritual Warfare

We believe that we are engaged in a relentless spiritual warfare; that as we strive to obey God's commands and preach the glorious Gospel of Jesus Christ to all whom we can, to "open their eyes, and to turn them from darkness to light, and from the power of Satan unto God" (Acts 26:18), that our adversary, the Devil, does all that he possibly can to try to thwart our efforts. Thus we are in the midst of a great war in which God's Heavenly forces are aiding, supporting and encouraging our efforts, and Satan and his demons are struggling to hinder and halt us. "For we wrestle [contend] not against flesh and blood, but against principalities, against powers, against the rulers of the darkness of this world, against spiritual wickedness in high places" (Ephesians 6:12).

Soldiers in the Lord's Army must therefore "put on the whole armour of God" (Ephesians 6:11), and learn to skillfully wield the powerful spiritual weapons which God has entrusted us with, particularly the "Sword of the Spirit, which is the Word of God" (Ephesians 6:17); for "the Word of God is quick [alive], and powerful, and sharper than any two-edged sword" (Hebrews 4:12). "For though we walk in the flesh, we do not war after the flesh: For the weapons of our warfare are not carnal [physical], but mighty through God, to the pulling down of strongholds" (2 Corinthians 10:3,4). No matter how much trouble Satan and his demonic minions may cause us, we are confident of victory, because God's Word has promised us, "Greater is He [Jesus] that is in you than he [the Devil] that is in the world" (1 John 4:4).

15. Prayer

We believe that prayer is the vital communication between every child of God and his or her Heavenly Father. Far from merely being a religious ritual or spiritual exercise, prayer is the means by which we enjoy sweet, intimate personal communion with the Lord. By prayer, we declare our love for God, and our dependence on Him and our submission to Him, and our desire to cooperate with Him in the fulfillment of His purpose. All those in our fellowships are encouraged to take time for personal private prayer daily, as well as to join the other members of their community in united prayer. In His Word, God promises to hear prayer and bless those who diligently seek Him, thus "men ought always to pray" (Luke 18:1). (See also Jeremiah 33:3; 1 Thessalonians 5:17; Hebrews 11:6; James 5:16; 1 Samuel 12:23; 1 Chronicles 16:11; Ephesians 6:18.)

16. Divine Healing

We believe that healing diseased and afflicted bodies was a major part of our Lord's ministry while He personally ministered on Earth, and that "Jesus Christ is the same, yesterday, today and forever" (Hebrews 13:8); that He still desires to restore health to the afflicted who come to Him in faith. Through Christ's suffering and atoning sacrifice on the Cross, God has made provision not only for the salvation of the soul of Man, but also for the healing of his physical infirmities, for "with His stripes [wounds] we are healed" (Isaiah 53:5). Divine healing is a privilege available to all who believe.

We do not consider a person's faith for healing as a test of fellowship or spirituality or a requirement for fellowship, but as a personal matter between the individual and God. We consider the Scriptural provision for healing a great blessing for those who can exercise the faith to partake of it, but in no wise condemn or hinder those who seek after medical alternatives for their afflictions. Regarding any such personal issues, our prescribed Scriptural outlook is, "According to your faith be it unto you" (Matthew 9:29). (See also Matthew 4:23,24; 10:1; Mark 16:17,18; 1 Peter 2:24; Matthew 8:16–17; Psalm 103:3.)

17. Fellowship of Believers

We believe that great spiritual benefit is to be derived from fellowshipping with other like-minded believers. Therefore, members of our communities are encouraged to not only take time for private prayer, Scripture reading and personal devotions, but for united prayer, united readings of God's Word, as well as united devotions and fellowship meetings, preferably on a daily basis.

Scripture exhorts us to "not forsake the assembling of yourselves together" (Hebrews 10:25), thus we endeavor to follow the example of the Early Church, whose members "continued steadfastly in the Apostles' doctrine and fellowship, and in breaking of bread, and in prayers" (Acts 2:42). Such times of united fellowship are not a drudgery or burden; they are enjoyable occasions in which we come together with the Lord for a time of spiritual refreshment, a time in which those participating are strengthened, encouraged, inspired, edified, instructed and commissioned by the Lord. "For where two or three are gathered together in My Name, there am I in the midst of them" (Matthew 18:20). And "if we walk in the light as He is in the light, we have fellowship one with another" (1 John 1:7). (See also Hebrews 10:25; Psalm 133:1–3.)

18. The Lord's Supper, or Communion

We believe that the Lord's Supper was instituted by Christ as a means for us to commemorate His death on the Cross for our sins, and that partaking of its elements is a profession of the believer's faith. The Supper consists of bread which is broken, representing how Jesus' body was broken for the healing of our bodies; and wine, which represents how Christ's Blood was shed for the remission of our sins. Scripture enjoins believers to periodically partake of the Lord's Supper, until Christ's Return, therefore it is the privilege of all who have spiritual union with Him to commemorate His sacrifice on Calvary "till He come" (1 Corinthians 11:26). Partaking of the Lord's Supper in faith, recognizing that His body was broken for our healing, can also be efficacious in the healing of the body, for "with His stripes we are healed" (Isaiah 53:5). (See also Matthew 26:26–28; John 6:51; 1 Corinthians 11:23–30.)

19. The Church

We believe that the Church is the Body of Christ, and not merely an ecclesiastical institution or organization; and certainly not a mere religious edifice or place of worship, as many presume, for "the Most High dwelleth not in temples made with hands" (Acts 7:48), and "God is a Spirit, and they that worship Him must worship Him in spirit and in truth" (John 4:24). We believe the Church is a spiritual entity composed of all born-again persons, irrespective of their affiliation with Christian organizations or denominations. (See Ephesians 1:22,23; 2:19–22; 1 Corinthians 12:12–14.)

20. The Great Commission

We believe the Great Commission which our Lord has given to His Church is to evangelize the world, to "go ye into all the world and preach the Gospel to every creature" (Mark 16:15). It is our conviction that this is the great mission of the Church and the explicit message of our Lord Jesus Christ to those whom He has saved; in fact, it was His final injunction to His followers before His ascension. We believe that this should be the born-again believer's primary purpose in life; to make Christ's love known to the whole world, and to seek to win others into God's Heavenly Kingdom. Whether or not the believer has received a formal ordination into the Gospel ministry from a denomination or institution is irrelevant, for we believe all Christians are ordained by God to preach His Gospel and win others to Christ, thereby bearing everlasting fruit for His Kingdom. "Ye have not chosen Me, but I have chosen you and ordained you, that ye should go and bring forth fruit" (John 15:16). (See also Matthew 28:19,20; Acts 1:8; 2 Timothy 4:2; 1 Peter 3:15; Proverbs 14:25; Acts 26:18; 1 Corinthians 9:16.)

21. Consecration

We believe that the Christian's life should be a life that is consecrated to the Lord, that is, a life which is utterly given and devoted to Him; not merely to do things for Him, nor to become something great in our own eyes, or in the eyes of others, but to "present our bodies a living sacrifice, wholly acceptable unto God, which is our reasonable service" (Romans 12:1), so that He may work through us and in us, "both to will and to do of His good pleasure" (Philippians 2:13). We consecrate ourselves to the Lord because we love Him because He first loved us, and we delight to belong to Him. (See Galatians 2:20; 1 John 4:19; Psalm 40:8.)

Knowing that Jesus has bought and purchased us with His Own blood, we recognize that our lives are no longer our own, but His. Therefore, we believe that we should "no longer live the rest of our time in the flesh to the lusts of men, but to the will of God" (1 Peter 4:2). Because our bodies belong to the Lord, and are the temples in which His Holy Spirit dwells, we do not believe in abusing them with drugs, alcohol, tobacco or other harmful and unnatural substances. "Know ye not that ye are the temple of God, and that the Spirit of God dwelleth in you? If any man defile the temple of God, him shall God destroy; for the temple of God is holy, which temple ye are. For ye are bought with a price: Therefore glorify God in your body, and in your spirit, which are God's" (1 Corinthians 3:16,17; 6:20).

We also believe that the life of the consecrated Christian should be a visible sample of the Lord's nature, "that the life of Jesus might be made manifest in our body" (2 Corinthians 4:10). Our Lord has enjoined us to "let your light so shine before men, that they may see your good works, and glorify your Father which is in Heaven" (Matthew 5:16). Thus, we consider that the degree to which a believer's conduct and behavior outwardly reflect the life and love of Christ to others, is a significant indicator of his or her inward consecration to God. (See Philippians 2:15; 1 Peter 2:12; 1 John 3:18.)

22. Separation from the World

We believe that the consecrated Christian is called by God to "be not conformed to this world, but be ye transformed, by the renewing of your mind" (Romans 12:2). We also adhere to the Scriptural admonition to "love not the world, neither the things that are in the world. If any man love the world, the love of the Father is not in him. For all that is in the world: the lust of the flesh and the lust of the eyes, and the pride of life, is not of the Father, but is of the world" (1 John 2:15,16). We take this to mean that the believer should not only avoid the unChristian pursuits and practices of the world, but that we should avoid conformity to worldly attitudes and ways of thinking as well. "Blessed is the man that walketh not in the counsel of the ungodly, nor standeth in the way of sinners, nor sitteth in the seat of the scornful" (Psalm 1:1).

However, while we believe that Scripture bids God's people to "come out from among them [unbelievers] and be ye separate" (2 Corinthians 6:17), we do not feel that this separation of the believer should be dictated by the sanctimonious or legalistic mores and morals of Man, but should rather be according to Biblical precedents and the leadings of the Holy Spirit, and according to the needs of those around us. When Jesus walked the earth, He freely ministered and reached out to those who were ostracized from the religious community of His day—a course of action which brought upon Him the contempt and condemnation of His selfrighteous pharisaical enemies, who derided Him for being "a friend of publicans and sinners" (Matthew 9:10–14; 11:19). Although we are "not of the world" (John 17:16), we are nevertheless in the world, where we should endeavor to live a godly life that reaches out to others, and follows the footsteps of Him Who came to this world to "seek and to save that which was lost" (Luke 19:10). (See also Ephesians 5:11,12; James 4:4; 2 Corinthians 6:14–17.)

23. Persecution for Righteousness' Sake

We believe that Christians who actively witness and live for Jesus Christ will receive persecution. Scripture clearly states that "all that will live godly in Christ Jesus shall suffer persecution" (2 Timothy 3:12). Jesus virtually promised that all those who fully commit themselves to Him will be persecuted: "There is no man that hath left house, or brethren, or sisters, or father, or mother, or wife, or children, or lands, for My sake, and the Gospel's, but he shall receive an hundredfold now in this time . . . with persecutions; and in the world to come, eternal life" (Mark 10:29,30).

Although we strive to obey the Scriptural admonitions, "if it be possible, as much as lieth in you, live peaceably with all men" (Romans 12:18), and "agree with thine adversary quickly, whiles thou art in the way with him; lest at any time the adversary deliver thee to the judge, and the judge deliver thee to the officer, and thou be cast into prison" (Matthew 5:25). We realize that it is inevitable that some of those who reject the Lord's message which we carry will likewise reject the messengers who endeavor to bring it to them. Knowing that the perfect and sinless Son of God was maligned, rejected, despised, and violently persecuted and crucified by a world that refused His truth and His love, we most soberly take to heart His warnings that "the disciple is not above his Master, nor the servant above his Lord. If they have called the Master of the house Beelzebub [the Devil], how much more shall they call them of His household?" (Matthew 10:24,25). "If the world hate you, ye know that it hated Me before it hated you. If ye were of the world, the world would love his own: But because ye are not of the world, but I have chosen you out of the world, therefore the world hateth you. The servant is not greater than his Lord. If they have persecuted Me, they will also persecute you. . . . But all these things will they do unto you for My Name's sake because they know not Him that sent Me" (John 15:18–21).

We know that "all things work together for good to them that love God" (Romans 8:28), including persecution. It is often a "blessing in disguise" which God uses for our benefit, to "try and test us" (1 Peter 4:12–14; Daniel 11:3–5); to disperse us into other areas that need our message, "When they persecute you in this city, flee ye into another" (Matthew 10:23; Acts 8:1); and to stir up interest in us and our message, "as concerning this sect, we know that everywhere it is spoken against" (Acts 28:22; Psalm 76:10). We therefore take heart from Jesus' words, "Blessed are ye when men shall revile you and persecute you, and shall say all manner of evil against you falsely, for My sake. Rejoice and be exceeding glad: for great is your reward in Heaven; for so persecuted they the prophets which were before you" (Matthew 5:11,12). (See also Philippians 1:29; Luke 6:26; John 16:1,2; Acts 7:51,52.)

24. Discipleship

We believe that it is a high privilege for a believer to affirmatively respond to Christ's challenge to follow Him as a full-time disciple. We also believe that Jesus' call to such full-time service remains essentially unchanged from that which He issued to the fishermen on the shores of Galilee long ago, "Follow Me, and, I will make you fishers of men" (Matthew 4:19). As was the case with the first Apostles and disciples, so we believe it is today; that the Lord has called us to wholly commit ourselves to Him, to follow His teachings and His example, fully devoting our lives to Him out of love and gratitude for His sacrifice for us. (See John 12:26; 13:15.)

It is our conviction from Holy Scripture that such discipleship entails:

a) Utter devotion and dedication to Jesus Christ, not merely "in word; neither in tongue; but in deed and in truth" (1 John 3:18). Discipleship requires laying aside one's own personal will and wishes in order to embrace God's divine will as revealed in His written Word. "If any man will come after Me, let him deny himself, and take up his cross daily, and follow Me. For whosoever will save his life shall lose it: But whosoever will lose his life for My sake, the same shall save it" (Luke 9:23,24).

On the one hand, the price to be paid in terms of self-sacrifice is so dear that we urge anyone who would consider heeding God's call to discipleship to most solemnly "count the cost" before endeavoring to embark on such a path. On the other hand, when we "consider Him that endured such contradiction of sinners against Himself" (Hebrews 12:3), and realize the immeasurable sacrifice and suffering that Christ endured to bring us Salvation, how can we give Him less than our all? (See Luke 14:25–33; Philippians 3:7,8.)

b) A commitment to win others to Christ ["bear fruit"], and to teach and train others to follow Jesus as His disciples. "Herein is My Father glorified, that ye bear much fruit; so shall ye be My disciples" (John 15:8). "Go ye therefore, and teach all nations . . . teaching them to observe all things, whatsoever I have commanded you" (Matthew 28:19,20).

c) A renouncement and forsaking of the vain pursuit of material wealth, as well as all other worldly and materialistic ambitions and endeavors. "No man that warreth, entangleth himself with the affairs of this life; that he may please Him who hath chosen him to be a soldier" (2 Timothy 2:4). The disciple is exhorted to "set your affection on things above, not on things on the Earth" (Colossians 3:2). Christ plainly set forth the rigorous terms of discipleship when He said, "So likewise, whosoever he be of you that forsaketh not all that he hath, he cannot be My disciple" (Luke 14:33). (See also Matthew 6:19–34; Mark 10:21; Hebrews 11:13.)

d) Making God's revealed will absolutely paramount in one's life, even when compliance with Scriptural injunction may conflict with the desires and designs of family, friends and loved ones. "If any man come to Me, and hate not his father, and mother, and wife, and children, and brethren, and sisters, yea, and his own life also, he cannot be My disciple" (Luke 14:26). [The usage of the word hate here is understood to mean "in the sense of indifference to or relative disregard for in comparison with one's attitude towards God.—The Amplified Bible, Zondervan.] (See also Matthew 10:34–38; 12:48–50; Luke 9:59–62.)

(The dictionary definition of "disciple" is "one who believes and follows the teachings of a master, and assists in the spreading of such teachings." Although it seems evident from the Gospel account that the ideal of discipleship is the course taken by the twelve Apostles who renounced all worldly pursuits for the privilege of being able to follow and live with the Master full-time, we acknowledge that there are varying degrees and levels of "following the teachings." We feel called to follow what we consider the ideal pattern of discipleship, that of the original Twelve. However, we recognize that pursuing this course is not possible for everyone. Scripture shows that besides the Twelve, there were others who obviously did not follow and live with Jesus full-time, yet who were still considered disciples; such as Joseph of Arimathaea, "being a disciple of Jesus, howbeit secretly, for fear of the Jews" [John 19:38]. We believe that the degree to which one commits his or her life to Christ is a matter of personal faith and conviction.)

25. Cooperative Communal Living

We believe that the New Testament's account of the pristine lifestyle of the Early Church offers us not only an historical narrative, but an exemplary pattern and model which God intended succeeding generations of believers to follow. The first Church's unselfish, cooperative lifestyle, in which "all that believed were together, and had all things in common" (Acts 2:44), not only proved to be exceptionally beneficial for the fledgling movement in terms of practical and economic concerns, but even more importantly, the close fellowship and spiritual unity fostered by such a lifestyle provided the early disciples with a needed spiritual haven of respite from the interminable hostilities of their religious enemies and the glaring idolatry of pagan Rome. Likewise, we today have found both the practical and spiritual benefits of cooperative communal living to be extremely advantageous in helping us achieve our goal of reaching all whom we can with the Gospel of Christ. (See also Mark 10:29,30; Acts 2:44,45; 4:34,35; Psalm 133:1.)

26. Children and Their Care

We believe that children are a wonderful gift of God with which He blesses and entrusts us, for "Lo, children are an heritage from the Lord; and the fruit of the womb is His reward" (Psalm 127:3). Therefore, it is our conviction that the physical, emotional, psychological and spiritual needs of children should be amply and competently met. We consider the care of the little ones God has given us to be a primary responsibility and a fundamental component of our daily lives and service to God, for which reason all members of our communities are encouraged to do their utmost to ensure that their children are reared in as healthy, loving, secure and godly an environment as is possible.

We believe that the training children receive in their early formative years will guide them all through life; that if we "train up a child in the way he should go, when he is old, he will not depart from it" (Proverbs 22:6). The Apostle, Saint John, expressed perfectly the sentiments every Christian parent should have in this regard: "I have no greater joy than to hear that my children walk in truth" (3 John 4). For this reason we strive to impart to our children a deep appreciation, respect and love for God and His Word, and the sacred principles contained therein, "bringing them up in the nurture and admonition of the Lord" (Ephesians 6:4). (See also Psalm 127:3–5; Ephesians 6:4; 2 Timothy 3:15; Proverbs 22:6; Deuteronomy 6:6,7; Psalm 34:11; 1 Samuel 1:28.)

27. The Sanctity of Life

We believe that human life is sacred, and it is the right of each person to be treated as an individual created in the image of God. Scripture makes it clear that God esteems the unborn as a person with an identity, not merely as a mass of fetal tissue. The Lord said to the prophet Jeremiah, "Before I formed thee in the belly, I knew thee; and before thou comest forth out of the womb, I sanctified thee, and I ordained thee a prophet unto the nations" (Jeremiah 1:5). The Psalmist David prayed, "My substance was not hid from Thee when I was made in secret, and curiously wrought in the lowest parts of the earth. Thine eyes did see my substance, yet being unperfect [not fully formed]; and in Thy book all my members [body parts] were written, which in continuance were fashioned, when as yet there was none of them" (Psalm 139:15,16). Modern fetology makes it undeniably evident that human life begins at conception, which means that the developing child deserves all the protection and safeguards that any of us enjoy. For all of these reasons, we are diametrically opposed to abortion. (See Genesis 1:27; 2:7; Psalm 139:14–16; Jeremiah 2:34,35; Acts 7:19.)

28. Civil Government and Religious Liberty

Although we believe that we are "strangers and pilgrims on the Earth" (Hebrews 11: 13), we also accept the Scripture's teaching that civil government is of divine appointment, for the interest and good order of human society. "Submit yourselves to every ordinance of Man for the Lord's sake. Let every soul be subject unto the higher powers. For there is no power but of God: the powers that be are ordained of God" (1 Peter 2:13; Romans 1:1).

Therefore, magistrates are to be prayed for, and the laws and ordinances of the land are to be conscientiously honored and obeyed; the only exception to this being in matters of faith, where obedience to a law of Man would mean disobedience to the Law of God. Our precedent for this position is taken from the Book of Acts, when the Apostles Peter and John were forbidden by the Sanhedrin to witness their faith in Jesus to others. (The Sanhedrin was the powerful Jewish tribunal which exercised both civil and criminal jurisdiction throughout the district of Judea from the time of Christ until the destruction of Jerusalem in 70 A.D.) "And they [the Sanhedrin] commanded them [Peter and John] not to speak at all nor teach in the Name of Jesus. But Peter and John answered and said unto them, 'Whether it be right in the sight of God to hearken unto you more than unto God, judge ye. For we cannot but speak the things which we have seen and heard'" (Acts 4:18–20).

Jesus Christ is King of kings and Lord of lords; and in any such cases where the laws or ordinances of Man would violate our faith or duty to witness our faith to others, our stance is the same as the Apostles, that "we ought to obey God rather than men" (Acts 5:29). (See also Romans 12:18; 13:1–7; 1 Peter 2:17; Matthew 22:21; 23:10; Proverbs 8:15,16; Revelation 19:16.)

29. Eschatological or Prophetic Considerations

(While we hold the following doctrines and teachings to be true and sound, they differ from the aforementioned beliefs in that they are not addressing dogma based on evident and clear-cut statements by our Lord, but are dealing with the rather more mysterious subject of Biblical prophecies, which, for the most part, are yet to be fulfilled. Therefore, as we recognize that these eschatological positions are considerably more open to interpretation than the previous statements, we do not call for the same degree of adherence to these teachings as to the more evident tenets covered earlier.)

We believe that we are now living in the time period known in Scripture as the "Last Days" or the "Time of the End", that is, the era which immediately precedes the Second Coming of Jesus Christ, when "the kingdoms of this world are [to] become the Kingdom of our Lord, and of His Christ; and He shall reign forever and ever" (Revelation 11:15). In brief, a careful analysis of Biblical prophecy has led us to embrace the following beliefs:

a) Prophecy Fulfilled. Many Biblical prophecies and "signs of the times" that specifically predict world conditions prior to Christ's Second Coming have unerringly been fulfilled within our generation, confirming that we are indeed living in the Last Days. "As it was in the days of Noah, so shall also the coming of the Son of Man be" (Matthew 24:37), for "evil men and seducers shall wax [grow] worse and worse, deceiving and being deceived" (2 Timothy 3:13). (See also Matthew 16:3; Matthew 24; 2 Timothy 3:1–.7.)

b) The Antichrist. Seven years before Jesus' Return, a powerful world leader known in Scripture as the "Beast", "Man of Sin", "Son of Perdition" or "Antichrist" will surreptitiously rise to power, gaining sufficient influence to "confirm a covenant" [peace treaty] (Daniel 9:27) with the primary antagonists in the Mideast, focusing on the centre of the crisis, Jerusalem. The ratification of this covenant will in all likelihood result in the internationalization of the city, with the Jews gaining free access to the Temple Mount, where they will restore their temple and resume animal sacrifices for the first time in nearly two millenniums. (See 1 John 2:18; 2 Thessalonians 2:14,9; Revelation 13:4,7.)

c) Great Tribulation. Three-and-a-half years after this peace initiative, the Satan-possessed Antichrist will break the covenant, abolish Jewish temple worship, declare that he alone is God, and demand all the world's veneration and worship. At this time he will institute a universal credit system, whereby none will be legally permitted to buy or sell essential goods, except those who bear this demagogue's mark or number, the "Mark of the Beast", in their right hand or forehead. These events will plunge the entire world into an unprecedented time of social chaos and religious persecution known in the Bible as the "Great Tribulation" (Matthew 24:21). Despite all the demonic fury that the oppressive Antichrist regime will muster against the Church, countless Christians will survive the Beast's onslaughts, boldly preaching the Gospel of Salvation until the Lord's Return. (See Daniel 9:27; 11:31; 2 Thessalonians 2:4; Matthew 24:15,21; Revelation 11:3–.6; 13:7; 12:11.)

d) The Second Coming of Christ. The three-and-a half-year period of Great Tribulation will be climaxed by the return of Jesus Christ to the Earth; "Immediately after the Tribulation of those days . . . shall appear the sign of the Son of Man in heaven; and then shall all the tribes of the Earth mourn, and they shall see the Son of Man coming in the clouds of heaven with power and great glory" (Matthew 24:29,30). All of the born-again believers will then be supernaturally delivered from their cruel persecutors by means of the Rapture, the miraculous event whereby their bodies will be gloriously translated and made like Jesus' Own resurrection body, as they rise to meet the Lord in the air. At this time, the deceased saved of all ages, whose spirits have been with the Lord in Heaven, will be reunited with their new glorified bodies which will be resurrected from their graves. "For the Lord Himself shall descend from Heaven with a shout, with the voice of the archangel, and with the trump of God: and the dead in Christ shall rise first: Then we which are alive and remain shall be caught up together with them in the clouds, to meet the Lord in the air: and so shall we ever be with the Lord" (1 Thessalonians 4:16,17). (See also Matthew 24:29,30; Revelation 1:7; 1 Corinthians 15:51,52; Philippians 3:20,21.)

e) The Marriage Supper, the Wrath of God, and the Battle of Armageddon. Following their Rapture and Resurrection, the saved will partake of the glorious "Marriage Supper of the Lamb" in Heaven, and appear before the Judgment Seat of Christ for rewards of service rendered on Earth. Meanwhile, God's angels of judgment will pour out His plagues and wrath upon the Antichrist and his followers, culminating in the Battle of Armageddon, when Jesus and the hosts of Heaven return to utterly defeat and destroy the Satanic Antichrist and his evil hordes. (See Revelation 7:9,13,17; chapter 19; 2 Corinthians 5:10; Daniel 12:2,3; Revelation 14:9,10; 16:1–21.)

f) Christ's Millennial Reign. Jesus Christ and His victorious Heavenly forces will then occupy and assume absolute control of the entire world, ruling and reigning over the survivors of Armageddon, and establishing the, Kingdom of God on Earth. Justice, equity and true righteousness will at last prevail; Satan will be imprisoned in the Bottomless Pit, all of Man's cruel and senseless wars will cease, and the Earth will be restored to its original paradisiacal state. This period will last for one thousand years, thus it is known as The Millennium. (See Daniel 2:44; Revelation 20:1–4,5; 5:10; Isaiah 2:2–4; 11:6–9; Psalm 46:9; Jeremiah 31:34.)

g) The Battle of Gog and Magog / The New Heavens and the New Earth. After the thousand years of the Millennial era have expired, Satan will be released from his prison for "a little season" (Revelation 20:3,7), to deceive those survivors of Armageddon who have refused to willingly submit to the Lordship of Christ and His reign of righteousness. These unregenerate rebels will again follow Satan, uniting in a futile insurrection which will culminate in the cataclysmic "Battle of Gog and Magog", in which God sends a supernatural flood of fire upon them. So vehement will be this conflagration, that the entire surface of the Earth will be melted, the seas will be vaporized and the atmospheric heavens will vanish. "The heavens shall pass away with a great noise, and the elements shall melt with fervent heat, the Earth also and the works that are therein shall be burned up" (2 Peter 3:10). God will then recreate the purged surface of the planet into a beautiful New Earth, with fresh new unpolluted atmospheric heavens. (See Revelation 20:79; 2 Peter 3:10–13; Isaiah 40:4.)

h) The White Throne Judgment. The unsaved dead of all ages will then be raised to appear before God at the awesome "Great White Throne Judgment", which is thus described in the Book of Revelation; "And I saw a great White Throne, and Him that sat on it, from whose face the Earth and the heaven fled away; and there was found no place for them. And I saw the dead, small and great, stand before God; and the books were opened: and another book was opened, which is the Book of Life: and the dead were judged out of those things which were written in the books, according to their works. And whosoever was not found written in the Book of Life was cast into the Lake of Fire" (Revelation 20:11,12,15).

i) New Jerusalem. God's marvelous Heavenly City, New Jerusalem, will then descend like a stupendous jewel from above to crown the paradisiacal New Earth. The Heavenly City is the glorious eternal Heavenly home for all of God's saved Children, the hope of all ages, where at last, "the tabernacle of God is with men, and He will dwell with them, and they shall be His people, and God Himself shall be with them, and be their God. And God shall wipe away all tears from their eyes; and there shall be no more death, neither sorrow, nor crying, neither shall there be any more pain: for the former things are passed away" (Revelation 21:3,4). (See also the remaining verses of Revelation chapters 21 and 22.)

30. Conclusion

We urge the people of God of all denominations and persuasions to stand by the Scriptural truths we hold in common, and to "earnestly contend for the faith" (Jude 3). May God bless you with His love! In Jesus' Name, amen.

Appendix B
Family Musical Literature

"Three Cheers for the Red, White, and Blue"

Turned my eyes westward toward the heavens.
Saw an eagle falling from the sky.
And all the eggs that she was droppin'
Were all in vain because there's no stoppin'

(Chorus)
Three cheers for the red, white and blue.
All your sins are coming right back down on you.
Three cheers for the red, white and blue.
You turned your back on God, now He's turned His back on you.

Take a good whiff of the air.
It's really something I do declare.
Your rivers and your streams are so full of pollution.
And in your streets I hear the cry of revolution.

(Chorus)

He brought them and He blessed them
To eat the good of the land.
But they've turned their eyes away from the Son of Man.

So here stand the Children of God
Shoutin' out their warning.
Turn away from your wickedness
'Cause you won't see rain until it starts pouring.

Three cheers for the red, white and blue.
All your sins are coming right back down on you.
Three cheers for the red, white and blue.
You turned your back on God, now He's turned His back on you.

"You Gotta Be a Baby"

Except a man be born again, he cannot enter into the Kingdom of Heaven.
Jesus said: Except a man be born again, he cannot enter into the Kingdom
of Heaven.
(Chorus)

You gotta be a baby, you gotta be a baby. You gotta be a baby to got to Heaven.
You gotta be a baby, you gotta be a baby. You gotta be a baby to got to Heaven.

As newborn babes desire the sincere milk of the Word that ye may grow
thereby.
As newborn babes desire the sincere milk of the Word that ye may grow
thereby.

(Chorus)

"Mountain Children"

Peaceful night while the moon is bright, love is in their hearts.
Breeze is blowing by the trees so high, singing to their God.

(Chorus)
Mountain children, yes we're mountain children. I will bless my colony.
Mountain children, mountain children Gypsies of the Lord.

Campfire glows while around they go, dance before their king.
Dancers shake their timbrels while the men they sing praises to their God.

(Chorus)

Morning comes, on the road again, happy caravan.
To another mountain, to another land, bringing peace to man.

(Chorus)

Abrahim, watch your children play, in New Jerusalem.
Babies born anew they claim the promise to manifest in them.

Mountain children, yes we're mountain children. I will bless my colony.
Mountain children, mountain children Gypsies of the Lord.

"Cry of Revolution"

There's a cry of Revolution in my country. There's a cry of hatred of idolatry.
And the cry comes from the hungry, from people just like
you, you and me, you and me, you and me.

All we like sheep have gone astray. We have turned everyone to his own way.
And the Lord hath laid on Him the iniquity of our sin, and set us free,
set us free, set us free.

Because they have no other way to follow, they'll turn to their weapons of war.
They'll burn and take our land, and suffer us to stand all alone, all alone,
all alone.

The Revolution for Jesus for love, the Revolution for Jesus for love.
The revolution to set us free, the Revolution for eternity,
The Revolution for Jesus, for me.
The Revolution for Jesus, for me.

"All I Want to Do Is Serve Him"

One day I took, I took an honest look. I tried everything,
I played every game in the book;
And I saw that there was nothing in this World to live for anymore.
Then one day, one day I heard about a certain Man who could work things out.
So I came to Jesus, you know He came in and He showed me the way.

Now all I want to do is serve Him.
Now all I want to do is serve the King.
That others may know Him and the power of His Love.

You know, the Kingdom of Heaven is like unto a merchant man seeking
    goodly pearls.
And when he hath found one pearl of a great price, you know he went and sold
    all that he had and he bought it.

He said, If any man, if any man will come after Me, let him, let him deny himself and take up his cross daily and let him follow, let him follow after Me.

You know He'd rather you, He'd rather you be hot or cold, (not lukewarm).
So yield to Him and you will be so bold, that you will win souls for the
    Kingdom of God's Son.

And all you'll want to do is serve Him.
And all you'll want to do is serve the King.
That others may know Him and the power of His Love.

"I Can Hardly Wait for the Day"

As I wait patiently for Him, His grace is poured out upon me.
And though you may say I'm bound by these walls, in my heart I'm free.
And I'll stay faithful to Him, no matter what men may do or say.
As I lift up my eyes upward, looking for that perfect day.

I can hardly wait for the day; I know it's not far away.
I can hardly wait for that day; I see Him coming in the clouds, to take me away
from this place.

As I look at my prison walls, they shine like diamonds in the night.
And though in a weak and wasted body, the Lord still fills me with His Might.
He says just a little longer, son, and I'll take you away.

The tears fall, my heart calls unto the Lord my strength.
Oh, my God, I've got the privilege to suffer such a little thing.
He was oppressed and afflicted, as they scorned Him to shame.
Jesus, thank all, my heart calls, unto the Lord my strength
Oh, my God, I've got the privilege to suffer such a little thing.
He was oppressed and afflicted, as they scorned Him to shame.
Jesus, thank You for counting me worthy to suffer for Your Name.

"I See My Lord Come Shining"

They say a man can't be a Christian, they say a man cannot be free.
And so they suffer persecution. Jesus said, they'll do it to you 'cause they
    did it to Me.
But I don't care . . .

(Chorus)
I see my Lord come shining from the West unto the East
Any day now, any way now I shall be relieved.

So they put me in a prison, they told me that I wasn't well.
And all day long I'm in affliction, they keep me locked up in a cell.
But I don't care . . .

(Chorus)

Down the hall there's a man, he's crying out loud. They torture him both day
    and night.
And all day long I hear him screaming out in pain, but he won't deny his Lord,
    Jesus Christ.
He don't care, cause . . .

(Chorus)

"God's Explosions"

That spark of inspiration
That lights that special fuse
Of the bomb of great accomplishment,
Ignites the precious few
Ordained by God's own power
Pent up within their souls
They wait for perfect timing
To really let her blow.
Sometimes they wait a lifetime
Before that fateful hour
To burst in blaze and glory
And light the sky with showers.

They change the course of history
Fulfilling God's own plan
And echo through the ages
To inspire the heart of man.

Change the course of history
Listen to the Lord.
Heavenly explosions
Echo around the world.

The king and psalmist David
Was a ruddy homemade bomb
As he smashed that burly giant,
As he praised the Lord in song.
And Jesus blew the darkness
Back to hell where it came from
And He died to set us free and
Blow us back to Kingdom Come.
And God is still exploding
And His bombs are still around
And like all His kings and prophets
We can't help but make a sound.
We'll blow like Krakatoa
If you try to shut us up
'Cause we're filled with God's hot Spirit
And exploding with His love.

Change the course of history
Listen to the Lord.
Heavenly explosions
Echo around the world.

"Peace in the Midst of a Storm"

When you're crying for all the times you've tried.
And you're tryin' to forget the tears you've cried.
You've seen so much pain and sorrow, you don't know about tomorrow
But you can have peace in the midst of a storm.

(Chorus)
You can have peace in the midst of a storm
You can have hope when you can't go on anymore.
Well, there's love to be found when your whole world's tumbling down
You can find peace in the midst of a storm.

Sometimes I feel like I know you feel, and my heart's reaching out for some
   thing that I know is real.

Then His love comes to me and it helps my mind to be in peace in the midst of a storm.

(Chorus)

"Battle Hymn of the Revolution"
Who will take the stand and heed the call from Heaven Above?
Who will join the band of David's Men, the Army of Love?
Called to live and die for the kingdom as we give our all to the Lord.
Lift up your sword, Look to Heaven's reward!
It's a revolution for Jesus and David our King.

(Chorus)
Loyal and willing, with whole hearts we're giving our lives for the Kingdom of God.
On every shore hear the thunderous roar as the Armies of Jesus march on.

Oh . . .
True to our nation with deep dedication we'll reach all the World with His Love.
Soldiers of the Cross, we will be faithful to His cause.

Who will face the foe and fight to free those caught in his snare?
Who will dare to go armed with faith and love and prayer?
We're the Endtime Army that's conquering hearts and minds and souls for the Lord
Lift up your sword! Look to Heaven's reward. It's a revolution for Jesus and David our King.

(Chorus)

Oh . . .
True to our nation with deep dedication we'll reach all the World with His Love.
Soldiers of the Cross, we will be faithful to His cause.

"Ballad of Aquarius"
From a dry and dusty land came the promise of a Man, who would water us again like a fountain.
In the time that was ordained Heaven opened and it rained, and the Spirit poured a cry of revolution.

(Chorus)
Aquarius, the name of the Shepherd of the Lame, pouring forth his waters like a fountain.

He is David of the End, and the Prophet of the Wind. The Spirit in the Man on the Mountain.

With a cry to get on board it was the prophet of the Lord with a warning to this wicked generation.
Came the warning, of a flood from a garment dipped in blood; it was Noah in the day of preparation.

(Chorus)

Well, take your hand, lift it up to the man who has called us from this system's world of madness.
Only truth can set us free! Jesus gives us liberty and He's watered us with oil and gladness.

(Chorus)

Well, you'd better praise the Lord, 'cause He's spreading forth His Word like a great and mighty wave of an ocean.
And the people that I see are a new and young army and they're spreading forth the fires of devotion.

(Chorus)

Glossary of Family Terms

1036er: From Matthew 10:36; parents or relatives who are negative toward The Family.

Babe: New disciple, normally "Babe status" lasts for the first six months in the movement. Sexual activity is prohibited and substantial study of the Bible and Family literature is required during Babe status. Returning disciples and those with moral or commitment problems can also be placed on Babe status.

Backslider: A person who ceases his or her commitment and leaves The Family.

Betrothal: Family marriage. It is often, but not always, accompanied by legal marriage in the System.

Bible name: New name taken by entering disciple to mark his or her separation from the System. Disciples can change their names at will and often do.

Breaking: Going through a difficult change or personal situation.

CTP: Consider the Poor. These are the various social welfare programs and ministries of The Family.

Catacomber: A secret disciple who must live out in the world until he or she is able to join a community.

Church of Love: Meeting of disciples with converts who are friendly to the movement but do not wish to join as full-time disciples. Meetings are for worship and the study of the Bible and Family literature.

Colony: Used for individual Family homes up to 1978.

Convert: One who accepts the message of salvation and prays to receive Jesus Christ as personal savior. Being a convert does not imply joining or supporting The Family.

DO: Disciples Only. Designation of literature and communities indicating they are restricted to full-time committed disciples.

Date: Time spent alone with someone outside of marriage. Normally implies some type of sexual encounter. However, young people can use the term without sexual connotation, sometimes referring to these meetings as "Word Dates."

ESing: Flirty Fishing while employed by an escort service.

Empty Wind: To clear out a home of all Selah or sensitive material for the purposes of security.

FAF: Family Aid Fund: homes donate 1 percent to a general fund used to aid members in times of distress or emergency.

Fish: A person who is a good potential convert. A person who was Flirty Fished by a member.

FFing: Short for Flirty Fishing.

Flee bag: Bag containing money, documents, and personal items necessary to sustain a disciple on the run from persecution.

Flirty Fishing: Engaging in sexual allure or sexual contact for the purpose of witness or developing support for the community.

Forsake All: Giving up all other allegiance and unneeded personal possessions at the time of joining the community. Also, a collection in every home of any surplus goods to be used by the community.

Get out: Scheduled time of communal recreation. Get Out is done out of doors as weather permits.

Goat: A person who is not a good potential convert.

Going mobile: A single family unit or small group of disciples living on the road for an extensive period of time without a permanent home.

Holy Ghost Sample: Invasion into public space by singing, dancing, and witnessing.

Holy Hole: A person willing to do anything, usually humble tasks, for community life.

HER: Home Emergency Reserves; a supply of cash held by every home to sustain the members in case of emergency, medical needs, or evacuation.

Inspiration: A time of group singing of Family and other Christian songs.

JJT: Jesus Job Time. Daily household duties of community life.

Jesus baby: Children fathered by men outside the community who were FFed.

Job 9:20s: Often humorous term used by the youth for self-justification when confronted with problematic behavior.

Kings: Persons supportive of the movement who provide substantial funds, goods, services, or protection.

Leadership: Disciples who hold positions of authority beyond the local community.

Litnessing: Sharing the message by passing out Family literature.

Make it work: The time couples spend living and working together as a trial period before marriage; usually six months.

Mated: Married in Family tradition. Normally, but not always legally married.

Mother Eve: Father David's first wife.

NWO: Needs Work On. Area of weakness in a disciple's personal life.

OHR: Open Heart Report. Formerly a part of youth training; young people were required to write out their views and personal weakness and read them in public.

On Fire: Particularly zealous or enthusiastic behavior; a positive term.

One Wife: Expression of communal responsibility of child rearing and general communal commitment.

Out of it: Not complying with standards of behavior. Not in tune with Family values. Not interested in or committed to the work of The Family.

Parent Time: Daily scheduled time for parents to be with their own children. This is usually a half hour to an hour each evening.

Personal Time: Weekly time spent by youth or adults with the shepherd to talk about significant life issues.

Pioneer: An area of new work. Also used to describe disciples who go into new areas.

Poison: Food, music, or entertainment that is viewed as unwholesome and not appropriate for Family homes.

Provisioning: Acquiring funds, food, clothing, and other necessities of life through direct appeal to the public.

Purge: Removal of outdated materials and literature no longer consistent with current Family policy or beliefs.

Push: Emphasis on a new concept or a new area of ministry.

RNR: Disbanding of the Children of God organizational structure in 1978. The name "Children of God" was abandoned and new name "Family of Love" was adopted.

Road trip: A time of traveling witness into new areas by a team of disciples.

Roman: A law enforcement officer.

Sample: Example. Used to refer to behavior, attitudes, or accomplishments that can serve as a positive or negative example to other disciples or the outside world.

Selah: Secret; used to refer to literature or locations not open to the public and generally on a need-to-know basis within The Family.

Selah Trash: Trash that must be burned daily for security reasons.

Sharing: A sexual encounter with someone within the community other than the marriage partner.

Sheep: One who is open to a gospel witness or receptive of Family teaching.

Standard: The basic requirements of good disciple life.

Survival: Each home maintains one to two months supply of food, fuel, water, and other necessities for survival in case of disaster, emergency, wars, or persecution.

System: The outside world generally held to be under the influence, if not the control, of Satan.

Team works: Group of elected disciples responsible for leadership and management of a local community.

Trial: A time of testing, personal difficulty, or doubt.

Underground: Keeping identity or location of disciples and Family homes secret.

Victory: In tune with Family values and aspirations.

Word Time: Specified hour of study of the Bible and MO Letters.

World Services: Headquarters for the international movement and home of Maria, Peter Amsterdam, and the highest levels of leadership.

References

Primary Sources

"The Family History." Unpublished.

"The Family of Love—Sin or Salvation?" GP #502R, June 1977.

"Return to Madrid." D.O. #61, Mar. 1978.

The Story of Davidito. 1982. Zurich: World Services.

The Book of Remembrance. Vol. 1. 1983. Zurich: World Services.

The Book of Remembrance. Vol. 2. 1983. Zurich: World Services.

The Book of The Future. 1984. Zurich: World Services.

Daily Bread. Vol. 8. 1984. Zurich: World Services.

"Our Heavenly Home." 1985. Zurich: World Services.

"Liberty or Stumbling Block." 1986. Zurich: World Services.

"Tightening Up Our Family." 1989. Zurich: World Services.

"Position and Policy Statement: Attitudes, Conduct, Current Beliefs and Teachings Regarding Sex." Apr. 1992. Zurich: World Services.

"PEN—Persecution End Time News." Oct. 1993. Zurich: World Services.

"The Ministry of Reconciliation." *New Good News,* no. 653, Oct. 1995. Zurich: World Services.

MO Letters

"The Old Church and the New Church!" ML #A, Aug. 1969.

"Scriptural, Revolutionary Love-Making!" ML #N, Aug. 1969.

"Abrahim The Gypsy King: The True Story of Our Spirit Guide." ML #296, Apr. 1970.

"I Gotta Split!" ML #28, Dec. 1970.

"Love-Making in the Spirit!" ML #N, July 1971.

"A Psalm of David!" ML #152, Jan. 1972.

"The Laws of Moses!" ML #155, Feb. 1972.

"The Great Escape!" ML #160, Apr. 1972.

"A Prophecy Against Our Enemies!" ML #188, Oct. 1972.

"One Wife!" ML #249, Oct. 1972.

"The Birthday Warning!" ML #215, Feb. 1973.

"Revolutionary Sex!" ML #259, Mar. 1973.

"The Goddesses!" ML #224, Apr. 1973.

"Shiners?—or Shamers!" ML #241, June 1973.

"Revolutionary Women." ML #250, June 1973.

"Old Bottles!" ML #242, July 1973.

"State of the World." ML #270, Sept. 1973.

"God's Only Law Is Love!" ML #537, Dec. 1973.

"The Flirty Little Fish." ML #293, Jan. 1974.

"The Law of Love!" ML #302, Mar. 1974.

"Witnessing!" ML #344, May 1975.

"Love vs. Law!" ML #647, July 1977.

"Our Declaration of Love." ML #607, Oct. 1977.

"Is Love Against the Law?" ML #648, Jan. 1978.

"Re-organization Nationalization Revolution." ML #650, Jan. 1978.

"God's Gift Is God's Work—Part 3." ML #756, Aug. 1978.

"Going Underground!" ML #750, Dec. 1978.

"The Devil Hates Sex!—But God Loves It!" ML #999, May 1980.

"Nudes Can Be Beautiful!" ML #1006, Mar. 1981.

"Fellowship Revolution." ML #1001, Apr. 1981.

"Glorify God in the Dance!—Caution & Importance for Your Erotic Videos!"
    ML #1026, July 1981.

"Their Last Resort." ML #1085, Oct. 1981.

"Go East: And Grow up with the Golden Triangle!" ML #1088, Jan. 1982.

"The Seven Fs of FFing." ML #1083, Jan. 1982.

"My Confession—I Was an Alcoholic!" ML #1406, summer 1982.

"Mass Evangelism!" ML #1510, Apr. 1983.

"Teen Terrors!" ML #1512, May 1983.

"I Will Set Up One Shepherd!" ML #1962, Jan. 1984.

"Revolutionary Discipleship!" ML #1965, Feb. 1984.

"Revolution for Jesus!" ML #1963, Mar. 1984.

"Sinless Sex!—God's Sex Position!" ML #1969, Nov. 1984.

"Sex for Babes?" ML #1909, December 1984.

"Interpreting Bible Prophecy! Rightly Dividing the Word of Truth!" ML #2210,
    Aug. 1986.

"The FFing / DFing Revolution—The Book Is the Hook?" ML #2313, Mar.
    1987.

"Moma on the New AIDS Rules!—It's Come to That!" ML #2346, Sept. 1987.

"Inside, Out of Sight! Get Off the Streets!—The No-More Sudden-Discipleship
    Revolution." ML #2385, Dec. 1987.

"The Word, The Word, The Word!" ML #2484, Nov. 1988.

"Flirty Little Teens, Beware!" ML #2590, Oct. 1989.

"In Tune with the Times!" ML # 2590, Oct. 1989.

"Go to the Churches." ML #2867, Nov. 1991.

"Consider the Poor!—Our New Ministry in the U.S. to the Poor!" ML #2755,
    Mar. 1992.

"When Teens Leave The Family!" ML # 2942, Sept. 1994.

"Go Ye Into All The World!" ML #2990, May 1995.

"Go for the Gold!" ML #2990, May 1995.

Secondary Sources

Barkun, Michael. 1994. "Reflections after Waco: Millennialists and the State."
    In *From the Ashes: Making Sense of Waco*, edited by James R. Lewis,
    41–50. Lanham, Md.: Rowman and Littlefield.

Bozman, John. 1998. "Field Notes: The Family / Children of God under the Love Charter." *Nova Religio* 2, no. 1: 126–35.

Bromley, David. 1998. "Listing (in Black and White) Some Observations on (Sociological) Thought Reform." *Nova Religio* 1, no. 1: 250–68.

Bromley, David, and Sydney Newton. 1994. "The Family: History, Organization, and Ideology." In *Sex, Slander, and Salvation: Investigating The Family / Children of God*, edited by James R. Lewis and J. Gordon Melton, 41–46. Stanford, Calif.: Center for Academic Publication.

Davis, Deborah. 1984. *The Children of God: The Inside Story.* Grand Rapids, Mich.: Zondervan Books.

Davis, Rex, and Jamers T. Richardson. 1976. "The Organization and Functioning of the Children of God." *Sociological Analysis* 37: 321–39.

Delgado, Richard. 1977. "Religious Totals: Gentle and Ungentle Persuasion under the First Amendment." *Southern California Law Review* 1, no. 51: 3

———. 1985. "Cults and Conversion: The Case for Informed Consent." In *Cults, Culture, and the Law: Perspectives on New Religious Movements*, edited by Thomas Robbins, William Shepherd, and James McBride, 111–28. Chico, Calif.: Scholars Press.

Enroth, Robert. 1977. *Youth, Brainwashing, and the Extremist Cults.* Grand Rapids, Mich.: Zondervan Publishing House.

———. 1990. "Jesus Movement." In *Dictionary of Christianity in America*, edited by Daniel Reid, 592–93. Downers Grove, Ill.: InterVarsity Press.

Geertz, Clifford. 1973. *The Interpretation of Cultures.* New York: Basic Books.

———. 1983. *Local Knowledge.* New York: Basic Books.

Hopkins, Joseph. 1977. "The Children of God: Disciples of Deception." *Christianity Today* Feb. 18: 18–23.

Hubbard, Jamie. 1998. "Embarrassing Superstition, Doctrine, and the Study of New Religious Movements." *Journal of the American Academy of Religion* 66, no. 1: 59–92.

Lewis, James R., and J. Gordon Melton, eds. 1994. *Sex, Slander, and Salvation: Investigating The Family / Children of God.* Stanford, Calif.: Center for Academic Publication.

Lynch, Zelda. 1990. "Inside the 'Heavenly Elite': The Children of God Today." *Christian Research Journal*, summer: 16–21.

McMannus, Una, and John Cooper. 1980. *Not for a Million Dollars.* Nashville: Impact Books.

Melton, J. Gordon. 1994. "Sexuality and the Maturation of The Family." In *Sex, Slander, and Salvation: Investigating The Family / Children of God*, edited by James R. Lewis and J. Gordon Melton, 71–96. Stanford, Calif.: Center for Academic Publication.

Miller, Timothy. 1998. "Academic Integrity and the Study of New Religious Movements." *Nova Religio* 2, no. 1: 8–15.

Millikan, David. 1994. "The Children of God, Family of Love, The Family." In *Sex, Slander, and Salvation: Investigating The Family / Children of God*, edited by James R. Lewis and J. Gordon Melton, 181–252. Stanford, Calif.: Center for Academic Publication.

Oliver, Moorman, Jr. 1994. "The Inquisition Revisited." In *Sex, Slander, and Salvation: Investigating The Family / Children of God,* edited by James R. Lewis and J. Gordon Melton, 137–52. Stanford, Calif.: Center for Academic Publication.

Palmer, Susan. 1994. "Heaven's Children: The Children of God's Second Generation." In *Sex, Slander, and Salvation: Investigating The Family / Children of God,* edited by James R. Lewis and J. Gordon Melton, 1–26. Stanford, Calif.: Center for Academic Publication.

Patrick, Ted. 1976. *Let Our Children Go.* New York: Dutton.

Richardson, James T. 1993 "A Social Psychological Critique of Brainwashing Claims about Recruitment to New Religions." In *Handbook of Sects and Cults in America,* edited by Jeffrey K. Hadden and David G. Bromley. London: Sage Publications.

Richardson, James T., and Rex Davis. 1983. "Experiential Fundamentalism: Revisions of Orthodoxy in Jesus Movement Groups." *Journal of the American Academy of Religion* 51, no. 3: 397–425.

Robbins, Thomas, William Shepard, and James McBride, eds. 1985. *Cults, Culture, and the Law: Perspectives on New Religious Movements.* Chico, Calif.: Scholars Press.

Robertson, George. 1994. "Island Pond Raid Begins New Pattern." In *Sex, Slander, and Salvation: Investigating The Family / Children of God,* edited by James R. Lewis and J. Gordon Melton, 153–58. Stanford, Calif.: Center for Academic Publication.

Shepherd, Gary, and Lawrence Lilliston. 1994. "Field Observations of Young People's Experiences and Role in The Family." In *Sex, Slander, and Salvation: Investigating The Family / Children of God,* edited by James R. Lewis and J. Gordon Melton, 57–70. Stanford, Calif.: Center for Academic Publication.

Sherman, Bithia. 1994. "To the children I hurt: you led me back to the arms of Jesus." Unpublished letter to World Services of The Family, Jan. 14.

Shupe, Anson D., and David G. Bromley. 1980. *The New Vigilantes: Deprogrammers, Anti-cultists, and the New Religions.* London: Sage Publications.

Singer, Margaret T. 1979. "Coming Out of the Cults." *Psychology Today* 72, no. 12: 72–82.

Smith, Wilfred C. 1959. "Comparative Religion: Whither and Why?" In *The History of Religions: Essays in Methodology,* edited by Mircea Eliade and Joseph M. Kitagawa, 40. Chicago: Univ. of Chicago Press.

Van Zandt, David. 1991. *Living in the Children of God.* Princeton: Princeton Univ. Press.

Vogt, Nancy R. 1998. "Correlates of Adolescent Sexual Activity in The Family, a Religious Group." Ph.D. diss., Fuller Theological Seminary.

Wallis, Roy. 1976. "Observations on the Children of God." *Sociological Review* 24: 807–29.

———. 1981. "Yesterday's Children: Cultural and Structural Change in a New Religious Movement." In *Social Impact of New Religious Movements,* edited by Bryan Wilson, 97–133. New York: Rose of Sharon Press.

————. 1987. "Hostages to Fortune: Thoughts on the Future of Scientology and the Children of God." In *The Future of New Religious Movements*, edited by David Bromley and Phillip E. Hammond, 80–90. Macon, Ga.: Mercer Univ. Press.

Wangerin, Ruth. 1982. "Make-Believe Revolution: A Study of the Children of God." Ph.D. diss., City Univ. of New York.

Williams, Miriam. 1998. *Heaven's Harlots: My Fifteen Years as a Sacred Prostitute in the Children of God Cult.* New York: Eagle Book.

Wright, Stuart A. 1994. "From 'Children of God' to 'The Family': Movement, Adaptation, and Survival." In *Sex, Slander, and Salvation: Investigating The Family / Children of God*, edited by James R. Lewis and J. Gordon Melton, 121–28. Stanford, Calif.: Center for Academic Publication.

Zablocki, Benjamin. 1997. "The Blacklisting of a Concept: The Strange History of the Brainwashing Conjecture in the Sociology of Religion." *Nova Religio* 1, no. 1: 96–121.

Index

Life in The Family: An Oral History Of The Children Of God was composed in 8.25/9.25 Trump Mediaeval in QuarkXPress 4.04 on a Macintosh by Kachergis Book Design; printed by sheet-fed offset on 50-pound Glatfelter Supple Opaque Recyled Natural, and Smyth-sewn and bound over binder's boards in Roxite B-grade cloth with dust jackets printed in four-color process and laminated by Thomson-Shore, Dexter, Michigan; designed by Kachergis Book Design, Pittsboro, North Carolina; published by Syracuse University Press, Syracuse, New York 13244-5160.